Against Humanity

The publisher and the University of California Press Foundation gratefully acknowledge the generous support of the Anne G. Lipow Endowment Fund in Social Justice and Human Rights.

Against Humanity

LESSONS FROM THE LORD'S
RESISTANCE ARMY

Sam Dubal

UNIVERSITY OF CALIFORNIA PRESS

University of California Press, one of the most distinguished university presses in the United States, enriches lives around the world by advancing scholarship in the humanities, social sciences, and natural sciences. Its activities are supported by the UC Press Foundation and by philanthropic contributions from individuals and institutions. For more information, visit www.ucpress.edu.

University of California Press
Oakland, California

Library of Congress Cataloging-in-Publication Data

Names: Dubal, Sam, 1986- author.
Title: Against humanity : lessons from the Lord's Resistance Army / Sam Dubal.
Description: Oakland, California : University of California Press, [2018] | Includes bibliographical references and index. |
Identifiers: LCCN 2017033917 (print) | LCCN 2017038132 (ebook) | ISBN 9780520968752 (ebook) | ISBN 9780520296091 (cloth : alk. paper) | ISBN 9780520296107 (cloth : alk. paper)
Subjects: LCSH: Humanity. | Lord's Resistance Army. | Insurgency—Uganda—Case studies.
Classification: LCC BJ1533.H9 (ebook) | LCC BJ1533.H9 D83 2017 (print) | DDC 179.7—dc23
LC record available at https://lccn.loc.gov/2017033917

Manufactured in the United States of America

27 26 25 24 23 22 21 20 19 18
10 9 8 7 6 5 4 3 2 1

For Hannah and Veena

It is impossible to *know* anything about men except on the absolute precondition that the philosophical (theoretical) myth of man is reduced to ashes.

Louis Althusser, *Marxism and Humanism*, 1964

Contents

List of Acronyms

ADF	Allied Democratic Forces
CAR	Central African Republic
CMS	Church Missionary Society
DDR	disarmament, demobilization, and reintegration
DP	Democratic Party
DRC	Democratic Republic of the Congo
FARC	Revolutionary Armed Forces of Colombia (Fuerzas Armadas Revolucionarias de Colombia)
FDC	Forum for Democratic Change
FRELIMO	Mozambican Liberation Front (Frente de Libertação de Moçambique)
GoU	Government of Uganda
GUSCO	Gulu Support the Children Organisation
HSM	Holy Spirit movement(s)
ICC	International Criminal Court
IDP	Internally Displaced Person(s)
JRP	Justice and Reconciliation Project
KAR	King's African Rifles
KICWA	Kitgum Concerned Women's Association
LDU	Local Defense Unit
LRA	Lord's Resistance Army (sometimes referred to as LRM/A, the "Lord's Resistance Movement/Army")

MSF	Doctors Without Borders (Médecins Sans Frontières)
NRA	National Resistance Army (pre-1995 precursor to UPDF)
NRM	National Resistance Movement (ruling political party, led by President Yoweri Museveni)
NUSAF	Northern Uganda Social Action Fund (a World Bank–sponsored development project for war-affected regions in the north)
PIH	Partners in Health
PRDP	Peace, Recovery, and Development Programme
RDC	Resident District Commissioner
RPG	rocket-propelled grenade
RUF	Revolutionary United Front
SPLA	Sudanese People's Liberation Army
UGX	Ugandan shilling (currency)
UNLA	Uganda National Liberation Army
UPDA	Uganda People's Democracy Army (also known as Cilil)
UPDF	Uganda Peoples' Defence Forces (see also NRA)
WFP	World Food Programme
WNBF	West Nile Bank Front

List of Characters

Aber   Worker-beneficiary at a Christian NGO catering to former LRA rebels. Makes dolls that are sold at a high profit to tourists and online shoppers in the Global North. Spent about five years in the *lum*.

Acen   Benjamin's wife. Spent a little less than a decade with the LRA. Her first two husbands in the LRA died, and she was accused of having a "hot chest" (*kori lyet*). She stayed a widow for some time before choosing to marry Benjamin—primarily because his disability meant that she would no longer have to fight but could live a more comfortable life in and around rebel bases.

Adong   Labwor's ex-wife, whom he courted and produced children with while both were in the LRA. They later separated after Amayo repeatedly abused her.

Akello Sabina   *Ajwaka* who does her work on the outskirts of Gulu town. A practicing Catholic, she was instructed by her *jok* to attend church on Sundays, causing discontent among some members of her church.

Alimocan   Labwor's former wife. She posed as though she had been an LRA rebel in the hopes of accessing humanitarian aid. A former banana seller, she left Labwor in mid-2013.

Aliya   Wife to a former LRA commander. Convert to Islam. She often complains of the prostitution, theft, and heavy drinking that goes on in the Gulu slum where she lives. By comparison, she feels life was better and cleaner in the *lum*.

Amayo   Labwor's elderly mother. A heavy drinker, she convinced Labwor to start drinking when he returned from the *lum*. She fights constantly with her sons and their wives.

Amito   Onen's youngest wife. Now at home and caring for their son, she awaits his return from the LRA after unhappy relationships with Anywar and Kidega. Co-wife of Gunya.

Amony   Otto's ex-wife in the LRA. Currently living abroad with their children.

Anywar   Amito's second husband, and first civilian husband after Onen.

Arac   Otto's ex-wife in the LRA. Younger than Amony. Did not stay with him as husband and wife after his return from the front lines, but continues to ask that he send money and clothes for their child.

Benjamin   Former LRA soldier whose leg was blown off by a landmine, after which he was relegated to work on supply and inventory. Lives with his wife Acen, whom he met in the LRA.

Gunya   Onen's senior wife. Former LRA soldier who hustles impatiently through life in Gulu town today. Co-wife of Amito.

Joseph Kony   Spirit medium and leader of the LRA.

Kidega   Amito's third husband, and second civilian husband after Onen.

Labwor   Former LRA soldier who struggles with recurrent drunken fits. Killed a leopard while in the *lum* and now coexists with its spirit. Captured in battle and brought back to Gulu, he has had a particularly difficult time living with his family members, who drink heavily and quarrel often. He is a friend to Otto, who lost Labwor's son, Odong, in an attack by the UPDF while the two were together in the LRA. Chose his pseudonym, Labwor, so that people would know that he is a *dano mager* (a wild/fierce person).

Lacambel   Host of the *Dwog Cen Paco* radio show.

Laduka   Worker-beneficiary at a Christian NGO catering to former LRA rebels. Pretends to be an evangelical Christian in order to receive preferential treatment.

Makamoi   Older man who served in the UNLA, UPDA, LRA (as both a fighter and a collaborator), and the UPDF. Tended to an LRA sick bay in which an injured Otto spent a significant period of time. Abducted his wife, Timkikomi.

Matayo   Former low-ranking LRA soldier. Born-again Christian with deep faith in God and the spirit of Joseph Kony. Serves as an assistant preacher in his community.

Min Amito   Amito's mother, a small-scale merchant. Widowed after her husband was killed by LRA rebels in a roadside ambush.

Min Onen   Onen's mother, a rural farmer. Unhappy with Mohammed after suspecting him of courting Amito, her son's wife.

Mohammed   Former LRA military policeman and clan brother to Onen. Suspected by Onen's family of trying to court Amito. Currently earns a good living working in Gulu town and farming on his rural land.

Musa Abunaba Lamgaba Former spiritual controller in the LRA. Left after more than two decades in the *lum* after suspecting an unfair plot was being concocted to have him killed.

Obwola Onen's brother and Min Onen's son. Lives in Palik with the rest of Onen and Mohammed's clan.

Odong Labwor's son, who was abandoned and left to die of hunger and thirst following a UPDF attack on an LRA camp. Otto had taken responsibility for Odong but left him behind to care for his own family in the chaos of the attack.

Ogweno Lakor A respected Acholi elder, highly knowledgeable about Acholi culture, history, and tradition. Critical of the government, he is (unlike Oyengo) not a part of Ker Kwaro Acholi. Performed reintegration rituals for returning rebels.

Ojara Amito and Onen's son. Born in the *lum* while his parents were together in the LRA.

Omony Catholic catechist. Childhood friend of Joseph Kony.

Onen LRA soldier still in the *lum* (as of early 2017). Father of Gunya's children. Awaited by Amito, the co-wife with whom he will likely stay if or when he returns from the front lines. Clan brother to Mohammed.

Opwonya Labwor's older brother, who was also briefly abducted by the LRA.

Otto Morris Labwor's close friend in the LRA. Spiritual technician and fighter for about two decades before he was unwillingly captured by the UPDF and returned from the front lines. Worked for Invisible Children, an anti-LRA NGO, even while maintaining fierce support for the rebels.

Oyengo A respected Acholi elder and member of the Ker Kwaro Acholi organization. Performed reintegration rituals for returning rebels. Often construes tradition to avoid criticizing the NRM government, which supports Ker Kwaro Acholi.

RV Wife of a former LRA commander. Spent about fifteen years in the *lum*. Originally a beneficiary of the NGO Eternal Salvation, she now works for them as a staff member.

Timkikomi Makamoi's spouse, whom he abducted and took as his second wife. After a brief separation, they now live together lovingly as husband and wife.

Yoweri Museveni President of Uganda since his 1986 overthrow of Tito Okello. Leader of the National Resistance Movement (NRM).

Acknowledgments

My name appears by historical accident and conventional necessity on the cover as the author of this text. I have merely absorbed, rearranged, and offered to readers the narratives, experiences, theories, and labors of others, some of whose names or identities appear below.

This work was financially supported through the years primarily by the National Science Foundation, with whom I was a graduate research fellow from 2012 to 2015 while a doctoral student in the joint medical anthropology program of the University of California at Berkeley and the University of California at San Francisco. The Andrew and Mary Thompson Rocca Scholarship in Advanced African Studies, from the Center for African Studies at the University of California at Berkeley, made archival research in the UK possible in June 2014. The staff at the British Library (London), the Cadbury Research Library (University of Birmingham), the Department of Manuscripts (Cambridge University Library), the Imperial War Museum (London), and the Rhodes House Library (Oxford University) were supremely helpful and patient in assisting me during that phase of my research. I thank the Uganda National Council for Science and Technology and the institutional review boards at the University of California at Berkeley and the School of Health Sciences at Makerere University for approving this project and allowing it to unfold with relative ease. A part of this book—a version of chapter 5—appeared as "Rebel Kinship and Love within the Lord's Resistance Army" in the Ugandan *Journal of Peace and Security Studies* 2, no. 1 (June 2016).

My principal debt remains with those former rebels and their families about whom this book is written. They welcomed me into their homes, feeding me meals of warm soft bread (*kwon*) and beans (*muranga*) and, when in season, offering me fresh mangoes from the trees in their compounds, which I ate to my delightful satisfaction. They let me work with them in their gardens, weeding and digging and harvesting and planting cassava, beans, millet, black-eyed pea leaves (*boo*), and other Acholi staples. They joined me in traveling on our motorbike, visiting old friends and searching for new ones across the grassy expanses of rural Acholiland and beyond. They shared with me intimate stories of their time as LRA rebels and of their civilian lives today, tolerating what must have seemed like endless questioning. *Wun lurema, amito waco-ni apwoyo tutwal me jolo wiya ki yom cwiny, calo dano me gang—me tedo cam, me winyo peny mega, me pwonya ki tam matut megwu. Ageno-ni acoyo buk maber—buk ma wacayo tito adaa i kom ngo ma otimme i kare ma wun wubedo i lum. Angeyo-ni dano mapol tye ka tic ki nying-wu calo dano ma odwogo ki i lum, tye ka nongo cente ki nying-wu nyo tye ka waco lok gopa ki nying-wu. Ageno-ni wutamo-ni atiyo maber ki nying-wu, ni ngo ma atye ka waco bot dano i lobo man ki buk eni bipwonyogi, biloko tam-gi, biweko lutela nongo yoo mapat i kwo eni—yoo me ngec, yoo me adaa. Yoo matir me konyo dano ma tye ka deno can, me pwodo dano ma tye ka kelo can. Atye kwedwu i lweny me giko can ma Rubanga tye ka lweny iye ni. An pe abedo i lum, bene muduku-na peke. Ento an lamony – lamony me adaa, me ngec. Wamede karacel i lweny eni.*

In Acholi, my deepest gratitude goes to Jimmy Odong, whose friendship, intelligence, curiosity, and meticulousness I greatly value, and with whom I found and continue to enjoy great intellectual camaraderie. Walter Akena, Janet Alimocan, Patrick Labanya Omot, Geoffrey Lakwonyero, Arthur Owor, Jackson Oyugi, and Padre Ramón Vargas assisted in this project in different ways. Daniel Komakech, Ongaya Acellam, and Opira Steven were lively and appreciated discussion partners. Father Joseph Okumu was a constant source of support and a willing soundboard for and historian of the ideas that developed in the course of this work. Much as I remained skeptical of the institution, not least for its close ties with the NRM government, Ker Kal Kwaro Acholi has my gratitude for explaining in its own way some historical Acholi social practices, welcoming me as an "Acholi son," and giving me the name of Otim, meaning an Acholi born outside of Acholiland. A variety of other organizations and their staffs, including Gulu Support the Children Organisation (GUSCO), World Vision's Children of War Rehabilitation Centre, and the Northern Uganda Youth Development Centre (NUYDC), also deserve thanks for their cooperation in my research, even as I profoundly critique their theories and actions in the pages that follow. Members and administrators of Golden Boda Boda and Gulu United Boda Boda Association generously taught me about the motorcycle taxi industry in Gulu district.

I was fortunate to have been a research affiliate at the Makerere Institute of Social Research (MISR) in Kampala, where Mahmood Mamdani, and in particular Adam Branch, have encouraged my work. I thank Adam for his kind attention to, continuing interest in, critiques of, and reviews of my work, which have been enormously helpful. I hope that my own work can inspire others in the way that his inspires me. Other scholars with whom I had the unexpected pleasure of discussing my work while in "the field" include Henni Alava, Tim Allen, Ron Atkinson, Jacob Doherty, Lioba Lenhart, Marissa Mika, Erin Moore, and Susan Reynolds Whyte. Part of what I refer to as the historical accident of my presence in this project is largely due to Michael Westerhaus, who first introduced me to northern Uganda. I owe Sverker Finnström and Ayesha Nibbe for their continuous and long-standing support. Most of all, I am deeply appreciative of and indebted to Adrian and Miriam Yen, whose companionship and support was and continues to be invaluable, and whom I am honored to call both friends and colleagues.

The intellectual environment in which this work was written, with the support of mentors and colleagues at the University of California at Berkeley and the University of California at San Francisco and beyond, was intensely stimulating. I am inexpressibly thankful that my closest advisers and mentors—Vincanne Adams, Nancy Scheper-Hughes, and Michael Watts—saw original value in this work and supported it from start to finish. That threads of their own work are present in this one is not a coincidence but a sign of deep respect and admiration. Paul Rabinow has been instrumental in shaping the way I think about "humanity." Louisa Lombard pushed me to think about the "bush" in more interesting ways. Seth Holmes, Charles Briggs, Deborah Freedman Lustig, and Christine Trost generously invited me to the Berkeley Center for Social Medicine at the Institute for the Study of Societal Issues, where I had the time and space to refine the manuscript. Erin Baines, Annie Bunting, and Chris Dolan gave me a forum to think more about love in coercive settings. The Anthropological Inquiry group of the Townsend Center for the Humanities provided an important space to discuss and rethink parts of the manuscript. This work has also benefited from the generous feedback of Lawrence Cohen, Mariane Ferme, Cori Hayden, Donald Moore, Martha Saavedra, and Ian Whitmarsh. Among those many colleagues who have helped nurture creativity and vigor in our collective work are Clare Cameron, Ugo Edu, Dana Greenfield, Ruth Goldstein, Patricia Kubala, Mukul Kumar, Heather Mellquist Lehto, Francesca Nicosia, Rachel Niehuus, Miguel Pérez, Maryani Rasidjan, Martha Stroud, Marlee Tichenor, and Jerry Zee.

I am grateful to many at the University of California Press who have helped bring this book to fruition. Danny Hoffman and Deborah Gould provided important suggestions to improve the manuscript. Naomi Schneider has been tremendously supportive throughout the publication process. Benjy Malings, Francisco Reinking, and Lindsey Westbrook assisted during its latter stages.

I perhaps would never have fortuitously ventured into and continued in academia were it not for James Ferguson, whose faith in me from my time as a first-semester freshman undergraduate student at Stanford gave me the confidence to take a thoughtful detour from one imagined path in medicine to create another. I thank him, Liisa Malkki, and Miyako Inoue for offering their continuous support and feedback over the years. Akhil Gupta, Purnima Mankekar, and Sunaina Maira have been loving friends and guides to me for many years. Jean Comaroff was encouraging as I attempted to balance writing with clinical duties. I am also grateful to my mentors and colleagues from my time at Harvard Medical School, in particular Ronald Arky, Lina Drada, Nathan Favini, Andrés Patiño, Shamsher Samra, and Beverly Woo, for trusting and validating my unplanned decision to take extended leave from medical school to pursue this work. I hope I can repay them in the years to come with unconventional and radical contributions toward envisioning and enacting a different kind of medicine.

My family—Bharat, Saroj, Dena, John, Veena, and Ryan—have been quietly supportive of my anthropological inquiries, and I thank them for their unwavering patience and understanding of my will to intellectual and political endeavor, irrespective of the specific content and rationales of those labors.

Finally, my deepest love and appreciation are reserved for several people without whom this work could never have appeared. Cristina Biasetto, Michael D'Arcy, Cole Hansen, Ya-Hsuan Huang, Jason Price, Raphäelle Rabanes, and K.S. have been critically productive colleagues, but more importantly, unbelievably supportive and loyal friends who have quite literally saved my life at various points. In particular, Jason has been constantly involved in my project, and a great inspiration for many of the ideas and forms contained herein. Hannah Appel has over the years, for reasons I cannot fully understand, given me astonishing levels of encouragement and critique, reading both my work and my mind in remarkable ways, and offering her optimistic, hopeful hand as a comrade in endless and uncertain struggle. I do not think I can ever pay back my debt to her—which is my life itself—yet I am happy in knowing that this is exactly as she would like it to be, in itself another piece of her radical wisdom. Veena Dubal has been everything to me—my most adamant supporter, my most reliable critic, and my closest friend. I am incredibly fortunate and proud to have her in my life, to be able to call her at once sister, friend, colleague, and comrade. Neither she nor I truly know how much she means to me.

1 Introduction

She is sitting on a worn papyrus mat. The shade of a towering mango tree shields her from the hot sun. She finishes making up her daughter's hair, her hands expertly weaving the strands in and out, twisting them together. Reaching for a knife, she begins to peel the skin off soaked cassava, preparing a meal for her children and elderly mother. Her daughter moves to stand behind her and now braids her mother's hair into cornrows. They watch as the neighbors' goats scurry across their homestead, past the rusty iron-sheet door to their hut.

Gunya is a woman in her late twenties who works as a waitress at a roadside restaurant. She lives with her family on this quiet homestead at the edge of Gulu town in northern Uganda. Soldiers of the Lord's Resistance Army (LRA) abducted her when she was eleven years old and forcibly conscripted her into the rebel ranks. Gunya spent a little more than a decade with the rebels before deserting. While there, she gave birth to a son with Onen, an LRA soldier who is still fighting in the "bush" (*lum*).

I take a deep breath, preparing myself for what I imagine will be a difficult first conversation with a woman I expect to match the description of what scholars, media, and NGOs have called "sex slaves"—young girls abducted by the LRA to be wives to rebels. I await a grim narrative about

rape, stigma, and victimization at the hands of what has been widely characterized as a violent, brutal army of inhuman rebels with an irrational
belief in the spirits possessing its leader, Joseph Kony. Indeed, as I come
to join her, it crosses my mind that she seems to embody a form of agent-
less, feminine victimhood. Such women who have returned from the LRA
are often spoken about, particularly by NGOs, as having become animals
in the *lum* and needing "re-humanization" on their return to civil society.

As we sit and chat for the first time, I am quickly disabused of my pre-
conceptions. Gunya identifies herself as a former LRA captain. Though
abducted, she expresses her continued support for the LRA and their tactics, admitting that she sometimes thinks of going back to the *lum* when
life becomes hard as a civilian at home. She tells me stories about using
rocket-propelled grenades (RPGs) to attack gunships and jet fighters of
the Uganda Peoples' Defence Forces (UPDF), the Ugandan national army.
She defiantly, almost proudly, shows me what remains of old bullet
wounds—scars faintly etched across both of her ankles. They are usually
hidden when she goes barefoot with a hoe to till her soil, the caked mud
concealing the bodily memories of her past from those around her. She
dismisses claims that the LRA are finished as a rebel force, insisting that
Kony is gaining momentum and will in the coming years return to Uganda
and overthrow the government. She dreams of the end of Ugandan
President Yoweri Museveni's reign, which began by coup in 1986. A change
in leadership, she hopes, will bring development and freedom to her people, peace of mind for her, and education for her children, whom she
wants to see grow up as doctors or lawyers. My respect for her suffering as
a victim is replaced with awe of her courageous agency and will to fight.

Over the course of a little more than a year, I became good friends with
Gunya, sometimes just hanging around at her home, other times joining her
for clan funerals. We often shared meals, and before we dug our millet bread
(*kwon kal*) into bowls of black-eyed pea or cowpea leaves (*boo*) and beans
(*muranga*), she always knelt before me, pouring water into a basin for me
to wash my hands, as was customary for Acholi women to do for men.
I joked with her that she, not I, should be the one attended to—as was the
case when she was an LRA officer and had house girls prepare her meals
and take care of her children. I insisted that she was the proverbial big man

between the two of us, but she laughed in disagreement. Nonetheless, I refused to take my first bite before she took hers.

I also frequented the restaurant in town where she worked. Her boss suggested to me that former rebels like Gunya were valued by employers for their strong work ethic, an ethic contrasted to that of their age mates who grew up during the war in refugee camps for internally displaced persons. According to the popularly circulated narrative, camp residents got "used to free things" and were prone to laziness, while rebels labored hard like brutes in the *lum*.

Gunya and I spoke regularly about Onen, who had remained with the LRA in the *lum*, and of the relationship they once had together, having courted each other when they met in the LRA. She knew that if he ever came back to Gulu, he would go live with Amito, another of his wives. Even so, she maintained contact with his family in rural Gulu District, taking their kids to see their paternal kin and the land that they will one day inherit by patriarchal right. Short on cash and without other support, she was also keen for his family to pay the fine due for unsanctioned sex (*luk*) for the children, who were born outside of formal marriage.

Gunya often impressed me with her military tactical knowledge and her fascination with weapons. She once mentioned that she enjoyed watching American war films, which played often in video halls in town, and asked me if I knew any. One night, I bought a bootleg copy of *Black Hawk Down*, a chronicle of the 1993 American military intervention in Somalia. Gunya and I sat down to watch it after the end of a workday. She gave me a running commentary on the battle scenes, critiquing the positioning of gunners on tanks and the imperfect techniques of rocket launchers aiming their RPGs at helicopters. "Mmm hmm," she nodded approvingly, when an RPG was shot at a cluster of American troops in the film. They are stupid to crowd together like that, she asserted. She called the American soldiers "lazy" and said that the LRA would have no problem dealing with the one hundred US military "advisors" deployed to central and eastern Africa in 2011 by President Barack Obama to fight the LRA on the ground.

One day in September 2012 I came to see her, excited to share the latest copy of *Rupiny*, a weekly Luo-language newspaper. Its cover story reported that the LRA had abducted fifty-five people in the Central African Republic (CAR). A picture of two LRA soldiers, said to be seventeen and twenty-four, caught Gunya's eye as she pored over the paper. They are not fighters, she said, but porters—people briefly abducted by rebels to help carry supplies and set up camps. She insisted that what they report in the paper is not what actually happens on the ground. She suspected the story was fake, but was nonetheless glad to hear that the LRA were still a strong force. Examining the content of the article itself, Gunya was struck by the description of a young child "rescued" by the UPDF. She did not see merit in his so-called rescue. Gunya worried about the kind of interrogation that this child would receive at the hands of the government soldiers, and lamented that he was taken away from his parents, who were likely LRA rebels in the *lum*.

"This child wasn't 'rescued,' but abducted and torn from his parents," she wryly remarked. Rather than envisioning the child as being a "captive" of the LRA, she wanted me to understand that to her, the LRA was his family, his life-world. Coming "home" to civilian life in Gulu would in fact mean a forcible separation from his family in the *lum*. While it was true that the LRA beat or killed those who tried to escape, there were also many who chose to remain with the LRA, and who were unwillingly captured even after having been themselves abducted into the LRA. The way in which "captivity" was imagined as a brutal violence from the outside did not always match the meaning it was given from within, particularly when contextualized within the structural violence of everyday life experienced by Acholi peasants and workers. Indeed, Gunya was one of many of my former rebel friends who had escaped or been captured but now lamented the conditions of life they experienced as they rejoined civilians in towns and villages across Acholiland. She and others wondered whether they would have been better off staying on the front lines in the *lum*.

As with all names that appear in this book, "Gunya" is a pseudonym. Gunya chose her pseudonym, which means "chimpanzee," because it reminded her of code names that rebels used for one another. She asked me to use it because, as she put it, "The LRA were there in the *lum* as gorillas [*sic*]. . . . It was gorilla warfare [*sic*] there."

This book is a collection of the lives of Gunya and other LRA rebels—lives that are too complex to be understood through the simple moral lens

of humanity. The rebels and their associated violence were often characterized as brutal and inhumane, but as I came to hear these stories, it
became clear that these characterizations did not well describe the ways
that rebels actually lived. The violence they had committed and the violence they suffered was not simply horrific, immoral, or "against humanity." When humanist accounts of the LRA and its violence give it cruel
names, speaking about "abduction" into and "captivity" within the LRA,
they hide away the meaning and complexity of that violence and of the
rebellion itself. The coming chapters tell a tale of the new forms of ethical
life that arose in the course of the rebellion—forms of life beyond humanity. Life within the LRA offered all kinds of transformative experiences.
Rebels forged new kinship relations. They reconstructed their relationships with God, as they witnessed miracles and reached new depths of
spiritual consciousness. They reconfigured their understandings of politics as they resisted and fought against the Ugandan government. Rebels
returning from the front lines of war often developed a more profound
discontent with the everyday violence of peasant life in Acholiland. These
experiences transcended the boundaries set by the notion of humanity,
and by doing so, brought the very category into question.

HUMANITY AS A PROBLEM, NOT A SOLUTION

I had no interest in thinking or writing about "humanity" before I began
long-term ethnographic research in northern Uganda in 2012 with former
Lord's Resistance Army rebels. Indeed, I came to Uganda expecting to
explore questions about violence and ethics—particularly the moral justification and condemnation of LRA violence: abductions, mutilation and
killing of civilians, and so forth. But I could not avoid the way in which
discourses about humanity constantly pervaded everyday conversations
and memories about the rebels, who were characterized as outside the
human in so many ways. "Humanity" appeared not only in official discourses and accounts of the war and the LRA, but also in the daily lives of
combatants themselves during and after the war.

Of course, "humanity" has always been a troubling issue for Africa. As
Achille Mbembe puts it: "Africa is never seen as possessing things and

attributes properly part of 'human nature.' . . . Discourse on Africa is almost always deployed in the framework . . . of a meta-text about the *animal*—to be exact, about the *beast*." As the absolute other to the West, he argues, Africa becomes a way for the West to define itself as different, to create a self-image that poses a problem to the "idea of a common human nature, a humanity shared with others" (2001, 1, 2).

The LRA were appropriated to fill this savage slot, against which the very definition of the human was produced and reproduced. They became irrational, brutal, Black animals committing inhuman violence. This depiction gained an unprecedented level of attention when the NGO Invisible Children launched a campaign called "Kony 2012," which sought to create enough pressure to arrest LRA commander Joseph Kony by the end of 2012. Invisible Children's campaign was brought to international attention through a viral video that has been viewed more than 101 million times on YouTube and set a record for the most ever single-day views of a YouTube video at more than thirty million. The video juxtaposes an image of Kony alongside Osama bin Laden and Adolf Hitler as an embodiment of pure evil. As a scholar-activist, I was compelled to intervene, and together with Ayesha Nibbe, I organized a group of scholars working in and around northern Uganda to piece together "Making Sense of Kony," a series of more nuanced academic accounts of Kony and the LRA. This project was partly motivated by a desire to complicate the black-and-white picture created of Kony, to disrupt the simplistic narrative of good and evil that had emerged through an activist campaign led by mainly white young Americans.

But scholars were not the only ones challenging this narrative. Rebels had also resisted their expulsion from humanity over the course of the war. For example, in a famous 2006 interview, Kony declared to a journalist who visited him in the *lum*, "I am a human being like you" (Schomerus 2010, 115). He was hitting back at discourses constructed by the West and by Ugandan President Yoweri Museveni that had expelled him from "humanity" as a savage, barbaric animal and terrorist.[1]

As I discovered in the course of my ethnographic research, this attempt to reclaim "humanity" was surprisingly common. A rebel friend of mine shared the picture in figure 1 with me and asked me to include it in this work. She explained that it was a photo of an LRA family in Sudan, resting

Figure 1. A family resting at an LRA base in Nisito, Sudan, in a temporary grass hut (*bolo*), having just arrived from Juba. The husband sits atop a box of AK-47 bullets. The woman is smiling at her husband and child. Photographer unknown.

in the rebels' Nisito base in a temporary shelter (*bolo*) after arriving from Juba. The father, holding his daughter, sits on a box of AK-47 bullets. His wife, sitting next to him on the ground, gazes longingly into their daughter's eyes. My friend reflected on the photo: "Some said the LRA were not human beings. Some people thought they were animals or some other thing. This [image] will help show that they were also human beings."

The question of the humanity of LRA rebels was an uncomfortable one that surfaced over and over again in my time in Uganda. "Do they see them as the rebels or do they see them as human beings?" a rehabilitation officer asked about her fellow staff who had been assigned to help defecting rebels "reintegrate" into civilian society. "They are the same human beings like us," she insistently answered. A hotel manager in Gulu once told me of former rebels, "They will all need some form of counseling," before quickly asserting that she was not discriminating against rebels, but rather

approaching them with the attitude that "this person is a human being."
My rebel friends who lived for long periods of time in the *lum* asserted that
they did not live with their fellow rebels in harshness or ferocity (*gero*), but
rather "like human beings" (*calo dano adana*). A former rebel speaking on
the radio airwaves, trying to convince current rebels to defect, urged her
former comrades: "Return home so that you can become a human being"
(*Dwogo cen paco wek odoko dano*). Friends of mine resisted this characterization. "[Civilians] think you eat human meat. They imagine you have fur,
your claws are long, and you don't have toes anymore . . . but people in the
lum are really human beings," one insisted.

This book is not about crimes *against* humanity. It is not about the
indictments of Joseph Kony and Dominic Ongwen—senior commanders
of the LRA—by the International Criminal Court (ICC) on charges of
crimes against humanity. It is not a story of enslavement, rape, inhumane
acts, or murder. It is not a story of the suffering, survival, or resilience of
former child soldiers abducted and forced to kill in the name of God. It is
not a story about how violent and animal-like former rebels are, or how
they should be humanized, reformed, and reintegrated into a peaceful
civil society. Nor is it an attempt to rationalize or explain a "bizarre," "irrational" rebellion through a scholarly uncovering of its history, politics, and
spirituality.

Rather, this book is about coming to terms with the problem of "humanity." The need to speak out and about the humanity of LRA rebels suggested that their standing in humanity was indeed under threat. A chorus
of voices—consisting of both scholars and rebels—sought to defend or
reassert the humanity of the LRA. In doing so, they echoed the sentiments
of anticolonial voices speaking back to the ways in which Europeans had
expelled Africans from humanity. Jean-Paul Sartre wrote of this resistance
in his preface to Frantz Fanon's *The Wretched of the Earth* (1961):

> The black and yellow voices still talked of our humanism, but it was to
> blame us for our inhumanity. . . . "You are making monsters out of us; your
> humanism wants us to be universal but your racist practices are differentiat-
> ing us." (xliii–xliv)

Rather than joining these voices in attempting to reclaim the LRA's
humanity, I instead aim to critically examine the very category of human-

ity itself. In the ethnographic material that follows, I show how claims to humanity are often too limiting, simplistic, and moralizing to capture the complexity of the social lives of former rebels. On this basis, I consider the possibility of being "against humanity," of recognizing it as a problem rather than a solution in ongoing struggles toward emancipation.

AGAINST HUMANITY

What does it mean to be "against humanity"? It is a question often posed skeptically to me. How can a reasonable person claim to be "against humanity," particularly in the aftermath of the Holocaust and the rise in the white, Euro-American consciousness of the category of the "crime against humanity" as an unassailable evil? After all, "humanity" has today been elevated to the sense of the highest moral good. Our global society prosecutes people it sees as committing crimes against humanity—including LRA commander Dominic Ongwen, who at the time of this writing sits in jail in The Hague, on trial by the ICC. Some of our most respected historical and peaceful world leaders, from Martin Luther King Jr. to Mahatma Gandhi, discuss ways to uplift humanity or to build faith in it.

To be against "humanity" is undoubtedly an unsettling proposition. In an attempt to deconstruct humanity, I should make very clear that being "against humanity" does not imply making a moral argument for genocide, ethnic cleansing, mass violence, rape, or similar so-called "crimes against humanity," directly or indirectly. It does not suggest camaraderie with mass killers. It does not entail a movement toward xenophobia and ethno-nationalism such as that which is currently gaining traction across America and Europe. Rather, being "against humanity" is a way to bring into question the kinds of work humanity is called upon to perform.

"Humanity" or the "human" has become subject to widespread scholarly critique and attention in recent years in different ways within a variety of disciplines, including Black studies, postcolonial/decolonizing studies, anthropology, and science and technology studies. A large literature in anthropology concerned with humanitarianism and human rights has extensively critiqued humanitarian action and reason in its various forms and practices. Humanitarian and human rights interventions have been interrogated for their logical aporias (Fassin 2012); eliding the political (Ferguson 1994); being complicit with military interventions (Fassin and Pandolfi 2010); commodifying and exploiting the suffering of others (James 2010); hampering the growth of true democracy (Englund 2006); and satisfying the needs of those who perform humanitarian work (Malkki 2015), among other analyses.

Rarely, however, do these critiques extend to humanitarianism's presumed philosophical root—humanity itself. By contrast, "humanity" is often an important organizing concept that ethnographers use to help readers understand forms of life that arise in the midst of violence and suffering. Medical anthropologists in particular tend toward the concept in their attempts to describe or narrate the "good" in generally grim tales of suffering, disease, illness, and pain, in ways that resort to the concept's affective and moral power.[2] This is not a new practice or usage as such, but one that has often been made absentmindedly through the lens of liberalism, as though humanity was a naturally occurring and universal category synonymous with the moral good. It is only in more recent anthropological work that humanity has begun to be thought of as a problem in itself (see for example Feldman and Ticktin 2010), given its dangerous deployments as a category with multiple meanings, a long history of exclusions, and a range of governmental effects. Though critical of the concept of humanity, Ilana Feldman and Miriam Ticktin contend that "almost everyone agrees that humanity should be considered sacred," and suggest that "we may not be able to do without [humanity] . . . because there does not seem to be any way to make it go away" (2010, 1, 25). In response to their claims, and based on what I learned from former rebels, I believe that there may be value in desecrating the category of humanity, and indeed in doing away with it completely. In this sense, my work attempts to fill in a gap between the pitfalls of existing attempts to heal the world based on the concept of humanity and a new horizon of alternative forms of progressive social action that eschew humanity.

In science and technology studies (STS), and specifically within what has been referred to as the ontological turn, the "human" is identified as a concept limiting anthropology from seeing and attending to alternative nonhuman worlds, worlds inhabited by creatures, spirits, cyborgs, or animals. In this turn, drawing from the work of Bruno Latour and including voices like Donna Haraway (2008), Eduardo Kohn (2013), and Eduardo Viveiros de

Castro (1998), there is concern for revealing the human as a biological concept or cosmological symbol that excludes broader perspectives of seeing the world, other ways of being. For Kohn, who writes toward an anthropology "beyond the human," "the goal here is neither to do away with the human nor to reinscribe it but to open it" (2013, 6). My approach blends both an ontological and a critical deconstructionist approach. Through the ethnography, I try to present alternative realities that I became familiar with in my time with my LRA friends that put pressure on the established form of thinking known as humanity.[3] Yet I also point to ways in which "humanity" creates really existing political and ethical problems in the world as an ideological tool constructed within particular material, sociopolitical, and economic conditions. In this sense, I identify my work as part of a militant anthropology both "against" and "beyond" the human.

My critique joins with "darker" voices in postcolonial/decolonizing and Black studies, which are, unsurprisingly, often neglected in scholarly discussions of humanity. For scholars like Alexander Weheliye, following the work of Sylvia Wynter, most current perspectives on post-humanism, particularly in animal studies, often exclude discussions of race and rarely consider "cultural and political formations outside the world of Man that might offer alternative versions of humanity" (2014, 8–10).[4] These perspectives usually take the human as universal and synonymous with Western Man, and with it, ignore the racist and colonial legacies that built this liberal concept. Sylvia Wynter (2000) refers to this Western bourgeois idea of the human as merely a specific ethno-class genre of being human, one that takes the name of the good and "over-represents" itself as if it were the human itself. This move falls within what Lisa Lowe calls "the violence of liberal universality" that "continues to be reproduced in liberal humanist institutions, discourses, and practices today" (2015, 7, 41). Following Saidiya Hartman, I am interested in the "forms of violence and domination enabled by the recognition of humanity," the ways that certain "encroachments of power" take place through humanity (1997, 6).[5] This book joins these and other critiques of white liberal humanity.[6] Yet while they seek to salvage humanity, I remain skeptical of the possibilities of finding genres of the human beyond the world of Man, of reinventing the human in a way that decentralizes Man, in ways that do not create their own forms of violence.

Being "against humanity" is a heuristic to think about the problems posed by the uses of humanity, a social construct much like "race" that must be critically interrogated rather than taken as a natural category.[7] It is an anchoring principle around which to rethink humanity and the missions that are organized around it, ranging from the International Criminal Court to human rights campaigns. It is part of an anthropological tradition that deconstructs categories like "rationality" and "development," molded by the lens of white Enlightenment social science.[8] And it is an attempt to break out of a prison that, like "human rights," chains us to specific notions of the good while disposing of alternative visions of freedom and justice— visions that often offer a clearer path to the common good.[9]

Drawing from James Ferguson (1994), I do not only seek to point out that humanity is a poor concept in empirically describing the richness and diversity of life, destroying with its moral prescriptiveness the meaning and truth that certain practices and beliefs bring to rebels (as "development" did to historical and political realities on the ground in Lesotho). I am also interested in pointing to the real effects that humanity has as a discourse and practice in this world—namely, expanding a certain notion of the good through which particular versions of time, violence, logic, being, and so forth become hegemonic and thereby unquestionable.

As I show in the coming chapters, humanity unsuccessfully attempts to monopolize control over compassion, justice, and the moral good. Indeed, under some of the most innocent and well-meaning uses of humanity lie moralizing agendas that obfuscate the experiences and social relations of life on the ground. A concept useful for simplification, binarization, and distillation, humanity loses its value when it denies meaning and value to experiences, thoughts, or actions that disrupt the smooth way in which it divides good from evil, purifying the complexity of experience through the lens of what are ultimately value judgments.

Humanity is not a neutral or non-ideological term. In the ways it is actually used, it divides the spectrum of violence into good and bad forms. When LRA rebels kill in a certain way, they are charged with crimes against humanity; when American drones kill in a different way, they are hailed as life-saving technologies.[10] Humanity divides forms of being into human and nonhuman, assigning proper spaces for each kind of being. Rather than embracing the continuity of animals and humans and their shared habitats, humanity proclaims one group sacred and excludes all others in both name and place. Because the LRA fought in the *lum* where animals and spirits roamed, they were disparaged as animals themselves, eating food meant for monkeys, not humans. Humanity also divides what is reasonable from what is unreasonable. When LRA rebels kill in ways not immediately under-standable to outsiders, they are seen as irrational and therefore inhuman. Humanity is a modern discourse and a modern philosophical feeling, not the inevitable end of human action against perceived injustice. For these reasons, it made little sense for rebels to think of or speak about their own killings in terms of humanity. These and other binarizations of thought and experience simply do not do justice to the lived realities of the LRA rebels that are told in this book. Here, being "against humanity" means beginning to think about the richness and diversity of human life that exists outside certain limited notions of the good—life beyond humanity.

The lives and experiences of the LRA rebels that are narrated in the chapters to come dislodge master narratives about humanity in ways that cut across these binaries. The construction of "humanity" as a moral senti-ment in line with the "humane" is revealed to be a peculiarly modern con-cept built against forms of "horrific" violence, including mutilation and forced marriage. Humanity as a form of being distinguished from animal-ity is questioned through LRA experiences in the *lum*. The Western con-cept of rationality as a key construct of the human, particularly compared to the (African) "savage mind," is critiqued through LRA magic and sci-ence. The ethnographic evidence breaks down humanity in these and other iterations. All the while, humanity unsuccessfully attempts to gov-ern or discipline the beliefs and experiences of rebels in different ways—including processes of re-humanization aimed at reintegrating what are seen as violent animals into a peaceful civil society of humans.

THE ETHNOGRAPHIC CONTEXT: UGANDA, ACHOLI, AND THE LORD'S RESISTANCE ARMY

Uganda is a landlocked country in east Africa bordered by South Sudan to the north, Kenya to the east, Tanzania and Rwanda to the south, and the Democratic Republic of the Congo to the west. It was colonized by the

British in 1894 and became independent in 1962. It is home to sixty-five legally recognized ethnic groups, including the Acholi, who are considered a Luo Nilotic group.[11]

Acholiland extends from north-central Uganda up into South Sudan. In Uganda, Acholiland is to some degree divided into East Acholi (consisting of the present-day districts of Kitgum, Pader, Lamwo, and Agago) and West Acholi (consisting of the present-day districts of Gulu, Nwoya, and Amuru). Topographically, Acholiland consists mostly of grassy plains and hills. The Acholi are ethnically bordered by the Karamojong to the east, the Langi and Iteso to the south, and the Madi, Lugbara, and other West Nile groups to the west. The majority of Acholi are agriculturalists working customary land—rural farmers whose daily work life focuses around caring for their fields. Among the staple crops grown are millet, sesame, potatoes, beans, groundnuts, and peas. In urban areas like Gulu town, trades of all kinds thrive. Many people in Gulu town hustle for a living, making ends meet in different ways. Popular working-class professions include motorcycle taxis (*boda boda*), petty hawking, and manual labor of all kinds. A petty bourgeois class includes civil servants and teachers, as well as traders who sell various goods, ranging from housewares to motorcycle parts. A more elite bourgeois class consists of organizational directors, government officials, and businesspeople who often travel to Kampala and other global metropolises, including London (where a sizable Acholi expatriate community lives). As a result of colonial-era evangelization by the British Church Missionary Society (CMS) and the Italian Verona Fathers (Comboni Missionaries), Protestantism and Catholicism are the most popular religions, though a small number of Acholi identify as Muslim. "Traditional" Acholi spiritual-religious beliefs (*tic Acoli*) are commonly held but often publicly hidden or disavowed.

On the whole, the Acholi have lived a fairly marginal existence at various points within the histories of pre- and postcolonial Uganda. They were not included as part of the territory of the original Uganda Protectorate in 1894 (Girling 1960, 150). The seat of industry and government was established in the south, and the British were initially uninterested in incorporating the Acholi—whose territory they found unimportant; whose work ethic they questioned (Girling 1960, 174–76); and whose political organization they found difficult to colonize, since they were not already neatly amalgamated into a chiefdom as the Baganda were in the south. Historically, Acholi men were recruited for military service into the colonial King's African Rifles (Finnström 2008, 61). They also became labor migrants working on plantations, industries, and other businesses and organizations in the south (Girling 1960, 178–80; Mamdani 1976, 52). Since 1986, under the presidency of Yoweri Museveni, the Acholi have felt particularly disenchanted and marginalized. This is partly explained by the feeling that Museveni has unevenly developed the country in ways that have excluded the Acholi. But more often the resentment stems from Museveni's response to and treatment of the Acholi throughout the course of the rebellion waged against his government by the Lord's Resistance Army.[12]

The Rise of the Lord's Resistance Army

The Lord's Resistance Army was formed in the late 1980s by Joseph Kony. Kony was born in the early 1960s in Odek, a sub-county in Gulu District in West Acholi. Kony's LRA rose to prominence in the aftermath of the defeat of other Holy Spirit movements in Acholiland, most notably that of Alice Lakwena, which resisted Yoweri Museveni and his National Resistance Movement/Army's (NRM/A) 1986 defeat of Tito Okello by coup (Behrend 1999, 23–26). Following their coup, the NRA committed mass violence in Acholiland, carrying out extrajudicial killings, raping men and women, and looting cattle in what has been seen as a form of retaliation for the Ugandan army's counterinsurgency campaign against the NRA in the Luweero Triangle in central Uganda. It was held that the Acholi soldiers in the army—many of whom fled back north following the coup—were responsible for the violence carried out in Luweero (see Finnström 2008, 67–75). Museveni, who hails from southwestern Uganda, has remained in power as president ever since his 1986 coup, and enjoys little support among the Acholi people.

How and why did the LRA arise? From a historical perspective, the LRA war has been interpreted as the latest iteration in a series of military struggles among different ethnic and regional groups for control of the national postcolony.[13] This struggle was often embodied through the ethnicization of the national army. Independent Uganda's first leader, Milton Obote, was seen to have filled his army ranks with members of his own ethnic group, the Langi, when he took power in 1962. When Idi Amin ousted Obote from power in 1971, Amin violently purged Langi and Acholi from the national army, replacing them with men from his own West Nile. By the time Yoweri Museveni began his "bush war" in 1979 to overthrow Obote (then in his second term), he filled his own rebel ranks with fellow Banyankole from southwestern Uganda. Museveni preached loudly against ethnic divides in national politics. However, in practice, his NRM vilified northerners, Nilotes, and Acholi—especially in retaliating against the Ugandan army, Obote's Uganda National Liberation Army (UNLA). Museveni's highest-ranking military officers in today's UPDF, many Acholi point out, are his own people; Acholi UPDF soldiers feel discriminated against and passed over for promotions to the highest levels of military leadership. Widespread distrust of Museveni and the NRM remains within the LRA and also among Acholi, with suspicion that Museveni is trying to steal Acholi land and destroy the Acholi people. Within this narrative, the LRA appears as the latest iteration of historical attempts at enacting violent regime changes in the ethnicized postcolony—a place where fair, democratic elections bringing about uniform sociopolitical change for all Ugandan ethnic groups are an exception rather than the rule.

More specifically, as other scholars have suggested, the LRA arose to meet the challenges of specific political and moral problems facing the Acholi people in the postcolony. Adam Branch argues that two particular political crises facing the Acholi spawned the spiritual rebellions in Acholiland after Museveni's 1986 coup. The rebellions, he suggests, responded to these two crises—the first, an "*internal* crisis stemming from the breakdown of authority within Acholi society"; and the second, "a *national* crisis brought about by the destruction of the political links that had tied the Acholi in the district to the national state" (2010, 25). The rebellions, Branch explains, attempted to solve these crises by instilling an Acholi political identity against the NRM/A—creating an internal Acholi order that sought to violently resolve the national crisis through military struggle. The rebellions have so far failed to achieve this order, leaving a rural Acholi peasantry—who lack a legitimate, mediating Acholi political authority—unrepresented at the national level.

This political understanding of the roots of the LRA should be supplemented by a more theological or moral understanding. As Heike Behrend describes, the Holy Spirit movements arose in the conflict between Acholi elders and returning soldiers retreating from Luweero in the immediate aftermath of the coup. Behrend argues that the returning soldiers had come back impure, haunted as they were by the spirits (*cen*) of those they had killed. They refused to undergo ritual purifications prescribed by Acholi elders, increasing internal discord by bringing impurity back to Acholi, and thereby provoking catastrophes such as AIDS, war, and drought (1999, 2). This violation of moral order catalyzed continual violence and suffering, and—Behrend argues—spawned the creation of the Holy Spirit movements to fight evil and restore purity to Acholi society. In this narrative, God had sent spirits to the sinful Acholi to save them from the evil that had infected them. In its initial phase, Joseph Kony—as a spirit medium—declared that he had been sent by God to "liberate humanity from disease and suffering," in part through fighting against all the evil in the world, including not only the NRA but also witches, spirit priests (*ajwagi*), and other authorities perceived as immoral (Behrend 1999, 179). According to this framework, Kony is a messenger of God, and the LRA are carrying out orders that, though often violent, are nonetheless divine.

A Brief History of Joseph Kony and the LRA

As long as Yoweri Museveni has remained in power, Joseph Kony has remained a rebel, fighting up to the time of this writing (currently about thirty years). As Behrend (1999) details, Kony began operating around his home of Odek in present-day southeast Gulu District. Raised a Catholic, he was said to have come from a family of spirit priests (*ajwagi*). At some point in the late 1980s, Kony became possessed by, or filled with, several spirits—Juma Oris, Silli Silindi (a female spirit), Jim Brickey, and Ing Chu, among others. A medium of these spirits, Kony initially focused on healing and preaching before being instructed to gradually build a rebel army consisting of brigades like Condum, Stockry, and Gilver. The LRA grew as a predominantly but not exclusively Acholi army.

My friend Labwor, a former rebel about whom we will hear more in the coming chapters, wanted me to set some misconceptions about Joseph Kony straight: "Kony is a human being, a person, who talks like we are talking now. He works not for himself, but follows the [spirits'] rules like we do. . . . When commanders die for failing to follow the instructions, it's the spirit that kills them. It's not Kony, because Kony doesn't fight in a worldly manner." Like many spiritual rebellions before it, the LRA was guided in its tactics, actions, and beliefs by the instructions of the spirits that spoke through Kony. New fighters, who were almost always forcibly conscripted rather than being recruited or self-volunteered, were anointed and purified before going to battle. Holy Spirit precautions or rules issued by the spirits governed the behavior of rebels. The spirits issued prophecies, directed fasts, revealed medicinal treatments, and otherwise helped and protected the rebels, who risked injury or death by breaking their rules and losing the spirits' protection. Certain rebels known as controllers and technicians mediated the spiritual aspects of the war, often from a sacred space known as a yard.

Taking to the "bush" (*lum*), the LRA carried on a war that has lasted more than thirty years.[14] In the early 1990s, Museveni launched military operations like Operation North against the rebels and began to organize extra-military community defense groups like the Arrow Brigades. The rebels became largely alienated from civilian peasants, whom they began to persecute and punish by mutilation and killing when and as they collaborated with or informed the government of their whereabouts, movements, weapon stores, and other strategic information. Peace talks in 1994 failed, and by the mid-1990s the LRA insurgency had become part of a proxy war between Uganda and Sudan. The Sudanese government, led by President Omar al-Bashir, supported the LRA with supplies and safe haven in response to Museveni's support for the Sudanese People's Liberation Army (SPLA). Continuing efforts to negotiate peace failed.

By the late 1990s, the Ugandan government began forcing civilians into internment camps or concentration camps—what they called "protected villages," even though they were hardly protected except by poorly armed and community-organized Local Defense Units (LDUs)—for "internally displaced persons," a poignantly apolitical term (see Branch 2011, 99–100). Camps were ostensibly meant to provide civilians with "safety" from rebel attacks, but were more widely understood as a strategic move to cut off rebels from resources.[15] Humanitarian organizations like World Food Programme (WFP) became complicit in this form of state structural violence. Such was the violence of this displacement that it was labeled by Ugandan politician Olara Otunnu (2005) as an attempt at genocide. Mortality levels in camps reached one thousand per week,[16] and people were largely denied access to their fields and homesteads, ruining livelihoods for years to come. Trawling through numbers documenting causes of death during the war, it struck me that while almost all accounts of the war were concerned with the spectacular violence of the LRA rebels—abduction of children, mutilation of body parts, "sex slavery," and so forth—the structural violence of the primary humanitarian-government apparatus, the so-called internally displaced persons camps, had inflicted deaths that, the numbers showed, far exceeded those caused by rebel violence.[17] In the words of a respected historian of Acholi, Ronald Atkinson, "The structural violence of camp life produced a far greater number of deaths than those caused by the LRA, just more quietly and unobtrusively" (2010a, 305). As important voices[18] critiqued government and humanitarian actors alike for participating in a form of what Chris Dolan (2009) termed "social torture," I wondered how and why the violence of the LRA had garnered more attention than that of the camps. In total about a million people lived in the internment camps, including most of the Acholi people (Branch 2011, 92). Many suspected the government of trying to grab Acholi land by displacing the people off of it (see Finnström 2008, 178–80). Indeed, during my own fieldwork, in a time when camps had closed, conflict over land had become an extremely important and sensitive issue.[19]

In 2000, the Amnesty Act was introduced as a way of encouraging defection by introducing blanket amnesty for all rebels fighting the Government of Uganda (GoU), including LRA rebels. By 2001, and after the attacks of September 11, the LRA found itself on the US Patriot Act's "Terrorist Exclusion List," blacklisted together with other "terrorist" groups like al-Qa'ida, Hamas, the Revolutionary Armed Forces of Colombia (FARC), the Revolutionary United Front (RUF), and the Shining Path (Sendero Luminoso).[20] In 2002 the Ugandan government negotiated with the Sudanese government to carry out Operation Iron Fist, destroying LRA bases in Sudan and forcing the LRA south and east into parts of Lango and Teso. In 2003, President Museveni referred the rebellion to the ICC, which in 2005 issued arrest warrants for LRA commanders Joseph Kony, Vincent Otti, Dominic Ongwen, Okot Odhiambo, and Raska Lukwiya on charges of crimes against humanity and war crimes.[21] Around 2005, the LRA began moving from southern Sudan into the Democratic Republic of the Congo (DRC), where they established bases at Garamba National Park (see Atkinson 2010b, 207). The last major LRA military operations in Uganda took place in 2004 (Allen and Vlassenroot 2010, 15).

Further peace negotiations took place in Juba from 2006 to 2008, but failed, and in December 2008 the Ugandan army, the UPDF, began Operation Lightning Thunder, bombing LRA camps in Garamba. From 2009 to 2015, the LRA split into several groups communicating primarily in person via messengers, across the Central African Republic (CAR), Sudan, South Sudan, and the DRC. In large part due to pressure exerted by various lobbying nongovernmental organizations, including Invisible Children, the Enough Project, and The Resolve, US President Barack Obama in 2010 signed the Lord's Resistance Army Disarmament and Northern Uganda Recovery Act, which provided military, financial, and logistical support for anti-LRA operations, including about one hundred troops sent to act as "advisors" in 2011.[22] NGO field intelligence analysts with privileged access to military and other informants estimate that the LRA in the early 2010s consisted of about 250 core fighters, having grown weaker over the previous six to seven years.[23] Reports on Kony's whereabouts suggested that he and his particular group of LRA fighters were periodically sheltered by Sudanese Armed Forces in the contested Kafia Kingi territory enclosed by South Sudan, Sudan, and the CAR, as recently as early 2013.[24]

As my former LRA rebel friends believe and convinced me, it is unlikely that the LRA will be eliminated anytime soon, whether or not the spirits are still speaking to or through Kony. Invisible Children's "Kony 2012" campaign failed in its goal to have Kony arrested. Shortly after the launch of "Kony 2012," its director, Jason Russell, was detained in San Diego for allegedly masturbating while naked on a public street and vandalizing cars before being hospitalized and diagnosed with "brief reactive psychosis." One rebel friend, together with whom I watched the "Kony 2012" viral video with Acholi subtitles, was convinced that Kony's spirits had something to do with Russell's breakdown. Most were confident that the LRA would outlast the US "advisors" and indeed all other forces conspiring against the LRA. Their predictions came at least partly true as, on December 15, 2014, Invisible Children announced that it would be shutting down in 2015, an announcement that came less than two years after its unsuccessful campaign to arrest Kony. "I know he might continue to fight for thirty years, even one hundred years maybe," one ex-rebel friend told me when I last saw him in July 2013.

I once asked Labwor how he wanted the LRA to be remembered in one hundred years, after we all have died. He instructed me to share this history:

> Write that when the LRA started as rebels [*adwii*], it was because of the disturbances that Museveni brought to people. Because government soldiers were defecating in cattle's mouths and in flour, sodomizing men, sleeping with women [rape], and were also using smoke to suffocate people in their huts. Because of this, the LRA went to the *lum* to fight. Kony was just a student at that time, and seeing all these bad things, he started fighting. He became a rebel leader of the LRA because he wanted to bring change and good leadership to Uganda. He was dedicated such that even if he were to be eaten up by guns [killed in action], he wouldn't mind it, as long as good leadership were to come. Fighting took many years—more than twenty now—and it's still going on. At some point, the government of Uganda solicited support from other countries to have a joint operation against Kony. But they failed to defeat Kony. This is something important that people should know. Even the ones born in the future will read it and know it.

The Inhumanity of the Lord's Resistance Army

Globally, within Uganda, and to a large extent within Acholiland, the LRA became known as an inhumane force operating against or outside the human. Upon signing into American law an anti-LRA bill in 2010, then-President Barack Obama reproduced a widely held global humanitarian and scholarly discourse about the LRA:

> The Lord's Resistance Army preys on civilians—killing, raping, and mutilating the people of central Africa; stealing and brutalizing their children; and displacing hundreds of thousands of people. Its leadership, indicted by the International Criminal Court for crimes against humanity, has no agenda

and no purpose other than its own survival. It fills its ranks of fighters with the young boys and girls it abducts. By any measure, its actions are an affront to human dignity. (Obama 2010)

In this narrative, the LRA committed inhuman(e) violence, killing and mutilating government collaborators and disobedient rebels, including with "primitive" weapons such as logs and axes, beating and hacking them to death. They operated in the *lum*, a dangerous space of nearly impenetrable vegetation filled with deadly animals and spirits. They fought "without a clearly articulated political agenda—or at least a very strange one," following the seemingly whimsical commands of spirits (Allen and Vlassenroot 2010, 11). When rebels defected or were captured ("rescued") by the UPDF, they needed to be "reintegrated" into a peaceful civil society, transformed from brutal killers into useful, productive citizens. Among the obstacles they were said to face in this "reintegration" included the problems of having been "sex slaves," having been victims of "rape," and/or returning with "unwanted" children from "forced marriages" in the *lum*. They were seen sometimes as perpetrators deserving of scorn and punishment; sometimes as victims deserving of charity and sympathy; and sometimes as both.

This was not merely a discourse circulating among international heads of state, humanitarian NGOs, or moralizing liberal scholars. It was also one commonly heard within Uganda, particularly outside of Acholiland. President Museveni and his National Resistance Movement (NRM) government often played up this image of the LRA as barbaric animals as part of what Sverker Finnström refers to as the "official discourse" of the war (2008, 100). Museveni has, over the years, called the LRA "terrorists" and "hyenas," using rhetoric that allowed him to collect foreign aid to fight the LRA and to enjoy relative impunity for his own crimes and those of his army and government.[25] This discourse was not used only by the Ugandan government. Acholi working and living in the capital Kampala routinely complained of being stigmatized and abused with the epithet "Kony" by Ugandans of other ethnicities, especially the Baganda. National papers—based in the south—often depict and speak of Kony as a primitive and violent animal living in the "bush."

Perhaps more surprisingly, Kony and the LRA had in many ways been expelled from humanity even by their Acholi kinsmen. Absorbing colonial discourses about humanity and anxious about prospects for modernity and development, many Acholi—including former rebels themselves—contested the humanity of the LRA through different avenues, including in imaginaries about the *lum* in which the LRA lived and in comparisons between LRA and state violence.

In both "local" and "global" imaginaries and discourses, the LRA has become the proverbial "heart of darkness," a violent specter against which certain notions of humanity and the good are constructed. Operating in the wild "bush," carrying out "brutal" killings, abducting and forcefully conscripting children—all without a clearly discernible "reason"—the LRA appear to most as inhuman monsters carrying out horrific and irrational violence. But if these notions contradict actually existing rebel cosmologies and experiences, what does one do with "humanity" in the shadows of their "inhuman" lives, experiences, and ideas?

This question has consistently posed a problem for scholars of and within northern Uganda. In struggling to deal with it, they have revitalized discussions of humanity and personhood. Many adhere to narratives in which the LRA have become inhuman or commit inhuman acts. Heike Behrend writes that the LRA "accelerated the process of dehumanization and despair they claimed to be protesting against" (1999, 189). Tim Allen (2006) has been outspoken in his support for the ICC and its indictments of LRA leaders on charges of "crimes against humanity." Indeed, he and Koen Vlassenroot have written about the possible killing of Kony by Ugandan forces as a hypothetical "lucky break," and have described the LRA as committing "horrific violence" and possessing a "weird spirituality" (2010, 12, 20).

Others are more critical when it comes to the (in)humanity of the LRA. Chris Dolan condemns the dehumanization of the LRA within a context of historical racism and ethnocentrism against the Acholi (2009, 202). Adam Branch attempts to explain how and why Westerners come to identify the suffering of Africans as the suffering of humanity, and then come to act based on the ethical demand of "humanity" (2011, 4–7). Sverker Finnström (2008, 225) refers to J.P. Odoch Pido's (2000) discussion of Acholi humanity and personhood in trying to understand the cultural context of when "child rebels" can be held as perpetrators morally responsible for their acts, rather than victims of abduction. Opiyo Oloya discusses how what he calls "child-inducted soldiers" tried to "free their humanness" by asserting themselves as human beings (*dano adana*), which he defines as the "Acholi cultural notion . . . universally recognized by all cultures as the 'human person,'" and which he compares to *ubuntu*, which "in the Xhosa and Zulu cultures of South Africa . . . describes the essence of humanness" (2013, 17, 21). Erin Baines cites Oloya and also draws a comparison between *dano adana* and *ubuntu*, using the concept as a humanist argument to complicate the "reprehensible" idea that formerly abducted men and women should be as responsible as orchestrators of the rebellion for the violence that was perpetrated by the rebels during the course of the war (2011, 490–91). In different ways, these and other scholars all attempt to push back against the manner by which the LRA have been expelled from "humanity," some through an explicitly humanist move that attempts to bring rebels back into the "human" as *dano adana*.

I do not share in discourses whereby the LRA are made part of or said to commit acts of inhumanity. But nor am I trying to "humanize" or "re-humanize" the LRA, to try to argue—as Finnström, Oloya, Joseph Kony, my rebel friends, and others do—that "terrorists" are also "human beings."[26] Instead of reclaiming the humanity of rebels, the chapters that follow expose some of the limits and instabilities of the concept of humanity, namely, dictating in moral terms how a life should be lived in ways that: claim universality; present as a science instead of an ideology; and dismiss the rich meaning of lives actually lived.

I am not suggesting that there is no cultural concept of personhood or "humanity" among Acholi. Nor am I arguing that rebels did not attempt to assert themselves as human beings in ways that resisted their expulsion. Rather, I aim to show that the intersection between these discourses and those of Western (in)humanity are constructed morally and in encounter—and thus by no means natural, universal, or stable. That is to say, they are discourses of humanity that are repurposed or reinvented to enter a discursive space to meet the shadowy demands of different discourses (colonial, modern, humanitarian, and so forth) originating in the West, including moral claims on technology, rationality, freedom, and so forth. Much like the concept of *ubuntu*, which Achille Mbembe (2011) suggests was invented to meet the demands of liberal discourses of humanity circulating internationally, *dano adana* or other concepts of

Acholi humanity are, I suggest, being mobilized to respond to specific demands that the discourse of humanity puts on them—a discourse that has, since at least the time of European colonization and Christian missionary attempts to make Men out of beasts, demanded a response in its own image.

I do not think it is worth engaging this demand of humanity. Rather than humanizing the LRA as a response to the friction between the LRA and humanity, I question the criteria of humanity itself. In this reversal of most scholarly approaches, I ask not how or why the LRA were or were not part of humanity, but—through a critical investigation of its defining criteria—why humanity would exclude the LRA. Instead of squeezing or reforming the lives, experiences, and narratives of my LRA friends into the normative framework of the human, I treat rebel lives as the norm and ask what can be learned from them. As the subtitle of this work suggests, there are important lessons that the LRA offers that might push us to reform or abandon inadequate concepts of humanity.

To be able to open this space, I positioned myself squarely on the side of LRA combatants. I refused to obscure my political sympathies or the way in which my knowledge was particularly situated. I wanted the rebels to be the revolutionaries they saw themselves to be, to overcome the injustice and poverty that faced them and the Acholi people—even though their mission had seemingly gone quite awry so far. This ethical stance allowed me to carefully hear complex stories and narratives that escape most humanitarian and scholarly accounts of the LRA. Many of these accounts start from a space of horror and/or pity at the Other's suffering and thus tend to focus on the tragedy of children becoming soldiers. My account starts from a space of empathy at the Other's attempts to challenge existing structures of power; thus, it tends to focus on the disjunctures between their worldviews and the ideological apparatuses of power that try to deny them. It provides a grounded, qualitative, and in-depth ethnography of insurgency not often found in political-scientific studies of civil war and rebellion.

Some readers may mistake this openness as an attempt to defend or apologize for the LRA, or to minimize the forms of physical and structural violence that they committed and suffered. I am often asked by critics engaging my work, "Where is the blood? Where is the violence? Where is the suffering?" I do not deny that suffering, pain, and deaths did take place. Indeed, my rebel friends and I lament them because they often detracted from other narratives of the LRA, bringing disrepute upon the rebels and their forms of being in the world, and often discouraging rebels who otherwise wanted to continue the struggle. I discuss LRA violence in some complexity in chapter 2. But I choose not to add to moral voices condemning or judging the LRA.[27] Instead, my purpose is anthropological: to show the damage done by crude presentations of the LRA through the discourse of humanity. I aim to offer accounts of the political lives of soldiers during and after the war—what they were fighting for, how they understand their lives today, and how they were harmed or misrepresented by human rights and humanitarian discourses.

SOME NOTES ON METHOD

The ethnographic material upon which this work draws stems primarily from thirteen uninterrupted months of research undertaken in and around Acholiland in northern Uganda, from July 2012 to August 2013, following a shorter spell of research from June to August 2009. I spent most of this time learning from networks of former LRA rebels who knew one another during their time fighting.

I started meeting former rebels through friends and family of theirs, creating several of what statisticians might call "snowball samples." Over time, these networks grew as they introduced me to other former rebels— their friends, their wives, their husbands, their children, their brothers, their sisters. The men and women they loved. The children they birthed and raised. The comrades they fought with together, side by side. In total, I met about sixty former rebels who became my teachers, and learned a great deal about many others who were killed in action or who were still fighting with the LRA. They included men and women who had spent varying amounts of time as or with the rebels, ranging from a few days to more than two decades, and with varying ranks, ranging from no rank up to high-ranking commanders. Not all of them appear in this book, which focuses primarily on a network of rebels who spent substantial amounts of time in the *lum*—roughly five or more years—but they all instilled different values and lessons in me through their stories, lives, and experiences. I chose to tell the stories of those who spent substantial time as LRA rebels because I found that more often than not it affected their memories, friendships, and present-day lives in more profound ways, not least of which included having rebel spouses and/or children born within the LRA. Taken together as a group, these rebels had participated in almost all phases of the war, including from the beginning and up until the present. Not all former rebels personally struggle with or engage in the questions I explore, but they are questions that almost all of them understand or relate to in different ways from their time in the *lum*, no matter how short or long.

While these rebels were often quite close together while fighting in the *lum*—spatially and spiritually—they scattered to different places after leaving the front lines of war. Many ended up in Gulu town, the largest urban settlement in Acholiland and where I permanently lived during the course of my work. Others returned to rural village lands or smaller towns and trading centers around the region, where I consistently visited them. In focusing on a group of friends and family rather than a specific site, my research became spatially wide, taking me through all seven districts of Ugandan Acholiland—Agago, Amuru, Gulu, Kitgum, Lamwo, Nwoya, and Pader.[28] As I was often interested in the past experiences and memories of my friends, much of the day-to-day ethnographic work consisted of long and usually private chats in my friends' homes. But it often involved participating in their day-to-day lives: hanging out with them at work—be it a restaurant where they served tables or a small shop from which they tailored; working on rural fields—digging, weeding, and harvesting; building huts; attending funerals and weddings; going to clinics for medical treatment; going to church; playing and watching football; sitting around drinking cassava gin and sorghum beer; watching movies; chatting around the fire at night (*wang oo*).[29]

In the course of everyday life, I also spent time talking with and learning from other people important to the lives of my friends—their civilian friends, families, employers, pastors, local government leaders, elders, and clinicians, among others. Through them, I made my way into new spaces, including rehabilitation centers, clinics, and churches. I made a point of visiting sites important to the LRA, including Awere Hill (Got Awere) in

Odek, where Joseph Kony grew up and first began to preach; grounds where battles and other military actions had taken place; sites of former LRA sick bays; as well as a concealed hill from which the LRA collected sacred soil known as "camouflage." I unfailingly read the two most prominent Ugandan daily newspapers, the *Daily Monitor* and *New Vision*, together with a popular weekly Luo-language paper, *Rupiny*.[30] I often listened to local radio, with particular attention to the weekly broadcasts of the Mega FM show *Dwog Cen Paco* (Come Back Home), aimed primarily at LRA soldiers with the purpose of encouraging them to defect.

My command of the Acholi language reached a level that allowed me to share in everyday conversations with my friends, although longer, complex stories and narratives often eluded me. For this reason, I worked together with a research assistant, Jimmy Odong, with whom I traveled and worked to ensure accurate transcripts and translations of the stories and conversations that appear in this book. Throughout the text, I offer readers the original Acholi of my English translations when translations are difficult, inexact, and/or when the syntax is important. At times, I use only the Acholi when I find that the concept or phrase is too difficult, for historical, political, and cultural reasons, to be translated into English. The glossary serves as a reference for unfamiliar Acholi terms that may come up in the text. I follow a conventional Acholi orthography, though at times I revert to the more phonetic of multiple possible spellings.[31] Responsibility for the precision and accuracy of the Acholi-to-English translations remains mine alone.

My real and perceived positionalities or subjectivities sometimes posed deep challenges to this work. I was often told that my questions were "deadly" to the Ugandan government and that I could be arrested as a rebel collaborator; accordingly, I took caution in choosing what I would talk about, with whom, and in what location. As a South Asian American, military-age man getting to know former LRA rebels, I initially encountered different forms of resistance and suspicion. At various points, I was accused of being an intelligence officer or spy for the United Nations Security Council or for the American government, both of which have opposed the LRA through indictments, arrest warrants, and/or military and financial support for anti-LRA activities.[32] Other times I was mistaken for a Ugandan Asian businessman looking to buy (or grab) land or sell motorcycles.[33] More commonly, in the aftermath of an enormous if fragmented humanitarian response, it was assumed that I was operating some kind of aid project that would provide money, jobs, and/or goods to beneficiaries. These impressions often wore off in time as my friends and others got to know me and what I was up to.

Time posed a different problem. This work remains limited by the present historical conjuncture or epoch—namely, one in which the war is ongoing. Because of this, certain truths or experiences could not be spoken; others have not yet happened. In my work, I attempted to stay close to what could be said and spoken of openly in this moment. Future work, perhaps when the war has come to some kind of resolution, may explore other important questions—including the positionality of former rebels now serving in the UPDF, a matter in which I was greatly interested but had difficulty exploring in depth.

It perhaps would have been easy to talk to former rebels by approaching NGOs that employed or benefited them. But I did not want to begin my work from or through an institution. In focusing primarily on the everyday lives, both past and present, of LRA rebels, I explicitly sought to deinstitutionalize my ethnographic work. Rather than working primarily within an institution or from inside a specific site, such as a hospital, clinic, or NGO—as Paul Farmer (1992), Vinh-Kim Nguyen (2010), Julie Livingston (2012), Peter Redfield (2013), and other medical anthropologists have recently done—I decided to center my work on different networks of former rebels. This was in part because I was already familiar with the kinds of discourses and practices at work within these types of institutions. But it was largely because I was interested in how former rebels negotiated, navigated, and understood these discourses as they lived their lives beyond the walls of such institutions. In this way, my work was a different form of "studying up,"[34] one that sought to understand not the inner workings of a controlling process or discourse, but rather how people experienced meaning under this kind of discourse—sometimes as resistance, sometimes as compliance, sometimes as obliviousness. Too often, I felt, did studies of such discourses end up reproducing their power by overstating their importance in the everyday lives of ordinary people. Following Harri Englund (2006), I tried to understand how LRA rebels lived amid these discourses. Their narratives and experiences not only deconstruct but also disempower the concept of humanity.

The ethnographic material was accompanied by archival work in both Uganda and England. Archival work in Uganda included study at the Makerere University Library (Kampala); the Uganda Society Library (housed in the Uganda Museum, Kampala); the United Nations High Commissioner for Refugees (UNHCR) Resource Center (Gulu); the Institute for Peace and Strategies Studies (IPSS) Library of Gulu University (Gulu); the Gulu Support the Children Organisation (GUSCO) archives (Gulu); the World Vision Children of War Rehabilitation Center archives (Gulu); the Human Rights Focus (HURIFO) library (Gulu); the Catechist Training Centre (CTC) library (Gulu); and the Comboni Spiritual Centre Layibi library and archives (Gulu). Additional archival work was undertaken in England from June to July 2014, studying documents and records pertaining to British colonial rule and missionary activities in Acholiland, within the Uganda Protectorate, and in other parts of east Africa. These archives included the Church Missionary Society (CMS) archive held at the Special Collections of the Cadbury Research Library, University of Birmingham (Birmingham); the Royal Commonwealth Society archive and other collections at the Manuscripts Department of Cambridge University Library (Cambridge); the Bodleian Library of Commonwealth and African Studies at Rhodes House, University of Oxford (Oxford); the Imperial War Museum Library (London); and the Manuscripts Collection at the British Library (London).

ORGANIZATION OF THE BOOK

A Note on Pictures and Anonymity

The pictures I decided to include on my own accord are sometimes of places or objects or activities that help the reader envision a situation in ways supplemental to words. Many are photos that I solicited as a practice of democratic ethnography. Near the end of my longer spell of fieldwork, I explicitly asked my friends if they wanted me to include photos they had or to take photos that they wanted me to include in the text. I collected many of these, together with the captions they wanted me to include, and have tried to insert as many relevant photos as possible. Uncertain of how the text may be used, and unwilling to risk my friends' safety, I have not included many pictures of people, despite their wishes to have them inserted.

Given that the war is ongoing at the time of this writing and that the Ugandan government could yet retaliate against former rebels, the names that appear in the coming chapters are pseudonyms. Almost all of my friends asked for anonymity and chose their own pseudonyms; only when my friends had no preference for what name was used did I provide one of my own making.

On the Character List

Unconventionally for an ethnographic text, I offer a list of characters at the beginning of the text as a reference. I include it primarily for reading convenience. The text may be read selectively rather than from cover to cover, and for those reading in this fashion, the list can be helpful to characterize unfamiliar people. This list should not be read as a way of fictionalizing, simplifying, fetishizing, or in any other way reducing or misrepresenting the people therein. Instead my attempt is to create a kind of accessible nonfiction that can be read by both specialists and non-specialists.

It may seem paradoxical that a book "against humanity" should focus on people. This is not a mistake or a thoughtless deferral to a traditional ethnographic method. Rather, it is a way of demonstrating through concrete stories, narratives, and experiences of people the ways in which humanity limits, imposes, mischaracterizes, moralizes, and/or fixes the meaning and values of people's lives. In practice, this "people-centered" approach is designed precisely to displace Man in the process of its movement.

Chapter Organization

In order to illustrate the problems posed by humanity, I deliberately organize each chapter around a particular criterion that has historically, philosophically, or otherwise been thought to constitute the idea of the human or humanity. The chapters are thus structured by the constraints of some existing notions of humanity, and struggle against them through ethnographic evidence. Each chapter embodies a particular dialectical conflict through which humanity is constructed and deconstructed, reproduced and negated against its others.

Rather than building a linear argument through the chapters, I posit them as stand-alone illustrations of my thesis against humanity, offering complex narratives of the instabilities and liminalities of life in times of unusual violence. For the reader's convenience, I often drop the ersatz quotes around "humanity" in the chapters that follow. However, it should be clear that "humanity" is a concept that is relentlessly contested throughout the text, without any guaranteed meaning, significance, or, indeed, value.

Chapters 2, 3, and 4 focus on rebels' wartime experiences, present-day memories of those experiences, and the transformative qualities of those experiences and memories. While memories and experiences of rebellion are also important to chapters 5 and 6, these later chapters are more attentive to the aftermath of the war, and in particular aspects of rebel lives and beliefs upon their return "home"[35] from the "bush."[36] This structure allows me to give a certain chronology to the story, one that appears to offer a transition break from violence to peace. The illusion of this break is destroyed when the return "home," rather than being a time of joy, belonging, and normalcy as is often imagined, is shown to be as or even more destabilizing and uncertain as the abduction to the "bush"—a reality that troubles the presumed opposition between violence and humanity. This destruction is highlighted in the interlude between chapters 4 and 5, which deconstructs and critiques "reintegration," the process by which returning rebels are presumed to be transformed from violent, lawbreaking, killer animals into peaceful, productive, citizen humans.

Chapter 2 explores how violence and humanity bifurcated into opposites in the course of the LRA war. This chapter investigates how it came to be that LRA violence was labeled as "dehumanizing" rather than "humanizing." It shows how the erasure of other moral frameworks by which to understand LRA violence led to its characterization as "against humanity" and thereby ignored the complexity and meaning of that violence. It offers alternative ways of understanding violence through ethnographic and historical evidence, drawing on narratives of colonial violence, mob justice, "traditional" violence, and LRA violence. It excavates ways of seeing and understanding violence outside the shadow of modern moral sensibility that split violence and humanity. It also explores the contours of this modern moral sensibility and the ways in which LRA violence was seen to violate it. Many of these violations disrupted modern expectations of the relationships that technology, reason, time, and development should have with violence. These violations were not felt merely by Western aid workers or scholars, but also by rebels and Acholi civilians as part of postcolonial wrenchings toward and anxieties about "reaching" modernity. As a result, the complexity and productivity of LRA violence was elided. It was not only condemned, but also seen to oppose modernity and humanity.

Chapter 3 investigates the ways in which humanity was constructed against animality through the space of the "bush" (*lum*). Whereas Acholi civilians and others saw the *lum* as a dangerous, evil space of animals, the rebels occupied the *lum* and came to endow it with very different meanings. In what became a contestation over what I refer to as an "anthropo-moral geography," the LRA collapsed an analytic separating animality and humanity, unsettling a spatio-moral definition of the human against animality. Rather than reinforcing a colonial-era notion of the *lum* that had been evoked through the course of the war, the LRA found the *lum* to be a site of life, sacredness, and development. In doing so, they dissolved some of the spatio-moral infrastructure of humanity itself.

Chapter 4 argues that the LRA transcended the question of rationality by binding together science and magic in their rebellion. Moving past a scholarly debate that either condemns LRA beliefs and actions as "irrational" (and therefore "barbaric" or otherwise inhuman) or attempts to explain them as "rational" (and therefore human), this chapter takes LRA beliefs and actions in their singularity in ways that expose the limits of "rationality" and "humanity" as concepts by which to understand them. Releasing "rationality" and "humanity" helps better conceptualize how the LRA held at once military and spiritual tactics; magical-prophetic and modern-scientific time; Christian and traditional Acholi religious practices; and spiritual and political reasons for fighting. By holding together logic and faith in this way, they transcended the category of "rationality" undergirding many concepts of humanity.

The interlude transitions away from the first part of the book, which explores the memories and experiences of rebels fighting in the war, including problems of violence, the *lum*, and beliefs/logics. It sets the stage for the second part of the book, which is more attentive to the lives of rebels who have returned from the front lines, including the problems of love, kinship, and politics that they encounter and negotiate in different ways. The interlude itself attends to the concept of "reintegration," whereby rebels leaving the front lines were to be reformed and readjusted to live peacefully among civilians. It highlights the ways in which civilians and NGO workers conceptualized rebels as animals needing to be humanized, and the ways in which rebels in turn resisted this disciplinary process. It shows that rebels did not want or need to have their heads "repaired," as was often assumed and said of them. Rather, it was civilians for whom the process of "reintegration" was ritually healing, allowing them the opportunity to heal their own sicknesses by projecting them onto rebels. Whereas the "reintegration" process offered rebels a chance at cleansing through the pure concept of humanity, I offer the interlude as a dirtying process of disintegration, rejecting with my friends the healing offered by humanity.

Chapters 5 and 6 are thus offered as dirtying experiences of healing from the injurious concept of humanity. Chapter 5 explores how new relations involving rebels were forged through rather than outside of or in the face of violence. These relations, which included marriages, brother- and sisterhoods, clans, and other forms of mutual belonging, challenged humanity as a form of kinship and as a sentimental community of humankind. Militant kinships drew boundaries between insiders and outsiders in a way that humanity cannot except by expelling other humans from humanity. Moreover, these kinships thrived with real meaning in the fertile ground of violence, even as they were condemned from the outside as forced, enslaved, or otherwise inhuman(e). Militant LRA kinships thus operated "against humanity" in the sense that humanity morally denied the meaning of these kinships and simultaneously drew boundaries of mutual belonging that excluded the LRA.

Chapter 6 engages recent anthropological debates that argue that categories like "victim" and "charity case" deny actors their political agency and reduce them to a form of bare life. By examining how LRA rebels remained political militants even as they accepted charity and humanitarian aid, this chapter shows how these anthropological debates ignore the complex ways in which rebels speak and act in the trenches of these kinds of discourses. Their experiences expose humanity as a concept historically constructed in the opposition of the "ethical" and the "political," a relationship that ultimately belongs to a particular experience of postmodernity. In the postcolony of Acholiland, "ethics" and "politics" had different meanings and could coexist. Rebels accordingly revealed humanity to be a premature fixer of political and ethical meaning, precluding dynamism and multiplicity of meaning in a global society in uncertain flux.

While there are indeed deeply meaningful forms of life that emerge in and often specifically because of violence, humanity does not help us understand these life-forms properly *analytically* because it tends to delimit norms that exclude these life-forms. Rather than approaching the LRA as a set of possibilities, humanity looks at the LRA as a set of problems, as a set of inhuman enemies needing reform. Humanity is evoked, in these cases, in ways that ask it to give meaning beyond, and indeed against, its scope of producing an ideological anthropo-morality that distinguishes between human good and inhuman evil. Humanity comes to represent the emotive force underlying the good–evil axes of humanity and its others (for instance violence, suffering, or animality).[37] What we risk in using humanity as this organizing concept is collapsing the science of medical anthropology (and indeed, social science at large) into a liberal, moral-affective framework—in other words, forsaking knowledge for emotion. Evocations of humanity ask us to abandon inquiry for an assumed shared feeling, a mutual understanding of the emotional imagery provoked by its name—a mutuality that may not be shared beyond a liberal humanist discourse.

In arguing that we should think beyond humanity, I speak not only to scholars in anthropology, political science, philosophy, and other disciplines, but also to liberal practitioners seeking a different world—NGO workers, activists, and clinicians, among others. The narratives and arguments presented in this book may help such readers recognize and rethink the ways in which humanity narrows the possibilities of what constitutes a moral life and thereby fixes the politics of liberal humanitarian interventions. Unanchored from the foundation of humanity, we might begin to formulate new ways of thinking and doing anthropology, medicine, activism, and intervention in ways that bring us closer to the common good. The concluding chapter explores anti-humanism as a possible vehicle by which to arrive at different and more radical forms of healing, including an anti-humanist medicine.

Thinking from the Demonic Ground of the Lum:
A Suggested Methodology for Reading

Following Laura Bohannan's (1966) reading of Shakespeare in the "bush," I invite readers to metaphorically imagine themselves in the *lum* with the rebels as they move through the chapters.[38] As explored in detail in chapter 3, the *lum* is the space that the rebels inhabit in the course of their war. One form of ethnographic reading is to enter into and think in the *lum*, as LRA rebels did. The chapters that follow accompany rebels in the *lum*, leave with them from the front lines, and then navigate life at "home." From the outside, the *lum* seems a "wild" space, feared for being violent, dangerous, and difficult to pass through. It evokes, even for Acholi civilians, the kind of "heart of darkness" to which Joseph Conrad refers. Yet I believe it is precisely the kind of "demonic ground" that Sylvia Wynter refers to in conceptualizing possible spaces from which to abolish the figure of Man.[39] Indeed, from within, the *lum* was not the evil, dark space of death that it appeared to be, especially when it was left behind by captured or defecting rebels. In fact, it was a space of life, in which rebels found love, made new families, and encountered the sacred. To think with rebels from the space of the *lum* is to be open to unexpected lessons from the LRA—lessons about forms of life existing beyond humanity.

2 How Violence Became Inhuman

THE MAKING OF MODERN MORAL SENSIBILITIES

We do not have a choice between purity and violence but
between different kinds of violence.

Maurice Merleau-Ponty, *Humanism and Terror*, 1969

Of the thirty-three counts facing Joseph Kony in the warrant of arrest issued in 2005 by the International Criminal Court (ICC), twelve were classified as "crimes against humanity."[1] The ICC described the LRA as

> directing attacks against both the UPDF [Uganda People's Defence Force] and LDUs [Local Defense Units] and against civilian populations; that, in pursuing its goals, the LRA has engaged in a cycle of violence and established a pattern of "brutalization of civilians" by acts including murder, abduction, sexual enslavement, mutilation, as well as mass burnings of houses and looting of camp settlements; that abducted civilians, including children, are said to have been forcibly "recruited" as fighters, porters and sex slaves to serve the LRA and to contribute to attacks against the Ugandan army and civilian communities. (International Criminal Court 2005, 3)

By abducting children to serve as soldiers, cutting off the body parts of their victims, and taking women as "sex slaves," among other acts, the LRA was seen through a modern discourse to act outside the moral limits of justifiable forms of violence. In doing so, they were said to have simultaneously attacked at its core a philosophical concept ("humanity") and removed themselves from its sphere of belonging.

Such characterizations became discursive truth about LRA violence, framed against "humanity," a modern, moral sensibility shaped by liberal thought, claiming universality, and cemented as what Hannah Arendt has called "inescapable fact" (1951, 298).[2] While this common sense circulated among controversial Western legal bodies like the ICC, as well as NGOs and most scholars,[3] many local civilians—themselves anxious about and expectant of modernity—also took on this modern discourse that pitted LRA violence against "humanity." Monsignor Matthew Odong of the Gulu Catholic Archdiocese said of continuing LRA violence in 2013, "Joseph Kony is our son from northern Uganda, but we condemn his barbaric acts against mankind" (Ojwee 2013). In a similar spirit, the Acholi and Lango Luo-language newspaper *Rupiny* exclaimed on June 5, 2013, in a summary of LRA violence: "People who work using the Holy Spirit—why do they kill people, cut people's body parts and commit 'terrorism,' all of which the creator refused!" (Ochola 2013, my translation). LRA violence was and remains widely understood in this framework—which circulates beyond its Western liberal roots—to be excessive, unusually brutal, and cruel: in a word, as the ICC puts it, "inhumane" (2005, 17).[4]

The experiences of my friend Otto speak to this conflict between a designation of certain forms of violence as opposed to humanity, and the lived experiences of those forms of violence. When I met Otto, he was nearly forty years of age and had spent more than two decades in the *lum* with the LRA. For many years he worked in the "yard," a sacred site within LRA camps that we will hear more about later. When I visited him in his rural village home, we sat inside his hut, the mud walls of which he eventually decorated by pasting old newspapers I brought for him from town. Lying on an old papyrus mat after working in his fields under the hot morning sun, he removed a gumboot from one leg while leaving the other—covering his prosthetic leg—on, casting the image of a small but intimidating man. Indeed, even after he lost his leg after stepping on a landmine in Sudan, Otto retained his reputation of being a feared fighter. "A rebel is a rebel [*Adwii dong adwii*]," he laughed, cursing the disability that limited the pace of his farm work, but remembering that he nevertheless moved very quickly in the *lum* on crutches. Otto still supported the LRA's fight, lamenting ceaseless corruption in President Yoweri Museveni's Uganda. He insisted that the LRA war was the only way out for a country that

Museveni had led for more than twenty-six years since his coup in 1986, and through many allegations of corruption and election fraud. Otto only regretted that he had become disabled and was unable to go back and fight, and had to live at home "like a woman."

He had had many wives in the *lum*, all of whom had left him. The eldest of his wives, Amony, whom he courted when they were both in the LRA, stayed with him briefly in Gulu after they were captured by the UPDF and brought back from the front lines. But Amony's family soon took her away and sent her together with their children to Western Europe, where she remarried and now lived. Though living on separate continents, Amony and Otto maintained a good relationship, calling each other on the phone every so often. Otto checked on his kids, who barely spoke any Acholi; Amony talked to Otto's mother and brothers, who all lined up excitedly in Otto's homestead to talk to her. Amony was not well liked by Otto's other wives, including Arac, who refused to stay with Otto when he returned home. Arac said he was too naive in listening only to the advice of Amony, who was harsh with the other women and got them punished for no reason. When he came back to Gulu from the LRA, and before returning to his village homestead, Otto worked for wages for several NGOs in town, many of which sought to dismantle the LRA, an agenda against Otto's wishes. While working in town, he stayed briefly with Labwor in a Gulu slum. Labwor and Otto were both low-ranking officers in the LRA. They often lived together in the *lum* and became good friends over their years as soldiers. Once, while Labwor had gone to look for food with a group of soldiers, he left his son Odong with Otto. While he was gone, the UPDF attacked their position. In the chaos of the battle, and in favor of caring for his own family first, Otto left Odong behind. Odong was never found again.

A discourse about the inhumanity of violence might simply mark Amony and Arac as "sex slaves," and Labwor and Otto as "abductees" or "captives." But the realities of their experiences and relationships, intricately constructed through affection and undercut by betrayal and jealousy, show an enormous complexity of life structured under violence but incomprehensible to notions of "brutality" or "inhumanity."

Often, this discourse offered little to make sense of multifaceted rebel experiences, doing violence to those experiences in the process of attempting to name them. Other times, it offered a language—such as "slavery"—

that matched the language used by rebels, but merely in form, not content. Otto, for example, was abducted as a child into the LRA. He self-identified as a slave (*guci*). Yet by this he did not refer to his experience of having been abducted and held captive by the rebels, as a hegemonic discourse might. Rather, he saw himself becoming a slave of God. "They are slaves—people who are enduring severe suffering [*Gin tye opii—jo ma tye ka deno can matek*]," he said of the LRA. But though they suffered in the *lum*, often without homes and food, walking thirty kilometers a day, and risking encounters with dangerous spirits (*jogi*) in the depths of forests, they were chosen by God to be His slaves and to undergo His tests. As the chosen people of God, these captives were, Otto and others often said, akin to the biblical Job, who kept praying to God even as his suffering deepened, before being healed and rewarded for his faith.

Reframing the question of "captivity" as a matter of God's will, Otto also questioned narratives that painted "captivity" as a time of total suffering. A Ugandan researcher for a well-respected NGO once told me that many ex-rebels began to "see and appreciate life after captivity" as a result of the "love, care, and guidance of NGOs" they received. Otto was not one of them. He did not see his removal from "captivity" as an entrance into a purer life-world. By contrast, returned to his village and digging in his gardens with a worn hoe, Otto was frustrated by the lack of wage labor available to him and fed up with government corruption. While grateful to have freedom over his daily life, he bemoaned the lack of unity or morality at home compared to the situation among LRA in the *lum*. Indeed, every day he wistfully remembered the *lum*, where he had spent almost half his life: "I can't forget about being in the *lum*. I sometimes think that if I weren't here at home, I'd be with the LRA in the Congo. But I think of it for a short time and get interrupted by other activities—gardening, burning charcoal, and so on. But when I sit freely, I think of it, on a daily basis."

In offering an emerging genealogy of a discourse, I question how and why "humanization" came to describe *less* physical forms of violence and "dehumanization" came to describe *more* physical forms of violence. In the specific case of LRA violence, how and why did physical spectacles of violence like mutilation, for example, come to be seen as a dehumanizing rather than a humanizing violence? In what follows, I make a historical and ethnographic case for how notions of modernity come with a discursive tyranny that sets violence against humanity, and inhumanity against morality. In the case of LRA violence, when certain visions of modernity went unfulfilled, violence became inhuman.

ACHOLI VIOLENCE IN THE COLONIAL IMAGINATION

To better grasp how certain forms of violence have become linked to inhumanity in northern Uganda, we must begin by examining early colonial encounters between Europeans and Acholi. British Church Missionary Society (CMS) and Italian Comboni missionaries, along with British colonial officials, left rich personal letters, memoirs, and reflections on their time in Acholiland, including thoughts about the "nature of the people" and their practices of violence. Drawing on archival records and other historical sources, I analyze significant examples of violence that occurred during the colonial period to show how their specific meanings and ethics—including as forms of anticolonial resistance, clan feuds, and claims to privilege—were selectively read and reinterpreted by colonial officials and missionaries. In these historical rereadings, that violence was recast as immoral and against humanity. I argue that such rereadings were only made possible when these violent events were seen through the troubling prism of modernity. The colonial period in Acholiland did much to cement modern judgments on forms of violence that had other, often forgotten or ignored meanings, producing a certain flavor of immoral violence.

I am not arguing that violence was endemic to Acholiland, nor am I suggesting that the Acholi were or became "inured" to violence. Nor am I showing that the Acholi lacked moral frameworks by which to differentiate ethical and unethical violence, or that these frameworks were entirely alien or relativistic to other moral codes. Rather, I show how violence committed by Acholi people for various reasons and with different moral frameworks came to be seen more or less uniformly as immoral and against "humanity." I attempt to excavate ways of seeing and understanding violence outside the shadow of modernity.

The British colonial governing apparatus encountered the northern part of the Uganda Protectorate not as an opportunity to exploit, but as a troubling problem.[5] The colonial government found its seat in the south of the country, in Buganda (the land of the Baganda, a single tribe for whom all of the nation-state has come to be named). For colonial administrators in the south, the relatively unknown northern part of the country was uneasy to manage and make useful. In his 1906 commissioner's report, Hesketh Bell spoke directly to the question of the supervision and place of the northern province within the protectorate, inclusive of stations at Nimule (present-day border town between Uganda and South Sudan), Wadelai (village on the Nile banks in West Nile), and Gondokoro (in present-day South Sudan). "The cost of the administration of this Province has been a heavy drain on the resources of the Protectorate while the results have been insignificant and disappointing," he lamented. Part of the problem was that the British found northerners, including the Acholi, to be unwilling to labor or produce for export.[6] "The natives carry on no industry of any kind, and simply grow enough millet and other grain or vegetables for their own support," Bell continued (Bell 1906a, 2, 4; see also Moyse-Bartlett 1956). Some officials suggested that the colonial administration should penetrate the region through taxes, support of existing chiefs, and the military force of the King's African Rifles (KAR), and create a civil headquarters at Patiko (in Acholiland, just north of Gulu town) with the intention of "bringing the Nilotic peoples under our rule" (Bell 1906a, 6). Bell offered deep skepticism toward this plan. Having traveled through the region himself, he found there to be little chance of its development without impractical costs for the administration. He encountered natives in the "most primitive condition" and "unwilling to submit to domination by chiefs"; poor soil; risk of disease; and poor roads—a general situation in which administrative costs outweighed the financial benefits of administrative development, and could only be undertaken as, Bell saw it, "purely a humanitarian work" (1906a, 9).[7] More so than other peoples of the Protectorate (for instance the Baganda and the Banyoro, whom Bell favorably names as being organized in chiefdoms and engaging in industry), the northern peoples were seen as savage, wild, and backward. Their humanity came into question because of the way in which modern eyes saw them not only as belonging to an older stage of society, but also as less than legible to colonial administrative apparatuses attempting to rule and extract capital. Noting their "absence of costume" and their inability to produce a surplus, Bell nonetheless offered that "after a more or less painful process of being tamed, [they] might ultimately be turned into a decent and law abiding peasantry" (1906a, 9).

Observations of natives by colonial officers and missionaries sometimes questioned whether or not the Acholi and other neighboring tribes belonged to humanity in the first place. Watching her reverend husband preach to a "dusky, dark crowd" of Langi, tribal neighbors of the Acholi, Ruth Fisher reflected that there was "hardly a ray of intelligence or *humanity* on their faces as they turned toward the figure on the ant-hill" (1914, 91, emphasis added). Many early colonial-era Europeans in the Protectorate, including trader Frederick Banks (1896–1905), referred to Nilotics not through a discourse of "humanity"; instead, they spoke of natives, savages, primitives, devils, children, tribes, and people. When "humanity" was mentioned, the Acholi were included as part of humanity, but only where "humanity" was a spectrum on which there existed "finer" and "lower" "specimens." This spectrum was divided into what Bishop of the Upper Nile Arthur Kitching called "two great blocks of humanity"—one, the Western "ruling races" of "exploiting progressive peoples," and the other, the "backward," "exploited," and "inferior races" (1928, 6). The "inferior races" included Congolese Pygmies, described by Bell as "one of the most primitive types of humanity,"[8] and Arab slave raiders, described by Military Administrator of Uganda Frederick Lugard as "that scum of all humanity" (1892, 835).

While placed into the "backward" block, the Acholi sometimes fit the role of the "noble savage." Big-game hunter Quentin Grogan described the Acholi as seeming "more intelligent and [as having] a more prepossessing appearance than the *miserable specimens of humanity* on the Nile banks."[9] Violence was one parameter that, when applied to the spectrum of humanity, structured it according to different moral qualities. Forms of violence came to define, in colonial eyes, whether or where a people might sit on the spectrum. As one example, Bell described the experience of a British sub-commissioner at Nimule who received the complaint of an Acholi man who came to him in an "almost complete state of nudity."[10] The man, a petty chief, complained that a rival had attacked his village, killing several men, stealing cattle, and taking three wives. The sub-commissioner, Bell reported, was unable (and perhaps unwilling) to act, since the chief's village lay outside his geographic jurisdiction, and advised the chief to attempt to regain his women and cattle himself. Three weeks later, the chief returned to the sub-commissioner and presented him with the dismembered hands of his killed enemy, which Bell described as the "horrid extremities." The sub-commissioner, "in spite of his long African experience," was "rather disgusted" and refused to accept the "beastly things," which the chief later deposited anyway on his porch. Bell reflected, both on the Acholi chief and on similar incidents in the Belgian Congo: "The cutting off of hands is a common form of punishment among all these primitive people and, while such a penalty horrifies us it has no such effect on the natives."[11] Those belonging to the higher "block" of "humanity," colonial Europeans, were separated from the lower "block" by moral outrage at certain forms and techniques of violence.

It was not that such forms of violence were inherently immoral, horrific, or against humanity; it was only through colonial eyes that they became so. Importantly, such eyes were selective. The violence committed by colonial officers themselves was not always seen as immoral, horrific, or against humanity. These forms of violence included the whipping of servants (Bell 1906b, 81) and tax debtors (Banks 1900, 54) with raw hippo hides; flogging subjects to elicit intelligence information (District Commissioner's Office Gulu 1913–14, 9); taking people and livestock captive (Delmé-Radcliffe 1901); and of course killing mutineers and others opposed to colonial projects (Delmé-Radcliffe 1901). Where this violence, committed against primitive resisters, was performed to meet colonial objectives, it was neither immoral nor against "humanity."

Yet the violence committed by those whose very "humanity" was in question, and who were proving troublesome to colonial governance, was often imagined as both immoral and against humanity, even where other imaginaries of that violence existed. One such example was the representation of the Lamogi Rebellion of 1911–12. At the time of my work in Acholiland, popular stories of the rebellion told of the Lamogi, a clan of people in West Acholi,[12] who fought with bows and arrows from the caves of Guruguru against the guns of the British. The people of Lamogi were seen, in the eyes of other West Acholi, to be backward.[13] "The people of Lamogi eat bats [*Lamogi mwodo olik*]," it was disapprovingly said, and a ridiculing story circulated of how the people of Amuru (the area of Acholi in which Lamogi traditionally reside) once attempted to hunt down the locomotive train that passed from Mombasa to Pakwach using nets and spears, thinking it a big animal. Labwor told me a narrative of the rebellion in which he claimed that the Lamogi people refused the development that the white people (*muni*) proposed to bring to them, in the form of roads and clinics, fighting as people who commit chaotic violence (*lutim aranyi*; today often translated as and for "terrorist") against "good things." Acholi peasants, it seemed, had internalized colonial styles of reading violence in modern terms.

By all scholarly accounts, the Lamogi Rebellion was an act of resistance to British disarmament of the Acholi (Adimola 1954; Girling 1960; Dwyer 1972). As a way of establishing their governance and of complying with the Brussels Act of 1890, the British administrators sought to register all firearms among the Acholi; those who registered their arms were to be able to keep them, while those who refused would have them confiscated (Adimola 1954). In an apparent miscommunication, the officers carrying out these orders engaged in pure disarmament of the Acholi. Following this mistake, a policy of complete disarmament was suggested, buttressed by arguments that it would ease colonial administration and reduce looting and robbery among the Acholi. The Lamogi, who had developed a reputation for resisting European orders, refused to disarm and were prepared to fight to retain their weapons. They did so from the strategic point of the Guruguru hills, where they camped and fought before dying in large numbers of bullet wounds, dehydration secondary to dysentery, and starvation. With no way out, they surrendered. The defeated Lamogi were marched to Gulu, about thirty miles away, passing through the lands of rival clans, including the Patiko, who had sided with the colonial administration against the Lamogi. In this march, as Andrew Adimola (1954) describes, the Patiko and other enemies of Lamogi settled their feuds with the defeated by killing starving men, kidnapping young women and girls to be their wives, and raping others, deepening tensions between the Lamogi and their rival clans.

The rebellion was witnessed by CMS missionary Arthur Bryan Fisher, who spent time across Uganda from 1898 to 1913/14, and his wife, Ruth, a fellow CMS missionary whom Arthur met in Uganda and married in 1902. Writing in 1913 to her children living in England, Ruth, stationed in Patiko among a rival clan of the Lamogi, spoke of the British response to the rebellion not as being primarily about resistance to the confiscation of firearms, but as a matter of whipping into shape a "very cruel," "savage," and "very wild lot" who stole both people (to be their servants and women) and goats:

> King Georges [sic] soldiers out here have just been out to fight some very savage people that live not very far from us. They are very cruel, they will not do any work but when a man wants some meat he steals a goat from his neighbours [sic] herd, and when he wants a servant he steals a little girl or boy, and when he wants to marry he waits about on the road and carries off the first woman he sees. So the soldiers went out to show them that their king would not allow these things to go on. . . . Now the officer . . . wants us to send a teacher to these people to tell them about God, for of course if their hearts learn to love God their wicked habits will soon be forgotten. (Fisher 1913 [March 22])

> These people are a very wild lot and love fighting. Last year they were fighting our English soldiers for many months. They hid themselves in enormous caves and when our soldiers came near they fired out at them. . . . But now they [have been] conquered, and our officer has just been round the country compelling them to give up their guns which have all been smuggled secretly into the country. Last week he brought in 1500 guns, but there are still a lot more that the people have hidden. He took a lot of their cows until they bring [sic] in the buried guns. So I dont [sic] suppose the people will fight any more. But they look very fierce and savage with their bodies painted in patterns with bright red paint, and sharp horns tied on their heads and pointed iron standing out like little spears on their lips. (Fisher 1913 [April 16])

A few months prior, upon their arrival in Gulu, Fisher had described her first impressions of the Acholi:

> The people are just the roughest blackies I have ever met. . . . They do not want clothes and say they are only a bother and hinder them when hunting and when fighting which they are often doing. The women paint their bodies with red clay and castor oil and look frightfully ugly. . . . One day when we came to a village over one thousand men and women came running to see us. . . . The men all had spears, and I was a little afraid because we heard they killed a man only a few days before we came. [As Reverend Fisher preached to them] it sounded splendid to hear that big crowd of armed savages all saying together the text that begins "God so loved the world." (Fisher 1913 [February 12])

Her descriptions, informed by a Protestant morality and modern, racist notions of civilization, mark the Acholi apart in terms of their appearance ("frightfully ugly," "very fierce and savage"), their weapons ("spears" of "armed savages"), their work ethic ("they will not do any work"), and the morally objectionable ends of their violence (abduction of women, robbery), while posing Christianity as a cure for these perceived ills.

Fisher's understanding of this violence was framed in a way that was disgusted by a perceived "inhumanity," as it might be put today. More precisely, this disgust was the product of the grating of a modern, racist sensibility. The Acholi, in her eyes, were cruel because they were not modern. They did not wear clothes, they were not productive laborers, they fought mostly with primitive weapons, and when they had modern weapons, they used them for (in modern eyes) primitive and immoral ends. And of course, while the vitality of the institution of colonial administration was primarily at stake in the rebellion, the rebellion was also about who could and who could not have access to modern technologies of violence. "Natives" were well aware of "the advantage and the superiority of guns over the spears and arrows to which they were accustomed" (Adimola 1954, 167). Their violence responded to the likely subordination they would endure without guns, implicitly recognizing and making claims to the modern. Ironically, as they fought for access to modern tools of violence, they were seen as non-modern, and thus cruel and immoral, designations that confirmed their lot as "armed savages" belonging to the lower "block" of humanity. In the case of the Lamogi Rebellion, a representation of violence as "against humanity," shaped by modern sensibilities, occluded the event's meaning as an act of anticolonial resistance or as a claim for modernity.

I have pointed out some of the modes by which, during the early colonial era, violence committed by Acholi in the region was constructed as "against humanity." In the frameworks of evangelizing Christianity and territorializing colonialism, certain forms of violence were read as primitive, savage, immoral, and opposed to humanity.[14] Since at least colonial times in Acholi, "humanity" has been tied to modernity, which often served to bifurcate "humanity" and "violence." As I discuss the question of the "inhumanity" of LRA violence below, this commentary on colonial violence should serve as a reminder of a longer history during which violence was made inhuman, becoming "cruel" or "brutal" because it grated against modern expectations of the forms, methods, contexts, and contents of that violence. In gesturing toward this genealogy, I point to a preexisting framework that was utilized to make sense of LRA violence, which, like colonial violence before it, was read and interpreted in ways inconsistent with and often silencing of other existing logics and moralities.

INHUMANITY, LRA VIOLENCE, AND THE EXPECTATIONS OF MODERNITY

Much like colonial violence before it, LRA violence was seen to lie outside of humanity. LRA violence transcended specifically modern moral values about the relationship between violence and technology, violence and reason, violence and time, violence and development, and violence and imagined communities. It was through the violation of these specific moral codes that "inhumanity" came to describe LRA violence. I argue that it is primarily through a *modern* moral rubric that violence and humanity bifurcate, and that this rubric constitutes the dominant framework by which LRA violence was judged as inhuman.

This sense that LRA violence was out of time in modernity was not merely a Western imposition—the violence of a naive humanitarian discourse or a national-state myth. As we will see, it manifested as part of postcolonial wrenchings toward, anxieties about, and expectations of modernity among rebels and Acholi civilians alike. In the context of failed development attempts and persistent postcolonial impasses, LRA violence was set against both humanity and the good through a modern mode of reasoning, eliding the complexity and productivity of that violence, and incorrectly laying the blame for ongoing violence in constructs such as "tribalism" or "tradition."

Morality and Technologies of Killing

"The sound of a bullet makes a spirit or shadow [*tipu*] run away," Labwor told me, as we chatted while working on his field at the beginning of a new growing season. I used a hoe to remove surface weeds, while he sprinkled rice seeds onto the cleared land. We had been talking a lot about violence around that time, with Labwor one of the few among my friends who was candid about the violence he himself had practiced. It was a subject he shared with some risk to himself, despite being lawfully protected from persecution under the Amnesty Act of 2000.

The issue of a certain type of *tipu*, vengeance spirits (*cen*), arose in our conversation. Labwor had for some time been possessed by the spirit of a fierce animal (*orongo*), that of a leopard (*kwac*) he had helped to kill in the *lum* while with the LRA. I asked him if he also felt haunted by the *cen* of the humans he killed while an LRA soldier. He replied that it was only the *orongo* that disturbed him. *Cen* has been described as the vengeance ghost or the troublesome spirit of a being killed who haunts or disturbs those responsible for the killing and who have not yet been brought to some form of justice or reconciliation (p'Bitek 1980; Finnström 2006; Baines 2007). In engaging the concept of *cen*, I do not seek a unitary cultural definition. Rather, I explore the ways in which people construct moral orders of violence through the concept.[15]

In my discussions with former LRA soldiers, respected elders, and others, a new dimension of *cen* became clear to me as people sought to make sense of LRA and UPDF violence and killings in the aftermath of the war through the concept of *cen*. In this process, and in a way similar to the violence of the Lamogi Rebellion, LRA violence became morally wrong not specifically because of its "inhumanity," but because of its supposedly more "primitive" technologies and practices of killing.[16] As Labwor told me, the sound of a bullet made a *tipu* run away. The bullet hit the person after the *tipu* had already run away. Elders and others largely agreed—*cen* feared guns and generally did not haunt a shooter.[17] Indeed, some suggested that pointing guns at those haunted by *cen* could chase the *cen* away, and that the shooting of bullets into the air at state burials was done to scare away any remaining *cen* from the deceased soldier, so that the *cen* would not be buried with her or him. On the other hand, *cen* did not fear other technologies of killing, including clubs and machetes (*pangas*) that the LRA were known to have used, and haunted killers employing less machine-like tools of violence.[18] In addition, so long as a soldier remained with his gun, he could continue killing, even angrily, and not fear *cen*. It is only when he left the battlefield and returned to civilian life that, without

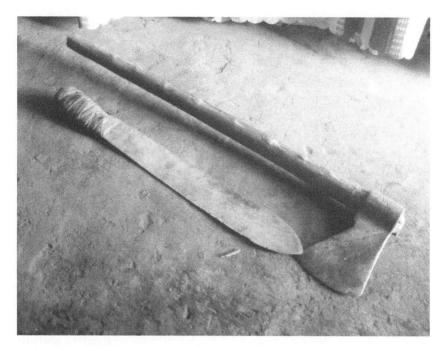

Figure 2. Machete (*panga*) and ax (*latong*), two tools used to kill people. Photo by author.

his gun, and assuming he was not taken through a cleansing ritual (*kwer*), *cen* might attack him.

Explanations for why *cen* acted this way varied. Labwor suggested that when using a gun to kill someone from a distance, the person killed does not see you, and so its *cen* cannot follow you; by contrast, when using a club or log (*dul*) to kill, the person sees you killing them, and its *cen* could then follow you. But, I asked Labwor, what if you snuck up on someone and killed him or her from behind with a *dul*, without being seen? Would you still be disturbed by *cen*? "Yes," he said, after some thought—suggesting that the tool of violence and its distance of use, rather than a visual obtained of the killer, determined whether or not *cen* would follow. Others disagreed. Indeed, it was widely known that *cen* physically stays in the eyes of the killer, because, as my respected elder and friend Ogweno Lakor told me, the killer had seen all the ways he killed with her or his own eyes, and re-saw these killings in a kind of flashback. It was common knowledge in

Acholiland that the last image one sees before dying is imprinted in one's pupil, and therefore, police investigations were said to involve examinations of the pupils of those killed, in hopes of retrieving images of the killer as evidentiary clues. Similarly, some suggested that there would be no *cen* involved in the killing of an innocent person judged criminal by mob justice, because so many people were involved that the innocent killed would not know exactly who killed her or him, and would not know whom exactly to haunt.

Modern technologies of killing challenged the way in which *cen* manifested, and in turn, how or even whether a killing would be socio-morally condemned.[19] When a killer employed modern techniques or technologies in enacting machine-like forms of physical and/or structural violence, especially from afar in both time and place from the killing, *cen* was less likely to be able to follow the killer. On the other hand, when a killer employed nonmodern techniques or technologies in enacting spectacular forms of physical violence, especially in close proximity in time and place to the killing, *cen* was more likely to be able to follow the killer. According to this logic, gunmen shooting anonymously and from afar avoided *cen*, but machete killers and club beaters killing up close and personal did not. What about those who set landmines that might explode sometime later, killing people whose deaths the killer might not even know of? Ogweno Lakor said that the heart of the killed did not see the killer's body, which was far away. How, he asked incredulously, could *cen* affect the one who set the landmine? No way, he insisted. Similarly, forms of killing by structural violence did not seem to bring *cen* upon structural killers. When new technologies and ways of killing arose with modernity, settled moralities of killing were disrupted. In this disordering, *cen*—as a manifestation of those moralities—confronted mainly killers employing non-modern technologies and forms of death, leaving aside those using newer or more unusual forms.

I posed the following case to Ogweno Lakor: What if a man, fatally sick with malaria, goes to a government clinic for antimalarial medication, but the doctor corruptly sold the government medication for his own private gain, leaving none left for the man, who dies? Would the man's *cen* haunt the corrupt doctor? Not unless the doctor directly kills the man, Ogweno Lakor reflected, through a failed operation on his body or an injected overdose of some drug. Then *cen* might follow. Another former rebel who listened to this case suggested that the malaria was sent by God and could not be blamed on the doctor.

In the face of modern forms of and ways of imagining violent killing, including by guns, landmines, and structural violence, *cen* is recruited as a concept that distinguishes moral from immoral violence. In this work, *cen* designates the violence of former LRA rebels as immoral and, by extension, non-modern. Another elder friend of mine, Oyengo, used the concept of *cen* to delegitimize and discredit LRA violence as outside legitimate norms of war because it involved killings of civilians who were also members of the same tribe (*kaka*) or community: "Where there is a battle between soldiers, there is no *cen* there. But the way Lakwena was killing—they arrested someone like you and killed you there, knowing this is Sam [not a soldier, and also knowing me personally as Sam]—there is *cen* here."[20]

This kind of characterization, in the eyes of many among the LRA, was seen as a technique by which they were marginalized and stigmatized, and the ascription of *cen* to the LRA was often seen as a kind of abusive epithet. *Cen* was less frequently used to explain the behavior of or apportion blame to state soldiers of the UPDF. Why, I wondered, did people tend to say that former LRA soldiers had *cen*, but not current or former UPDF soldiers? "People just spoil the name of Lakwena with *cen*. The UPDF also have *cen*. . . . But people, when they think of the LRA, they tremble and they fear, saying that the LRA have *cen*," Labwor insisted, constructing a moral framework in which *cen* functioned to apportion blame to objectionable but not unobjectionable forms of violence.[21]

His claim was not only a defense of LRA violence (or, more precisely, a critique of UPDF violence), but also a de-modernization of UPDF violence: "They [the UPDF] kill in all sorts of ways [beyond using guns]. They kill in the same way as Lakwena. They smoke people [to death] inside their huts [as Lakwena did]." Others, like my friend Matayo, understood Labwor's claim by its opposite: "[People say the UPDF don't get *cen*] because of the kind of killing. The UPDF kill with guns, and the LRA kill with sticks and the rest." For Matayo, *cen* was a way of marking the marginality of those already socio-spatially marginalized:

> Both the LRA and the UPDF who have killed are likely to be affected by *cen*. There is no exception, but the UPDF are said not to have *cen* because they

fight and kill in battle and return to live together with the community. But the LRA remain in the *lum* and don't stay with people—so people see those who return to the community don't have *cen*, but not those who do.[22]

Indeed, it was said that people with *cen* in their eyes were more likely to go mad and continue to kill others until the *cen* was chased away. Another former rebel friend of mine suggested that this structure of blame could be inverted were the LRA to finally take state power: "If some UPDF are around, they [civilians] don't say anything [about *cen*]. But if the LRA overthrew the government, you won't hear the issue of *cen* being with the LRA—the stigma against them will transfer to others [the UPDF]."

Cen also involved an individual moral assessment and show of strength, made by the killer himself. Labwor insisted that if a killer showed mercy or sympathy (*kica*) for the one she or he killed, the *cen* would attack her or him. While with the LRA, Labwor often set landmines along footpaths and roads that the LRA traveled on. He explained:

> I was a good mine planter myself—mines of all kinds. The Arabs' mines, the UPDF's mines, grenades, et cetera—I planted them along the roadside. If it detonated, they would all go off, and if it was in the midst of battle, many enemies [*lumone*] would be killed. If I kept thinking about it, the *cen* may have attacked me, but as a soldier, I don't think of it.[23]

Seeing killing as a duty of his profession, he saw no moral quandary in bringing death to his enemies: "I didn't feel pity. As a soldier you don't need to feel pity or worry—that was the army." But, he acknowledged, those who experienced moral anxiety about killing risked the haunting of *cen*:

> If you are sympathetic, you'll be attacked by *cen*. If you set a landmine and think it will kill someone, the *cen* will come to you if indeed someone is killed, because the person has been thinking of it a lot. It can even attack the manufacturer of a landmine if they fear, even if the person is not Acholi. . . . Even mine producers from Italy—if they keep thinking about it, that the mine could kill—and if it does kill, the *cen* attacks them.

Indeed, it was said that *cen* was more likely to attack women, because they were "weaker" than men.[24] Matayo suggested that this "sympathy" or inability to see the killing as a matter of "duty" was perhaps more precisely about whether or not one felt one had a legitimate reason to kill. He also hinted that "sympathy" was more likely to manifest in killings of close proximity because of the opportunity for the killer to hear the killed's pleas and cries:

> If shot [with a gun, from a distance], the person dies without cursing [*lamo dog*], without saying "you killed me for no reason." They don't say anything, and just die, and then no *cen* follows. But if they are killed in a horrible way, for example with the stick . . . then they die screaming, cursing, and seeing you who is killing him well. Then the *cen* follows [you].[25]

Although proximity was important, others suggested that the duration and quality of the pain produced by the technology of killing also affected whether or not *cen* haunted the killer. "If you kill without using a gun, the death is painful and it will bring *cen*," suggested a former rebel who spent a brief time in the *lum*, and who believed death by gunshot or landmines was not painful compared to stabbings by knives, *pangas*, and bayonets, or clubbing people to death with logs.

Cen socially operated as a means of demarcating moral from immoral violence, or more precisely, violence that was socio-morally reconciled from violence that was not. This was readily apparent in the ways in which people talked about *cen* as primarily following killers (and their kin) who were genuinely guilty or responsible for their killing, who killed unjustly, and who committed acts of spectacular violence in close proximity rather than acts of structural violence from afar.[26] This rubric of morality generally coincided with a rubric of modernity that, more often than not, also coincided with a rubric of the legality of violence. Put simply, modern technologies of killing, such as through guns or landmines, were less likely to create *cen*, and simultaneously were more commonly associated with the "legal" state violence of the UPDF than the "illegal" rebel violence of the LRA. When speaking of *cen* haunting former LRA rebels, then, one reconstructed LRA violence as immoral, non-modern, and illegal. Underlying the concept of *cen*, then, was a moral framework for violence that distinguished the good from the bad on the basis of technologies of killing— moral judgments that reflected social anxieties about delays in and impediments to development.[27] Amid these anxieties, LRA violence that used "primitive" rather than "modern" technologies of killing was condemned.

The Moral Uncertainty of the Beyond

The problem of *cen* highlights the technological and technical dimensions by which LRA violence was seen to fall outside of modernity. This section focuses on the problem of Kony's spirit (*tipu*), showing the way in which irresolvable uncertainties about the future and the beyond displaced LRA violence from the domain of modernity and, in so doing, excluded it from the domain of the good. Drawing on narratives by a community that debated Kony's *tipu* and remained uncertain as to its character, I suggest that an important barometer of the (im)morality of LRA violence was pure faith, unadulterated by rational designs for the future, logical and planned timescales, or evidence-based data as to the nature of the *tipu*.

It was common knowledge in Acholiland, among all social and economic classes, that Joseph Kony remained or had been in the past possessed by some kind of spirit. There were strong debates, however, as to whether or not that spirit was a holy spirit (*tipu maleng*) or a feared or respected spirit (*jok*).[28] During the time of my work, Christianity, traditional religion, and other beliefs coexisted in tension. *Jok*—an important figure in pre-Christian, precolonial Acholi religion—had become, publicly, an immoral, bad spirit, often equated by evangelical Christians to Satan. Villagers were reticent to acknowledge their belief in *jogi* lest they come across as non-modern, and the shrines (*abila*) associated with that belief were no longer publicly displayed but carefully hidden, if maintained at all. At the same time, churches had monopolized the concept of *tipu maleng* for Christianity. In this context, the very naming of Kony's spirit as either *jok* or *tipu* became an act in which one passed moral judgment on the meaning of LRA violence itself, as either devilish or divine.

There were three main forms in which people identified Kony's spirit, two morally negatively and one morally positively. Negatively, some believed that Kony was possessed by an evil *jok* that committed senseless violence. Positively, some believed that Kony was possessed by a *tipu maleng* that directed him to commit violence that, although painful and difficult to understand, was part of God's will and plan. In between, another group of moral skeptics believed that Kony was *once* possessed by the *tipu maleng*, which revealed prophecies to him and allowed him to perform miracles that they saw with their own eyes. But as they saw it, the spirit left him over time, thereby stripping meaning from subsequent LRA violence. Naming the spirit was an implicitly politico-moral act that revealed one's stance about the LRA; at the same time, it was also an epistemological declaration that revealed one's stance vis-à-vis modernity.

"Some say Kony doesn't have *tipu maleng*, but I know he *does*. They say he has *jok*, but that's a lie. Kony has *tipu maleng*." My friend Matayo was one who believed that Kony had, and remained with, the *tipu maleng*. This manifested not only in his naming of the spirit, but in his choice of verb for how that spirit acted. He carefully observed the distinction in the way in which *tipu* and *jok* were said to inhabit the body, saying that Kony was a person "filled with heart/spirit/mind" (*dano ma opong ki cwiny*, suggestive of *tipu*), not a person "possessed" (*ido*, used primarily for *jok*). "I know he [Kony] might continue to fight, more than thirty years, even one hundred years maybe." I asked quizzically if he would never die. "People with *tipu* are like God. God can protect them and they have energy," he replied. Matayo spent almost a decade with the LRA, serving as a low-ranking officer. Throughout his time in the *lum*, he was visited in dreams by spirits who gave him revelations about the war. Matayo was generally quite observant of LRA rules, but when he one day touched a bloody piece of cloth, against these rules, he knew that divine punishment would come to him. Soon thereafter, he stepped on a landmine and his leg was blown off.

After being released from the LRA due to his injury, Matayo returned home and became a devout evangelical Christian. He served as a deacon in his village church, and faithfully began each of our chats with a prayer. Together, we spent countless hours combing through the Bible, as he tried to explain the LRA war in relation to biblical passages, stories, and figures, among them Sodom and Gomorrah, Noah, Elijah, and Moses.

Kony's killing of Acholi civilians in retaliation for their lack of support, he suggested, was precisely the story of Sodom and Gomorrah (Genesis 19). Kony had come to help the Ugandan people, Matayo said—he told them so, that they needed to come to him. But they continued to disobey and so he mutilated, killed, and burned their huts, just as God had destroyed Sodom. In other passages, Kony became Noah, who was sent by God but thought mad by people, who only realized the madness as truth too late. Kony became Elijah, with Museveni as Baal (1 Kings 18), and

Matayo disparagingly noted that Museveni fought using *jogi* and *ajwagi* while Kony fought using God. Kony became Moses, receiving promises and guidance from God, and slowly but patiently led Ugandans to a promised land, as Moses did for the Israelites. If Kony were to win the war, all kinds of moral ills would be contained, ranging from smoking to drinking to prostitution.

Matayo's utter faith in Kony, in part bolstered by what he saw Kony do over the course of a decade in the *lum*, required no evidence; no certainty about the future, nor any moral judgment of the present; and no delimited length of the war, a criterion important to rational modernists. Many of them opposed the war, often insisting it had gone on for "too long." But Matayo's belief executed a different temporo-morality of violence, in which its length and severity were both unknowable and bore little consequence in relation to its divine origins and design.

Those who believed Kony had *jok*, or else believed he had *tipu maleng* but lost it, reasoned using modern rationalities. Some saw the scope of the violence and immediately calculated that it was inconsistent with the acts of God (perhaps, as some former rebels suggested to me, forgetting the biblical story of Job). Others, including former rebels, who suspected that Kony lost the *tipu*, made judgments that they saw as rational logic, but that others might have called a loss of faith. Prophetic deadlines by which the LRA were to have overthrown the government would pass without results. Kony's *tipu* no longer appeared in front of the soldiers, but "behind the scenes" or in Kony's dreams. RV,[29] whose husband was an LRA commander and who spent a long time with the LRA, reflected: "Around 1994, I realized the spirit had stopped appearing to him, when he started to talk to people about dreams he had. I was also surprised he told people to go dig in gardens—why? Is this no longer a war to overthrow the government? The direction seemed to have changed, if we were being given plots to dig [instead of fighting]." In deciding to abandon their faith in the *tipu*'s presence and goals, they made rational, personal decisions that privileged experiential evidence over wavering belief. This was not always an entirely black-and-white decision, however. Mohammed retained faith in the *tipu*, but left the LRA because he felt its design was too big for him. He reflected: "I couldn't wait for the *tipu*. I didn't want to waste my time there, but I knew the right time for the *tipu* was far away. The time for fulfilling it was far away, but that doesn't mean I disagreed with what the *tipu* said. I returned because so many from our home were already in the *lum* [many of his clan brothers were abducted and serving in the LRA], and we couldn't all stay there. So I returned."

In the shadows of modernity, pure faith, as opposed to logical reason, allowed one to apply a different moral calculus to LRA violence which, rooted in the beyond, made sense of a violence that others saw as senseless. Modern discomfort with the moral uncertainty of the beyond framed LRA violence as senseless, and therefore inhuman.

Violence, Out of Time

If modernity was indeed the key parameter by which LRA violence became inhuman(e) and thus evil, then the inability of LRA violence to fit modern temporalities was central to this process of inhumanizing this violence. In other words, LRA violence failed to humanize partially because it was, in modern eyes, violence "out of time"—anachronistic, obsolete, and incomprehensible to modern expectations of, sensibilities about, and experiences of time. From this perspective, and as artifacts of modernity, deaths became useless deaths; violence dragged on rather than moved forward; and civilians grew w(e)ary of and disconnected from guerrillas.

The LRA war seemed to have simply come at the "wrong" time. Civilians, having already witnessed the failure of Alice Lakwena's rebellion to overthrow Museveni's nascent government,[30] and somewhat confident that Museveni could in fact bring lasting social change, were not ready to join Kony in the *lum*. Although that sentiment seemed to have been changing during my fieldwork, especially among young men disillusioned with the real possibility of living impoverished futures, even the idea of guerrilla warfare as a method of overthrowing Museveni seemed outdated. Indeed, many fighters remembered that life in the *lum* grew more difficult when the UPDF began using helicopters to fight them, forcing them into more jungled areas for protection. The American military, who aided the "hunt" for Kony at the time of my work, were said to be using advanced technology to locate LRA groups living in large swaths of jungle and forest in central Africa. It is certainly remarkable that, at the time of this writing, Kony had been in the *lum* for more than thirty years—a fact that Matayo said made him the "world's greatest rebel." But the idea that he could win the war through guerrilla warfare and with limited technological support (though possibly abundant spiritual support) seemed outdated to modern eyes.

Perhaps more grating to modern sentiments was the way in which the war was perceived to have dragged on for nearly three decades. Many former rebels pointed to this sentiment as a modern problem—of people today being in a hurry, wanting to see immediate results without any suffering. Some blamed this rush on the influence of money, of people hustling to make quick cash. But they stressed, over and over, that this war was not one that should be expected to end quickly, nor in accordance with particular human deadlines, such as those issued by the UPDF or by American NGOs such as Invisible Children, who launched an unsuccessful "Kony 2012" campaign to have Kony arrested by the end of 2012. They warned that this war, directed by spirits, could continue for another thirty or one hundred years, particularly with certain prophecies yet to be fulfilled. Those modernists who wanted a quick resolution, it seemed, lacked patience.

The Death of Killer Names and the Eclipse of Ethical Violence under Modernity

> All the men with moi names
> And those with "killer" marks
> On their backs
> And on their arms
> Will be hanged for murder
> Okot p'Bitek, *Song of Ocol*, 1985

In historical Acholi practice, it was common for warriors and soldiers (for example those fighting in the King's African Rifles in World War II) to be given killer or hero names (*nying moi*) after having killed an enemy and undergone a *kwer* ceremony. As described by E. T. N. Grove (1919; who refers to *ñiñ toñ* or "spear name"), F. K. Girling (1960), Okot p'Bitek (1980), Angelo Negri (1984), and others, these names were given as a kind of noble title or reward for having killed a foreign enemy (*merok*).

Returning to their village lands with a body part of the killed, such as beard clippings, ears, and sometimes heads, which would be gathered in the clan ancestral shrine (*abila*) (Girling 1960, 103–4), killers underwent the ritual of *kwero merok*, requiring the participation of someone who had himself previously undergone the ritual and received a *moi* name. In the course of this ritual, the spirit of the killed was cleansed so as to minimize its disturbance of the killer, and afterward, the killer received a *moi* name that reflected some detail of the killing, such as who, how, when, where, or why he killed.[31] Such ceremonies were celebratory, in contrast with the solemnity of *kwer* conducted to cleanse killers of *cen* or other spirits of clan members. Killing an absolute enemy was a moral good and constituted an ethical form of violence.

By the time of my fieldwork, however, *nying moi* was uncommonly bestowed and an uncomfortable subject for discussion. The LRA did not give *nying moi* to its soldiers, and clan elders were reluctant to bestow *nying moi* on those who had killed in the course of the war. Why had the moral tradition of killer names faded in Acholi? I argue that the eclipse of *nying moi* is best understood as a consequence of the modern reconfiguration of the boundaries of ethical violence, determined in various parts by the dominant paradigms of the nation-state and its laws, Christianity, and international human rights. Taken together, these paradigms constitute a modern mentality in which *nying moi* became "backward" and embarrassing, as p'Bitek (1985b) suggests in *Song of Ocol* (an excerpt of which appears above as the epigraph for this section). In this poem by one of east Africa's most famed poets, and one of Acholi's most celebrated sons, Ocol, a modern, educated Acholi man and the son of a chief, responds bitterly to his traditional wife, who laments the way that he has forsaken the traditions of his people. Lamenting and lambasting stagnating traditions like superstitions, ancestral shrines, and *nying moi*, Ocol underscores the modern assessment of *nying moi* as a "primitive" celebration of what in modern law might be understood as criminal murder.

Ogweno Lakor was philosophical when it came to the subject of the death of killer names. "Human rights has finished *nying moi*," he suggested, noting that killers of enemies felt shy and scared to report their killings to elders (as would be required to undergo *kwero merok*), fearing police arrest or the guilt produced through Christian teachings against killing.[32] "[The killer] feels guilty and tries to shy away from telling others so that he's not looked at as a sinner. And today, people see killing as something that is *dong cen* ["backward," literally "remaining behind"]—so people don't brag about it as they used to do before. When they kill, people feel shameful and shy."

Aside from shifts in moral feeling corresponding to the influence of secular and Christian religions, shifts in kinship under the nation-state meant that killing a non-Acholi was no longer a certain criterion for earning a *moi* name. Elders often expressed concern that, for instance, an Acholi killing a Muganda (a member of the Baganda, a Ugandan ethnic group) required not *kwero merok* (a celebratory cleansing of foreign enemies)[33] but a mournful reparation with kin members (*culo kwor*), under the assumption that the Acholi and the Muganda are "brothers" under the Ugandan state. I asked Ogweno Lakor why people did not receive *moi* names in the course of the LRA war. "There is no *moi*," he declared. "Can you have *moi* with your brother? [Rhetorically] You can't kill your brother and get *nying moi*. There is not any *kwer* in Kony's war."

This sentiment arose from the well-known fact that much of the war saw Acholi fighting Acholi—with a predominantly Acholi LRA fighting the UPDF, whose front-line soldiers often included many Acholi. But Oyengo, who often pandered to government lines on the war—in part because the government funded Ker Kwaro Acholi, the organization of Acholi elders and chiefs of which Oyengo was part—suggested, "Even the Baganda are brothers to the LRA. There's no *nying moi* in that. This needs paying of reparations [*culo kwor*]." I pressed Oyengo on this question. Would an Acholi killing a Munyankole (a member of the Banyankole from southwestern Uganda, Museveni's home region) not constitute the killing of a *merok*? Oyengo was torn between a customary Acholi logic of kinship and a modern nation-state logic of kinship:

> You can *kwer* and get *moi*, but it's not okay to do it, because we are all from Uganda. [The Munyankole is] not *merok* because this is a Ugandan person within our home—it's not good to *moi*. You can *culo kwor* for such a person, the Munyankole you killed in battle, if there are some other Banyankole around who you know, you can go to them and say, "I killed one of your people while fighting, so if you accept I can *culo kwor*." If they accept, they can receive the *kwor* and eat it.

In reconfiguring a traditional *merok* as a brother under the modern framework of the nation-state, Oyengo also rewrote Acholi linguistics, reconfiguring networks of kinship and enshrining the logic of the nation-state as a cultural logic. Accepting that *moi* could be given to UPDF who were fighting in Somalia or in Sudan, but not against fellow Ugandans, meant aligning traditional Acholi ethics of violence with the ethical violence of the nation-state, a purely modern move.

In addition to the influence of the question of the nation-state, *nying moi* was difficult to bestow because of the modern technologies of warfare alluded to in an earlier section. Explained Ogweno Lakor:

> The killings that someone can gain a *moi* name from is when the killing has happened from the battleground, the real battleground, like that of the World War, where you killed the other one in a confrontation in battle. You shoot the person and when you shoot the person, you cut the body part of a person and return with it—not like this one here, where people just shoot without seeing where they are shooting, and afterward, you walk past that place and you see dead bodies and have to assume who you killed [because of the nature of the warfare, you are not exactly sure who shot whom]. It is hard to *kwero moi* for this. The *kwer* for *nying moi* is done when the person is sure that he's the one who really shot the person, not any other person.

When the enemy was killed from afar with modern technologies, encounters between the killers and the killed were not face-to-face. One was less certain of one's responsibility—and honor—in the killing. Accordingly, the practices of naming by which both moral condemnation (in the form of *cen*) and moral praise (in the form of *nying moi*) was given became much more difficult in the practice of modern warfare and the use of modern technologies of killing.

In the context of the fading away of *nying moi* amid a growing concern with modernity, the LRA also did away with *nying moi* as part of a general forsaking of, and even attack against, traditional Acholi religion or "Acholi work" (*tic Acoli*). Musa, a longtime spiritual controller, told me, "We do God's work [*tic pa Rubanga*; Christianity], not *tic Acoli* [Acholi work, or traditional Acholi religion]. We didn't rely on traditions and there were no *moi* names." The LRA abandoned not only *nying moi* as an immoral traditional practice, but also ancestral shrines (*abila*), witch doctors (*ajwagi*), and spirits (*jogi*).[34]

In reproducing elements of modern frameworks, the LRA disrupted an older morality of violence and attempted to replace it with modern state forms. Otto suggested, "Instead of the *moi* name, they gave ranks to give morale to soldiers." Indeed, the bestowal of ranks was perhaps the most modern of substitutions for *nying moi*, particularly in the formalized structure of the army that the LRA employed. There were LRA captains, lieutenants, colonels, and so forth.

Gunya described the way in which she gained a rank, chronicling a practice very similar to that of *nying moi*.[35] During a surprise LRA attack on a Dinka barracks in Sudan, Gunya killed a Dinka commander—a killing that, she emphasizes, she *knows* she herself did (as opposed to killing from afar): "I shot him and even removed his pips, and went back with them to the defense, and was given a rank. From [being previously a] private, I became sergeant."[36] Even without *nying moi* given, her practice of collecting the pips from the killed remarkably mirrored that of the collecting or snipping of a body part to take home in the process of receiving a *nying moi*. Such imbrication of a traditional practice into this modern morality suggested that perhaps the LRA had not in fact fully exceeded a traditional morality of violence.

In the eclipse of killer names (*nying moi*), the boundaries of ethical violence were reconfigured in modern terms. With the collective pressures of human rights, Christianity, modern law, modern technologies, and/or LRA regulations, *nying moi* as an ethical commemoration of violence no longer made sense.

LRA Violence through Fanonian Eyes

> Irrepressible violence is neither a storm in a teacup nor the reemergence of savage instincts nor even a consequence of resentment: it is man reconstructing himself. . . . Offspring of violence, he draws every moment of his humanity from it: we were men at his expense, he becomes a man at ours. Another man: a man of higher quality.
>
> Jean-Paul Sartre, preface to *The Wretched of the Earth*, 1961

LRA violence came to be characterized as "inhuman" through its friction with a rubric of modernity, composed of specific expectations of the technologies, temporo-certainties, and ethico-moral boundaries of violence. While these expectations echoed colonial sentiments, they also represented postcolonial expectations of the humanizing qualities of liberatory violence as described by Frantz Fanon and others. Fanon describes decolonizing violence in terms of man re-creating himself in the birth of a new humanity. Under the violence of colonialism, "the 'native' is declared impervious to ethics, representing not only the absence of values but also the negation of values. He is, dare we say it, the enemy of values. In other words, absolute evil" (1963, 6). Fanon's violence takes aim at colonial ethics and sentimentality. But it retains, indeed privileges, the colonizer's cosmology of modernity. Much as Fanon decries Western values such as individualism and the "white man's Church," he is surprisingly complicit in chastising the colonized for their "negation of common sense" and "'head-in-the-sand' behavior" when they engage in practices he sees as self-destructive (1963, 17). Among the objects of his critique are internecine feuds, religion, dance, spirits, possession, and "magical superstructure," which he characterizes as typical of "underdeveloped societies" and in which he claims people lose interest during liberation struggles.

While an important figure in postcolonial Africa at large, Fanon holds a particularly special place in the historico-intellectual development of Ugandan violence, having been the subject of President Yoweri Museveni's 1970 university thesis. Sixteen years before he took power in his "bush war," Museveni, then a student at the University of East Africa studying under Walter Rodney, was part of a delegation that traveled to Mozambique and observed and interacted with FRELIMO (Frente de Libertação de Moçambique) fighters. Returning from his trip, he wrote an impassioned dissertation entitled "Fanon's Theory of Violence: Its Verification in a Sub-Sahara African Territory," in which he follows Fanon in condemning "escapist mechanisms" such as a "metaphysical world" that have nothing to do with the "rationalized, cold struggle" that he envisions the colonized must make. Describing the death of old customs of the Makonde people, replaced by revolutionary military culture, Museveni nods approvingly with Fanon: "This is as it should be; modernizing ourselves is what we want" (1970, 45).[37]

So, even through Fanonian eyes, LRA violence could never humanize its perpetrators. By lieu of its apparent engagement with metaphysics, "magical superstructure," tribalism, and internecine feuds, LRA violence belonged to an irrational past, excluded from a modernity that promised the rise of the oppressed's humanity. And yet, as we will see, LRA rebels often conceived of their violence in very rational and often very cold terms—but not in ways that fit the other modern conditions of humanizing violence.

Not limited to LRA violence, much postcolonial violence in Uganda can be described essentially as struggles with the terms of modernity. From the moment the British left Milton Obote with the prime ministerial keys to power in 1962, the Ugandan state has been the object of a series of coups and insurgences in attempts by rebels to take over power for their own political group,[38] during which more than one million people were killed in what A. B. K. Kasozi describes as "the Ugandan holocaust" (1999, 6). Kasozi's explanation of the social origins of violence in Uganda from independence in 1962 up to 1985 describes this violence as a failure to achieve or adjust to several ideal aspects of modern nation-states, including a strong, united central government—free of ethnic and religious factionalism, unequal distribution of its resources, and poorly educated leaders—and with its own indigenous class structure, economic production, and common language. He explains:

> Precolonial moral values were built on the roots of traditional beliefs, religions, and social organizations. With the establishment of the colonial state, morality, law, and social behaviour were derived from Euro-Judeo-Christian values. Although remnants of traditional beliefs still influenced social behaviour, they were increasingly undermined. It was hoped that the African leaders who replaced European officials would either carry on and enforce the moral fabric they inherited or create a new moral code, a new African belief system, from which a national social fabric could be woven. But they failed. (1999, 13)

While the exercise of power was at stake for those seeking it, I suggest, following Kasozi, that what has prevented a definitive resolution is this impasse in resolving the problem of modernity, particularly as embodied in the requirements of the modern nation-state. This impasse was clearly articulated during the celebrations of Uganda's fifty years of independence in 2012, around which time pessimistic citizens and columnists suggested that the "Independence dream" (Mpanga 2012) eluded a nation that,

Figure 3. Rusted AK-47 magazine and two bullets abandoned in a former UPDF defense. Benjamin, a former LRA soldier, found these in 2010 in his garden while digging. Photo by author.

divided, prone to violence, and having failed to industrialize, remained "forever teenagers" (Kalyegira 2012). Some suggested that Uganda would have been better off under the colonialists (Kanana 2012; Akaki 2012) rather than the "inhuman NRM leadership" (Mafabi 2013). In the midst of this cynicism, one columnist urged Uganda to "reach out for the life vest and escape the wreckage of pessimism" through entrepreneurial capitalism (Nyamugasira 2012).

"Humanity" falls within the terms of this problem as part of the imagined "new African belief system," out of which philosophies of "African humanism," such as *ubuntu,* were crafted. In such pan-Africanist attempts to find (and thereby invent) African roots to modern problems, postcolonial intellectuals like Fanon re-chained themselves to modernity by attempting to articulate "native" African versions of it. In the eyes of these modernist African visions, LRA violence could never realize the dream of "humanity" promised to the postcolony, unmodern as it was in its spiritual, religious, and tribalist currents.

PHENOMENOLOGIES OF PERPETRATED LRA VIOLENCE

Let us now explore LRA violence in the concrete, from the perspective of those who committed it. How did they remember their actions in terms of modernity and humanity? Though cast into a network of spirit possession and internecine feuds in theory, LRA violence on the ground was often quite reasonable and rational.

Most of my former LRA friends did not look back with much fondness on the violence they committed. Many felt "bad" (*marac*) about it in retrospect, and did not agree with the manners or methods of the violence. They insisted that they were simply following orders, distancing themselves from the more "brutal" killings or mutilations. Indeed, many cited a common LRA ethico-moral discourse about violence, which suggested that those who committed wrongs in the form of immoral violence had already been punished by the *tipu maleng*, by being killed or injured in the course of battle. That my friends had returned home unscathed proved, in this discourse, their innocence.

To the extent that my friends were willing to talk about the violence they committed, it proved very difficult—even for close friends—to speak openly about it. There was always something held back, usually replaced by a meek, commonly circulated narrative about regret, reconciliation, and forgiveness. This was not an easy topic for former rebels to discuss with a military-age American man in the midst of an ongoing war in which the US government actively fought against the LRA; and in which the pieces of paper assuring government amnesty were not in fact reassuring that they might not yet be prosecuted, persecuted, or otherwise abused for having been LRA soldiers.

Nonetheless, even in the midst of expected regret and displeasure, there were unexpected moments of happiness, joy, pleasure, and relief in killing or mutilating. These emotions were often framed in the context of being soldiers whose lives were constantly at stake; of being frustrated soldiers whose orders to civilians were not being followed; of being sympathetic in performing some kinds of violence versus others; and of being Acholi soldiers with different forms of kinship to different objects of their violence.

Labwor was one of the only people who spoke quite candidly to me about the violence he committed: "A new soldier [*lamony*] should first be injected with the urine of a lion [referring to a proverb about bravery]. I experienced this when I first arrived in the *lum*. There were fifty strokes of beating to welcome me. It was part of trying to bring anger in you who is to become a fighter. Anger is needed to fight well." Labwor remembered the violence he saw and committed early in his time in the *lum*:

> In Uganda, when I was being abducted, I saw children being killed. They were abducted from Omel and tried to escape at night. In the morning, they were followed and killed. They were still young. They couldn't walk fast in the *lum*. They were caught, brought back, and ordered killed. We who were abducted went to kill the children. One girl cried and said they shouldn't be killed, and the commander added her to those to be killed, and so she was also killed for sympathizing. We were selected to go kill them, and after the killing, we dipped our hands in blood to show that we participated in the killing. We did it because if we hadn't, you might be the next to be killed. We did it before it reached us.

How did he feel about it?

> I felt good. But at first, I felt bad, when I first clobbered them. It was painful. But afterward, when I thought about it, I realized I shouldn't have felt painful, because these children shouldn't have escaped. Who would have stayed and worked [had everyone been allowed to escape without penalty]? Why leave the rest and only they are to escape? Then I didn't feel pain.

A true soldier, Labwor set aside his initial pain at committing violence for the orders and requirements of soldier-rebels. "The enemy [*adwii*][39] has zero tolerance. The issue of sympathy, of other feelings, is not encouraged. You put them aside and you do your work. . . . *Adwii* thinks of self-protection, that if you don't kill a person, you'll be killed. They follow whatever orders are issued." In fact, over time, Labwor felt that violence became a part of him, and he began to enjoy it: "The first time [I killed], I tolerated it, but then it normalized because it becomes like a part of your body. An *adwii* is injected with the urine of a lion. You're supposed to be fierce [*ger*], so you do it because you think you might also die next, so why not do it happily? You don't know when you'll die." Laughing, Labwor recalled various acts of violence he committed—killing enemies (*lumone*) in battle; abducting civilians and killing them if they tried to escape; burning houses with people inside them; locking people inside huts and letting them die of starvation; cutting off the penises of Karamojong and other peoples they fought.

I wondered if he saw these as particularly brutal forms of violence (*tim gero lataya*). "No," he insisted,

> not even cooking body parts or cutting off penises. This is done when the person has done something very serious. Sometimes if you tell the person to do something and he doesn't follow it, the next time you give them a very serious punishment . . . because [you] are tired of warning a person several times. [Rebels] want the killing to be more painful to people remaining in that area. If they aren't killed in a special way, it is not as painful to people there, and the privates [*lutino mony*] also expect that they [themselves] could die, so they want these deaths to be more painful than his own death—to be more painful than the death he is going through, his own suffering [*can*].

Indeed, given the stress of his own life being constantly at grave risk, it was no surprise to hear Labwor speak of killing government collaborators and civilians disobeying LRA orders not as a process of becoming human, but as a release, a pure relief: "You become relieved that this stubborn person that has been disturbing us a lot—at least today, I've finished him. You feel relieved." But much as Labwor himself felt comfortable killing those he felt to be enemies threatening his life, he was uncomfortable stabbing people to death. It was common, he explained, for killings to be ordered without the use of bullets or gunshots, both for purposes of concealment and for preservation of ammunition. *Lutino mony*, he suggested, had to find alternative ways of killing. Some used logs. Others used bayonets.

Labwor's personal experience of being stabbed with a bayonet made it difficult for him to inflict that violence on others. When he had just been abducted, he and a group of new abductees had been sent to a potato garden to harvest food. The commanding officer at the time felt they took too long in the garden and suspected that they were plotting their escape. To punish them, he pierced their hands with bayonets, leaving scars that remained with Labwor. Labwor felt he was being wrongly punished, as he had no intention of escaping. The commanding officer was later punished for acting out of turn in stabbing these new recruits, receiving three hundred strokes of the cane. With the memory of his own stabbing by bayonet, Labwor preferred to kill using logs. "Killing a person with a log isn't hard [*Neko dano ki dul pe tek*]," he reflected, and was less painful than killing them by stabbing them with a bayonet—with four thrusts into the right side of the rib cage, then four thrusts into the left side of the rib cage, and a sometimes prolonged death. Better, he said, to have the person to be killed lie face down, and strike them with a log on the back of the head. They died immediately, he noted, especially if you hit them on a specific spot on the back of their head. Labwor repeated a kind of moral sympathy of violence that many former LRA rebels spoke to me of—that of mercy killing, of preferring to kill people to let them "rest" rather than mutilating them and having their suffering continue.

These sympathies extended, Labwor explained, to civilians guilty only by association, who were killed for having been together with someone who committed a wrong against the LRA—those who had inherited wrong (*bal alaka*). He found it painful and difficult to kill these civilians. But for those who made the LRA suffer and put LRA lives at stake, Labwor found not pain but indeed pleasure in killing them, particularly in unusual or special ways: "I enjoyed it so much, really. It's nice to kill in this way, especially those who have intentions of killing you. You have to kill for it to be heard for some time, that it becomes historic. You can kill in any way that scares people who remained, even if it's chopping them into pieces, leaving only the skin of a person, or using a bayonet." He described being part of an LRA group that captured a team of UPDF soldiers. The LRA soldiers split the soldiers into two groups, chopping off the arms of those in the first group, and gouging out the eyes of those in the second group. For Labwor, the reasons for this kind of violence had nothing to do with "magical superstructures" as Fanon or Museveni might imagine for the LRA. It was a tactical violence meant to scare the UPDF, to make them fear the LRA and not follow them so closely: "They imagine how they'll be dealt with by the LRA if they [the LRA] get hold of them, so only those with a desperate desire for money would stay in the UPDF, but the others would go back home."

These forms of violence were also rationalized by Labwor and others by the imagination of what could or would be done to them if they were captured or arrested:

I imagine if I were to be arrested by him, he would do much more to me than I'd do to him. Most UPDF killed the LRA from the *lum*, so if I [kill him], I feel I've saved my life. Why can't I be happy about that? Generally, the UPDF do terrible things to the LRA once they are arrested, so the LRA do the same if they arrest the UPDF. I'm happy because I feel I'm saving my life. For example, informants who ululate [to alert the UPDF of LRA presence] and the UPDF come and kill the LRA—you see the effects visibly with LRA dead. The only way to stop them is to scare them to stop continuing to ululate—so we cut lips, legs, et cetera, so that others would stop collaborating.

These descriptions of LRA violence sounded in their content much less like an "escapist mechanism" condemned by Fanon, and much more like the "rationalized, cold struggle" Museveni spoke admiringly of, and which was based in military tactics and strategy, however unpleasant they seemed. In discussions about mutilations and killings of civilians, former rebels of all kinds of political tastes emphasized reason above all—there was a reason for every mutilation, a reason for every killing. For the LRA, there were in battle few "innocent" civilians among a sea of friends and enemies.

Yet since the content of LRA reason was encased by the form of a "magical superstructure" (a topic we will revisit), it pre-violated the terms under which violence could be human or humanizing. LRA violence was thus confined to inhumanity by virtue of this and other forms of dissonance with modernity. Below, I illustrate what is lost when LRA violence is condemned to inhumanity, a discourse that reduced lived experience to limited imaginations of that experience. When LRA violence is characterized as inhuman, and thus absolutely evil, horrifically shocking, and belonging to the denigrated realms of other-than-humans, such as devils or animals, it becomes difficult to see other important moral capacities of that violence.

LRA VIOLENCE IN LOCAL IMAGINARIES: MORALITY AND THE UNMAKING OF INHUMANITY

When LRA violence is not opposed to humanity, how else can we make sense of it? In the final part of this chapter, I explore some of the ways in which LRA violence held meaning, richness, and reason for Acholi civilians who lived close to it. I contextualize LRA violence with some unexpected stories—stories of civilian support for the rebels, of praise for their violence, and of comparative forms of "cruel" violence, including mob justice and state violence. These stories, which emerge in both ethnographic Acholi accounts and NGO reports, give brief pause to the frequent ascription of exceptional cruelty and inhumanity to these spectacular forms of violence, resisting the ways in which discourses of spectacular violence elide the meaning, context, and effects of that violence. They remind us what forms of understanding and significance of violence are hidden from the sight of modernist, humanist eyes.

Sitting under a large mango tree on Sunday morning, May 19, 2013, the community of Lukodi gathered for its annual memorial prayers, commemorating the anniversary of what had come to be known as the Lukodi Massacre of 2004. According to the 2011 report of the Justice and Reconciliation Project (JRP), on that day of May 19, 2004, the LRA "raided the village of Lukodi, and carried out a massacre that led to the death of over sixty people" (Justice and Reconciliation Project 2011, 5). On the report's cover appears a poignant quote from a "Lukodi massacre survivor," who says, "By the time the LRA left, the whole camp was littered with dead bodies as if they had been on a hunting spree. They killed people as if they were hunting animals and not human beings." The report tells us, "The affected community can only guess what may have instigated the massacre or who should be held responsible, as no accountability mechanisms are in place. They continue longing to understand what happened" (5).

What is surprising about the report is how it remains almost blind to its own data in the form of several pages of explanation, including testimony from a former LRA rebel involved in the attack, of how and why the LRA attacked Lukodi: "Information would flow quickly from the civilians to the soldiers regarding the movements of the LRA. The LRA started to perceive the population of Lukodi as a group of Government collaborators because of such cooperation. They blamed the community for several incidents" (Justice and Reconciliation Project 2011, 10). It then goes on to describe one civilian whose report to the UPDF led to a rebel death and the capture of an LRA weapon; another civilian whose loud alert of the clandestine LRA presence led to the rebels coming under heavy UPDF fire; and a rebel from Lukodi who deserted the LRA, taking their gun with him. Whereas the meaning and context of the LRA attack as a retaliatory violence was quite clear, the report nonetheless represents the LRA attack as illogical and senseless, voiding the meaning of its violence in order to re-create it as inhuman.

In the eleven months before these memorial prayers, I had spent a lot of time in and around Lukodi, a small trading center north of Gulu town, with friends who had been LRA rebels. Their understandings of what happened in Lukodi coincided with that of JRP, seeing the attack as retaliation for civilian actions against the LRA. One noted that an LRA weapons store had been reported by a Lukodi civilian to the UPDF; others said that an LRA rebel had been killed by a civilian. Most were less concerned with the LRA attack than with blaming the UPDF for creating the civilian camp around (rather than protected by) their barracks.[40] They lamented what had happened, but held onto the contextual significance of the violence as a necessary evil, neither senseless nor inhuman.

It took some time for the multidenominational prayers to begin. The church pews that had been taken outside under the giant tree began to fill, slowly, with local residents, and then later with NGO staff and beneficiaries. A Catholic priest began to tell a story of how he was briefly abducted by the LRA and taken to the *lum*, where he was asked to help lead prayers. He recalled that Kony said that Jesus was in the *lum*, but, he asked the congregation, was he really? He dismissed Kony's claim to be a messenger of God, saying it was just a bad or evil spirit (*tipu marac*) that Kony had. Citing Mark 13:14, he warned of people who claimed to speak in God's name but only had intentions to deceive—not only Kony, but also corrupt pastors, particularly from Kampala.

After the Catholic priest finished his sermon, a prominent Anglican bishop took the floor. The bishop was from Lukodi, where he maintained a large field of his own, with cattle and cash crops. He apologized for arriving late, blaming it on car trouble, and briefly commemorated those who were killed in the 2004 attack. I expected him to give a sermon that mirrored the JRP report—to speak of the brutality and senselessness, perhaps even inhumanity, of the violence perpetrated by the LRA. I also suspected he might condemn Kony in Christian terms as a violent and superstitious primitive.

To my surprise, the bishop barely spoke ill of the killings. He chastised the congregation for wrongly seeing these killings as suffering (*can*). There

Figure 4. Lukodi Memorial, in disrepair. Photo by author.

were only two forms of *can* in Lukodi, he claimed: first, that people were lazy and did not want to work, and second, that they lost their faith and did not put their prayers into practice. If they did not work hard, he mused, more would die of poverty than those who died at Kony's hands. For him, the attack was relatively insignificant, unworthy of even being seen as suffering, much less imbued with the heavier moral weight of "inhumanity."

He urged people to stop quarreling over land, and illustrated his point with the remarkable story of a young man who persisted in digging in land that, he was warned time and again, was not his own. He was eventually arrested by the LC3 [the chairman of the sub-county] and caned. "His ear is in his buttocks [*Ite tye i dude*]," the bishop said. The young man was told to stop digging on land that did not belong to him, and he did not listen until he was caned.

The bishop then, to my surprise, favorably compared the caning of this young man with the canings that Kony [the LRA] used to administer. "The Acholi are stupid [*Acoli ming*]," the bishop proclaimed, and *needed* to be caned. "This guy was beaten. Kony got them used to sticks, because people's ears are in their buttocks [*Kigoyo jal-i. Kony onyebogi ki odoo pien it dano tye i dudgi*]." People did not listen to Kony, just like this young man did not listen to people who told him not to dig on land that was not his. It was not until the police and LC3 came and beat him that he began to listen. To my amazement, the bishop used this narrative not only to recast LRA violence as sensible and moral, but also to draw on it as a model for enacting positive social change. His sermon departed from an established Acholi Christian tradition in which such violence was generally seen as immoral and against humanity.

The bishop was not the only one who imagined LRA violence in more intricate ways, beyond representations that cast it as immoral and inhuman. Many elders pointed out to me that "traditionally" (by which they meant before the introduction of the religion of white men and modern government systems), Acholi people used machetes (*pangas*) to cut and kill others, to avenge the deaths of their own people. They killed animals, burned houses, and abducted young girls and brought them back with them. The modes of killing were the same as the LRA's—the only difference, I was told over and over by civilians, was that the LRA killed people for no reason (*nono*), without any offense committed against them. People had, one elder told me, "forgotten" the old kinds of killing before religion and modern law, only learning them again from Kony—as did, we discussed, one man in the nearby district of Pader, who had recently cut off part of a woman's upper extremity in a land wrangle.[41] Recalling the Acholi chief who brought the hands of his dead enemy to the sub-commissioner, these forms of killing were justified and moral in contemporary frameworks. If a discourse of "humanity" indeed existed prior to colonial encounters (a possibility of which I am skeptical), they were also surely "human(e)" killings.

Others traced LRA modes of killing to different violent practices in postcolonial Uganda. In the eyes of historian A. B. K. Kasozi, post-independent Ugandans had begun "to live in an almost Hobbesian state of nature" as they endured "dehumanizing violence" (1999, 5, 13). General Idi Amin, I was told by elders comparing him with the LRA, also mutilated people—dissecting their bellies, removing their internal organs, and sometimes eating them. It was Amin who brought back mutilation and killing, after people had forgotten about it. Some talked disparagingly about the Karamojong, a tribe in northeast Uganda that served as the savage other to the Acholi, who were thought to commit brutal violence because they were, in this elder's words, far from the government and its law. If you do not know the law, he said, you are like an animal (lee), and you do not know that killing is bad. In the postcolony, colonial moral frameworks of violence had been assimilated as "local" ones. Postcolonial violence like mutilation could then sometimes be condemned as excessive in terms of humanity, rather than in other terms, or possibly not at all.

Where "inhumanity" connoted an exceptional immorality of forms of violence, many saw LRA violence in the aftermath of, and in moral response to, state violence committed by NRA (now UPDF) soldiers around the time of Museveni's coup. Most people were able to (often angrily) narrate, either firsthand or through family stories, acts of violence committed by the NRA against Acholi civilians in the late 1980s and early 1990s, including sodomy of men, rape of women, defecating into the mouths of dead cattle, defecating into flour stores, and burning huts and granaries. At Bucoro, people were killed by being pushed into a pit and then set on fire. An elderly witness to this violence said, "They killed them for no reason [Gineko nono]," echoing what civilians came to say of LRA violence years later. Otto recalled NRA violence with anger, lamenting that he was already with the LRA in the *lum* when these things happened to civilians at home. He claimed he would have destroyed the soldiers who were enacting such violence himself if he could have. Indeed, he was proud to say that "we" [the LRA] killed most of the NRA who were committing sodomy against men. If one were to go looking for the specific perpetrators of sodomy in Bucoro and elsewhere, Otto claimed, one would have difficulty in finding any of them still alive—implying that the LRA executed them all. To the extent that the LRA had at least some justification in responding to NRA violence, it was difficult to see LRA violence as fully "inhuman."[42]

Moral justification, rather than the physical or spectacular forms of violence, came to construct not only LRA violence outside of discourses of humanity, but also violence such as mob justice. A recurrent form of communal punishment in Acholiland, mob violence often took the forms of beatings, spearings, or cutting up of people and not uncommonly ended in the death of the accused if objectors, including police or government, did not intervene. Thieves were among the primary targets of mob justice. "The thief tires people [*Lakwo oolo dano*]," one man told me. He described the nuisance posed to communities by thieves who were not dealt with by the police and who, despite being warned time and again (like many objects of LRA violence), continued to steal, until one day they were caught and simply killed. Unhappy with corruption and other inadequacies of existing government and policing, in which thieves might continually bribe police for their release, many resorted to mob justice as an alternative to the weakness or inability of existing governance and law to address their concerns: "It's said to be a community affair . . . there is some mercy at first [when the thief commits his first theft], but if it continues, we just finish [kill] him."

By contrast, born-again Christians and other religious people, I was told, did not involve themselves in mob justice because of the biblical teaching that people should not kill. They, not unlike colonial-era missionaries witnessing similar forms of violence, saw the ones participating in mob justice as animals that went mad (*lee ma opoo*). While religious folk were caught in scriptural dilemmas, many lower-level and local government officials were caught in the middle of two forms of justice. A friend of mine, an LC1 (lowest-level government leader, representing a parish), described how a mob once beat him for protecting a thief from being lynched. Hit in the chest by a brick, he was injured and hospitalized. However, if he had participated in the beating himself, he might have been arrested by the police as a killer for encouraging and committing mob justice. The LCs were, in essence, caught between community justice and state justice, between different moral codes that represented mob violence differently.

I suggested to the LC1 that perhaps, instead of killing a thief, one might just cut his hands off so that he could never steal again, as a kind of lesson similar to what the LRA did to government collaborators and informers. "It's better to kill [him]," he insisted, saying that the thief would have you arrested because he would know it was you that cut off his hand. So instead, he should be killed. Such violence toward suspected thieves was not unusual. The mayor of Gulu municipality at the time of my work was elected in part because he was seen to have taken a strong stance against crime while acting as an affiliate of the office of the Resident District Commissioner (RDC), the president's ears and eyes into every district. His technique of reducing crime was to hammer six-inch nails into the heads of thieves, which, people saw gratefully, reduced theft rates. That his violence was moral, I suggest, prevented it from becoming "inhuman," however spectacular its form.[43]

In the midst of other forms of violence, however, LRA violence put most civilians in a difficult position. Museveni was roundly reviled in Acholiland, and it initially struck me as a paradox that more people did not willingly join the LRA in their rebellion against Museveni. Indeed, young men who had never been part of the rebels would sometimes brazenly tell me that they wished they were there in the *lum* with Kony, fighting Museveni; others who were abducted at a younger age and escaped home wondered, many years later, if they would have been better off staying in the *lum*. It often struck me that had the rebellion begun in 2012 instead of in 1987, large numbers of Acholi men would have joined the LRA (or at least, they claimed they would have); indeed, in early 2013, Acholi ministers publicly warned their constituents against starting another rebellion ("Minister Warns Acholi" 2013; "Acholi Cautioned" 2013). With the passage of time and the worsening of life under Museveni, LRA violence seemed less immoral, and by extension, less inhuman.

Those who lived through the war told a different story—of being caught between the violence of the LRA and that of the government. Many attributed the lack of large numbers of men joining the LRA voluntarily to several causes: first, unlike the NRA/UPDF, the LRA offered no salary; second, when or if people tried to join the LRA, they risked being killed, in part because the LRA were very careful about spies infiltrating the ranks; third, many feared being killed in the course of fighting, often citing the difficulty of life in the *lum* as an impediment to joining the LRA (indeed, occasional hunger and famine, along with fatal disease, afflicted the LRA over their years in the *lum*). It is not difficult to understand the reluctance of civilians to support the LRA; as mostly rural peasants largely content producing food on their own clan land, Acholi villagers had too much to lose in a rebellion, and too much personal and kin-oriented concern to agree to lose it. These considerations made the rebellion immoral and senseless, easing its representation as cruel and inhuman violence. There were also spiritual and temporal concerns that spoke to other forms of discomfort, as we will see.

So, much as some civilians found moral reason in LRA violence, as they did in mob justice or in precolonial forms of violence, others understood LRA violence as immoral and cruel, operating outside of existing frameworks of understanding and entering into the realm of "inhumanity." One example of what came to be seen as brutal and senseless LRA violence took place in Omot. The Omot massacre of 2002 was arguably the most spectacular of LRA attacks, given the form of violence that was perpetrated there. In October 2002, the LRA retaliated against a rebel named Abong who deserted with the LRA's weapon and returned to his land in Omot, a sub-county in East Acholi. There is strong tension between East and West Acholi, a tension that existed before but grew during the war. The LRA were perceived as largely a West Acholi force, given that most of its leaders were from Gulu (including Kony, from Odek sub-county of Gulu District). They were largely shunned in East Acholi, where they garnered very little support.

Following Abong, a group of LRA soldiers arrived in Omot and killed about twenty-eight civilians. A few bodies were selected to be chopped up, with legs and arms placed in boiling pots in the middle of the road—a practice that, unlike the chopping of hands, had no known historical or traditional precedence in Acholiland. The cooking was, as the current LC1

Figure 5. Omot Memorial. Photo by author.

of the area described to me, an act meant to serve as an example to other LRA who might run off. But it was also a form of civilian education. My friend Mohammed, a former LRA military policeman, opposed the violence at Omot, asking rhetorically how a person could be cooked in a pot, as though a fish—implying that such violence was in some way dehumanizing. But, he reflected, rebels knew that in the areas where such brutal violence was committed, civilians started to do what the LRA said, when they had not before. Though an effective tactic, this cooking of body parts—unlike many other forms of LRA violence—finally threatened to transcend all existing boundaries of moral sense-making, and in doing so, entered local discourses of inhumanity.

In Acholi, people variously described the violence in Omot to me as "a thing done fiercely/cruelly/harshly, anyhow or in any way" (*tim gero lataya*), "a bad thing done fiercely/cruelly/harshly, uselessly" (*tim gero marac ma konye pe*), and "a painful thing done fiercely/cruelly/harshly" (*tim gero malit*) and that in attempting to explain the violence, "there is no understanding of it" (*niang mo pe iye*). By contrast, a JRP report written in English on the Omot massacre describes the rebels' actions as "barbaric" (Justice and Reconciliation Project 2010, 13), re-presenting this violence, through the term's etymology, as uncivilized and backward. Recalling the colonial-era discourses explored at the beginning of this chapter, this kind of representation similarly threatened to preclude a richer telling of violence through other moral frameworks.

THE VIOLENCE OF MODERNITY, OR THE MODERNIZATION OF VIOLENCE

> I am not aware [of reports that Kony had been killed] but
> that would be very good news for *humanity*.
> UPDF Lieutenant Colonel Paddy Ankunda, 2014[44]

In this chapter, I elucidated the ways in which LRA violence was made humanity's other. LRA violence became "inhuman" because of the ways in which it was positioned to exist against or apart from modern reasoning, including moral certainty, temporo-morality, and prescribed remedies for postcolonial malaise. These expectations of modernity coalesced into a moral sensibility known as "humanity." When these peculiarly modern expectations of violence went incompletely fulfilled in the context of a spiritual postcolonial rebellion, the resulting friction grated against the moral sensibility of "humanity." In this process, LRA violence was not only condemned but also "dehumanized," and blamed on "tradition," "tribalism," and other concepts against which modernity constructed itself. When the LRA failed to satisfy modern expectations of violence, their violence became at once bifurcated from both modernity and humanity.

Under the discourse of inhumanity, the full complexity of meaning and context of LRA violence was ignored. Rebels, elders, bishops, and indeed most civilians largely did not read LRA violence as inhuman as long as it drew on existing and/or conceivable moral frameworks through which it made sense. For example, when it drew moral justification from or as a response to state violence, or was akin to mob justice, it resisted characterization as "inhuman." When such frameworks were exhausted, as in the

case of the Omot massacre, LRA violence began to interrogate the boundaries of what was considered "human(e)" violence. But more commonly,
LRA violence was opposed to humanity only after a discursive erasure of
alternative moral frameworks of understanding. As an analytic, "humanity" offered little to morally frame or understand LRA violence.

   In the next chapter, I approach a different other to humanity—
animality—through an understanding not of LRA "guerrilla warfare" but
of "gorilla warfare," exploring the ways in which LRA fighters were seen—
and saw themselves—as wild animals living in the space of the *lum*.

3 Gorilla Warfare

LIFE IN AND BEYOND THE BUSH

This chapter interrogates one way in which Acholi civilians delimit the borders of humanity—through a simple, common-sense division between the "bush" (*lum*) and the "home" (*gang*). According to this prevailing wisdom, the "bush" is the bad space where animals live, and the "home" is the good space where humans live. The LRA rebels came to challenge what humanity really meant by virtue of living their lives for years in the *lum* while engaged in what they called "gorilla warfare." In doing so, they assaulted the normative ontological categories used by civilians to divide humanity from its others, showing by virtue of their own lives the amount of interchange between animality and humanity.

This chapter begins with a brief history of the origins of the *lum-gang* binary, followed by a thick description of the ways in which Acholi civilians construct these binaries in practice within the context of the LRA war. I then offer up, by contrast, the experiences and stories of former militants who lived in the *lum* as "gorillas"—human-animals that disrupted the normative humanity of *gang*. Their stories pry open these binaries for investigation, offering an ethnographic critique of certain logics that have been shared more or less contiguously by colonial-era big-game hunters, today's Acholi civilians, and NGO and development workers, among others. My approach begins from the civilian understanding of the concept of *lum* but slowly moves into the existential and phenomenological world of the LRA militant in the *lum*—a world in which some of these binaries begin to break down, unable to neatly confine the density and fluidity of experience and thought. Through the eyes of LRA rebels, being against humanity means questioning some of the very conditions by which their civilian counterparts understood humanity—including its proper space, morality, and level of development. Confronting the terms of humanity in this way opens up a space to think about possibilities of a moral life beyond humanity.

"THE BUSH": ANTHROPO-MORAL GEOGRAPHY AND THE CONSTRUCTION OF HUMANITY

I had no interest in animals before beginning to work with former LRA rebels, much less the philosophical or practical becomings of human-animals, nor—even worse—in engaging racist images of the animality of dangerous Black men in heart-of-darkness places like the *lum*. But in spite of my preexisting intellectual and political commitments, it became clear during the course of my research that I had to attend to a certain tension that existed not only in humanitarian discourse but also in Acholi civilian discourses around the question of the humanity, or lack thereof, of LRA rebels. This tension pitted humanity in opposition to animals. Much of it arose around the question of the morality of a space—*lum*—and was framed, to my surprise, in binaries pitting the *lum* against the home (*gang*), animals against humans, evil against good, and so forth.

Lum *versus* Gang

Lum (used hereafter in place of "the bush") is a central organizing concept by which Acholi civilians make sense of a particular space and its relation to morality and humanity. In the Acholi imagination, *lum* is loaded with a specific *moral* meaning and a specific relation to the *human*. It is best approached with what I would call an anthropo-moral geography, a study of a space in its relation to the specific concepts of the human, the animal,

Figure 6. Walking in the *lum*, between a river and a homestead near Palaro, Gulu District. Photo by author.

and the moral. The Acholi imagination of the *lum* is largely nonhuman and animal, and more often an evil or bad space than a good or clean space.

By the Acholi civilian definition, the *lum* is a space in which humans do not live or where human settlements do not exist. In this way, *lum* is antonymous to home or homestead (*gang*). People may make temporary visits to the *lum* for a variety of reasons. They may enter the *lum* to hunt; to gather firewood; to collect grass for thatching the roofs of huts; to tie goats and cattle to graze; to exorcise spirits; to defecate and urinate, if they have no latrine; to throw away and/or burn trash; or to seek refuge from danger,

---

Table 1 Comparison of "home" or "homestead" (*gang*)
and "the bush" (*lum*)

---

gang (*home*)	lum (*grass or bush*)
place of humans	place of animals and spirits
good	bad
clean	dirty
sacred or pure	profane
visible	hidden
domestic	wild
safe and peaceful	dangerous and violent
developed	backward or "left behind"
rational	irrational
easy to live in	hard or cruel to live in

---

among other reasons. But they do not permanently settle there. Indeed, when an Acholi household compound (*dyekal*) is first established, it is carved out of the *lum*. Existing grass is dug up or cut, and the remaining dirt is pounded down by foot over time to create a compacted, dry ground.

If one lets his compound (*dyekal*) grow grass or weeds and fall into disorder, he is considered irresponsible and reprimanded with the lament, "his compound has become *lum*" (*dyekalle odoko lum*). Men known to be chronic drunks are among those who are accused of this negligence, a moral condemnation that bears resemblance to colonial accounts discussed below.

Anthropo-moral Distinctions between Lum and Gang

The distinction made between human and nonhuman in the realm of *lum* is closely accompanied by other moral distinctions (table 1). These general divisions include: what need not and what need be feared or respected; what is clean and what is dirty; what is sacred[1] and what is profane; what is visible and what is hidden; what is sane or rational and what is wild or irrational; what is safe and what is dangerous; and what is developed and what is undeveloped or "left behind" (*dong cen*). I will address the conceptual origins of these categories below. What is critical here is to observe how these divisions reflect existing norms in an Acholi anthropo-moral geography. That is, opposing the conceptual spaces of *lum* and *gang* allows civilians to produce and reproduce notions of humanity defined by morality and space.

THE HISTORICAL CONSTRUCTION OF THE *LUM* IN ACHOLILAND

Much, of course, has been said about the meanings and connotations of the term "bush," particularly in British and Australian colonial history and in relation to notions of development, civilization, morality, and cleanliness, among other social concepts. But the "bush" has a particular meaning in the context of Acholi history, having been solidified in the colonial era. The division between "home" and "bush" that most Acholi rely on today is not a natural, static distinction. Rather, it originated in the context of a colonizing mission to civilize animalistic heathens.

Colonial officers and missionaries who spent time in Acholiland from the late 1800s up to independence in 1962 were among those who developed a moral distaste toward the *lum* as a space of and for wild animals. In their first visits with what are now known as the Acholi people, Europeans did not call them Acholi but rather Ganyi, Gang, or Gangi people, a name almost certainly derived from *gang*, which refers both to "village" and "home." F. K. Girling suggests that this name was given to the Acholi by Langi and Banyoro neighbors, and distinguished them as "sedentary agriculturalists" from the wandering hunters known as Kidi, who of course would be more likely to inhabit the *lum* (1952, 14).[2] That one original name of the Acholi was likely derived from *gang* suggests a fundamental description and definition of the people through a space other than *lum*.

For colonialists, the bush took on negative connotations, particularly as a space lacking Christian moral good, civilization, and order. This was seen most clearly in colonial accounts of the clearing of *lum* for stations and compounds. Arthur Kitching, who together with Albert Lloyd created the first Church Missionary Society (CMS) post in Acholiland at Patiko in 1904, wrote of the clearing of *lum* for their station there: "This change from thick grass to clearing, and from anarchy to order, is parabolic of the change coming over the ideas of the people: old suspicions of the white man are giving way to confidence, heathen jungle is receding before the entry of new ideas, and the ground is being broken up for the sowing of the Gospel seed" (1906, 372). Here, the clearing of *lum* physically removed both grass and the spiritual evils within it, including "anarchy" and "heathenism."

Beyond the question of morality, the "bush" or "grass" was in practical terms, too, a formidably difficult space. European travelers might camp temporarily but not permanently in it, in part because it was so challenging to traverse. Quentin O. Grogan, a hunter seeking ivory in colonial Acholiland, described "bad march[es] in long grass," that was "awful for walking through," and abandoning elephants who entered into bush "so thick [that they] did not consider it worth pursuing them" (ca. 1908–11). Charles Delmé-Radcliffe, among other soldiers, lamented the difficulty of passing through the *lum* of Acholiland with his troops as they pursued Sudanese mutineers within the Uganda Rifles, battalions of the colonial army known as the King's African Rifles (KAR): "This country is formidable—grass 8 feet high and everywhere swamps [illegible] for miles, heavy rain, forest everywhere and no tracks" (1901).[3]

While British officers and big-game hunters did not envision the space as natural for themselves, they certainly believed that the *lum* was the right space for a so-called primitive people such as the Acholi whose place in humanity was still in question. The governor of the Uganda Protectorate, Hesketh Bell, on a trip through the Nile Province in 1906, reflected on the physical appearance of these "savages," as he called them: "While they would probably appear very remarkable in Piccadilly or in the Row, *here, surrounded by tall grass* and leaning on their spears, *they look almost appropriate*. They have cleared quite a large piece of ground as a camp for me and have built a hut that looks like a huge beehive for my accommodation" (1906b, 104, emphasis added). In colonial eyes, such so-called savages were one with the *lum* in which they were supposed to have lived, within structures resembling the homes of nonhuman insects. Meanwhile, colonial officers like Bell lived only on cleared ground in preferably different forms of housing.

As the Acholi were seen to be fit to live in the *lum*, they were logically seen to be able to fight better within it. Many Acholi were recruited as soldiers (*askari*) into the KAR, where they were seen as different creatures. In his 1956 history of the KAR, Hubert Moyse-Bartlett demonstrates how Africans were imagined, by virtue of difference in their physical nature, to be more adept at "jungle warfare" than their European commanding officers:

> In many aspects of jungle warfare African troops proved outstanding. Their great physical strength enabled them to make long marches across rough country, carrying mortars, ammunition, and other heavy loads. . . . Their eyesight, especially at night, and their sense of hearing when in the jungle, were markedly better than those of Europeans. . . . Some senior officers thought the clumsiness of Europeans in thick bush a liability, and preferred to entrust reconnaissance, as apart from fighting patrols, to the leadership of Africans, despite their lower level of intelligence. (1956, 682)

In the postcolonial period, of course, this form of warfare became commonplace, as countless rebel groups, including the LRA, went "to the bush" as they sought to, among other purposes, overthrow existing regimes.

It is difficult to historically untangle the origins of the *lum-gang* binary and its related features. Certainly, colonial influences helped establish or deepened this binary, often sorting Acholi into the *lum* category and Europeans into the *gang* category. But that does not mean that this division was only a colonial creation or imposition. It also drew on and changed parts of Acholi civilian ontology that colonists ostensibly "discovered" in the course of their early encounters. One clue that points to an extra-colonial history lies in the nickname given by Acholi to Delmé-Radcliffe, mentioned above in his pursuit of Sudanese mutineers. He was dubbed "Langa-Langa," or "were-lion," a name that even his European colleagues began to use to refer to him in their writings. Moyse-Bartlett explains that "the distances he covered during the night marches of his military patrols earned him locally the name of Langa-Langa ('were-lion'), as the tribesmen thought it impossible for a mere human to traverse the bush so quickly under the cover of darkness" (1956, 85). Sir John Milner Gray notes of Delmé-Radcliffe, in the third part of his history of Acholi, "He was accordingly credited with the ability to turn himself into a lion and pass through the bush in this form" (1952, 132).[4] There was, it seems, a precolonial restriction on the nature of human behavior in the *lum*; when Delmé-Radcliffe exceeded them, he could no longer be considered by the Acholi as only human, but rather part human, part animal. Entering the *lum*, he was no longer fully human.

THE CONCEPT OF *LUM* IN THE ACHOLI CIVILIAN ONTOLOGY

The concept of *lum* has remained external to humanity in postcolonial Acholiland. Through the course of the LRA war, the *lum* existed in a process of mutual transformation with the LRA itself. In other words, the social imagination about the LRA was shaped by the fact that they lived in the nonhuman *lum*; likewise, the social imagination about the *lum* was shaped by the fact that the violent LRA lived in it. As intertwined concepts, the LRA and the *lum* mutually transform and co-create each other. In the Acholi civilian imagination, *lum* has subsequently taken on a more sinister meaning as a space not only of inhumanity, but also of dirt, madness, and non-modernity.

The Dirt of the Lum

"All the things that are in the *lum* are bad [*Gin ma tye i lum weng raco*]," my friend Akello Sabina, a practicing spirit-priest (*ajwaka*), once said to me, articulating a common cultural spatio-moral dichotomy. Acholi villagers often describe *lum* as "dirty" or "dark" (*col*, pronounced ideophonically in Acholi with a grating, unpleasant sound that embodies its meaning as fundamental depravity). It is seen as a wild and difficult place to live in, where one is exposed to cruel elements such as rain or famine. This is often cited as a reason why more Acholi did not join the LRA voluntarily—while many were sympathetic to the struggle and wanted to see President Museveni overthrown, they did not want to suffer in the rain and hunger they imagined existing in the *lum*.

By virtue of staying in the *lum*, the LRA were also seen as being immoral, evil, or ostensibly bad. "The first thing that comes to mind [when I think about *lum*] is that it's a bad place, and that's why people regard those who return from the *lum* [the LRA] as bad people," Akello reflected. Specifically, the LRA were seen as being dirty or impure for having stayed in the *lum*.

In reception centers—where many former rebels were processed after having been captured or having deserted—it was common for rebels' dreadlocked or grown-out hair to be shaved clean. Reception center staff justified this practice by citing the dangers of lice and dirt picked up in the *lum*. Rebels' clothes were also burned in a ritual meant to symbolize "the complete change from the past life to the new one," both "burning away the past ways of life" and "burning away the past memories."[5] Gunya remembered when she went through this procedure at the reception center: "They [the reception center staff] burned [the clothes], saying it's the dirt of the *lum* [*cilo me lum*], [and that it was being burned] so you become a good person [*dano maber*]. . . . They said the clothes were like the dirt from the *lum*, and they wanted it to remain there [in the *lum*]. Since we were home . . . we should get rid of dirt in the *lum* and become new people. They also shaved our hair clean, and we grew new hair at home."[6]

On the other side of this relationship, *lum* has taken on the characteristics of being not only the dangerous site of vengeance spirits (*cen*), but also a site that is fierce (*ger*) and merciless (*kica pe*), and a place where people's hearts turn dark. In everyday life among young men in Gulu town, those who show no mercy to others, perhaps playing a series of punishing moves in a card game outside a roadside shop, might well be asked, half-jokingly, "Were you in the *lum*?!" From the standpoint of disease and dirt attributed to the *lum*, the LRA became more impure; from the standpoint of the imagined horrors and evils attributed to life as a rebel, the *lum* became more impure, adding to the imagined sacredness of *gang*. As the reception center ritual suggested, moving from the *lum* to *gang* meant a transformation from dirtiness to purity, creating "new people" out of what were seen as bad and dirty animals.

Nonhuman Creatures and the Lum

> Children who were abducted, but were not forced to commit atrocities, who were not forced to have children; they have a *more human than an animal mind.*
>
> Reception center characterizing "low risk" children returning from the LRA (Gulu Support the Children Organisation 2002, 15, emphasis added)

If the *lum* is not the space of humans, it is certainly the space of others—animals, spirits, and nonhuman creatures of all kinds. Whether *lum* is used to refer to the grass surrounding one's compound, or to the larger areas of *lum* (often designated as *tim*, vast stretches of *lum* that include hunting grounds and, in the legal framework of the modern nation-state, national parks), it is treated with caution because dangerous animals may lurk within it. In the *lum* near the compound, one might come across snakes or stinging ants; in *tim*, one may come across wild animals (*lee tim*), especially fierce wild animals (*lee tim mager*), even ones that can kill (*merok*), such as lions or hippopotamuses. Entering into these areas requires a degree of vigilance and a weapon with which to defend oneself. Friends often lent me a spear or ax to carry in case we encountered danger while walking through the *lum* to go fish, swim in streams, or check hunting traps in more rural areas. And if there are worries about entering *lum* or *tim*, so too are there worries about what may come out of it. In West Acholi near the boundaries of Murchison Falls National Park, farmers fear the incursion of animals into their homesteads, be they elephants that eat crops from their fields or predatory cats that kill and feast on their livestock.

In the Acholi civilian imagination, performing and suffering violence in the *lum* pulled LRA rebels out of the human and into the wild and the animal. It was thought that the LRA suffered through living conditions not meant for human beings. A well-known weekly radio show aimed to encourage LRA defection, entitled *Dwog Cen Paco* (Come Back Home), often drew on this notion.[7] In a broadcast on June 13, 2013, the host, Lacambel, spoke in apparent sympathy to LRA rebels still in the *lum*, whom he sought to lure back home: "I know how you sleep there [in the *lum*]. The desired Acholi home is one with a urinary shelter, latrine, and houses for sleeping—not sleeping under trees anyhow. These are things needed for being human." The wandering of the LRA in the *lum* without settled homesteads removed them from the social category of humanity. This inhumanity was, in the civilian imagination, expressed in the rebel body—cut up from walking through the *lum* and thinned from hunger. *Lum* is indeed very difficult to pass through, often cutting the skin of those who attempt to traverse it. Radio messages and songs urging the LRA to leave the *lum* and return home (*gang*) advise fighters that "the grass is

Figure 7. Some leaves of wild plants eaten by the LRA in the *lum* (left to right): *pobo*, pumpkin (*okono*), and *larwece*. Photo by author.

cutting you for no reason" (*lum tye ka ngoli nono*). A June 6, 2013, broadcast of *Dwog Cen Paco* reminded rebels of the pain they feel when their skin is scratched and pricked by thorns in the *lum*.

The body's figure is equally imagined to be dehumanized by the hunger that rebels face from time to time. The LRA have indeed eaten wild plants and other wild foods considered fit for consumption not by humans, but by wild animals. Many former rebels painfully remembered times of hunger in the *lum* during which they were forced to eat wild plants, leaves (such as the *pobo*, pumpkin leaves [*pot okono*], and *larwece*, pictured in figure 7), and roots—whatever they could get their hands on, wondering if they would survive or die of hunger. On the June 6 broadcast, Lacambel contrasted bodies thinned and scratched in the *lum* to that of Otim, a former rebel joining him in the studio that night, who, Lacambel told his listeners, had grown fat and now had smooth skin. "They are now staying where humans are supposed to stay, not where animals are supposed to stay. Because if someone stays where a human is supposed to stay, his body cannot be the same as the one who is staying where animals are supposed to stay," Lacambel remarked of Otim and other former rebels, attempting to entice more LRA out of the *lum*.

Even respected figures in the peace talks between the LRA and the Government of Uganda, such as Catholic priest Carlos Rodríguez Soto— who was arrested and abused by the government after being accused of collaborating with the LRA—draw on this association between the *lum*, animality, and the body of the LRA rebel. Throughout his reflections on the war published in 2009, Soto describes rebels as animals: he compares one, Onekomon, to a wildcat ("His fingernails were outgrown.... He reminded me of a big cat ready to attack his prey, pondering first the calibre of its claws" [8]); speaks of a certain area as being "infested" with rebels (122); and is reminded of Saint Francis of Assisi's speech to a man- and animal-eating wolf when, as part of peace talks, Catholic Archbishop John Baptist Odama spoke "with great humility and sincere affection to rough armed men [LRA rebels]" (151).

Aside from animals lurking in the *lum*, one must also be careful of spirits. Certain categories of evil spirits known as *gemo*, traditionally thought to be responsible for infectious diseases such as measles, smallpox, and the plague, stay primarily in the *lum* and can attack those who walk carelessly into the *lum*.[8] Other bad spirits are also said to stay in the *lum*.[9] When a spirit-priest or witch doctor (*ajwaka*) is possessed, it is not uncommon for more than one spirit to possess the *ajwaka*. Some are good spirits and others are bad. An *ajwaka*-to-be will often run to the *lum*, where bad spirits are chased away and left behind there with food to eat, while the *ajwaka* returns home with good spirits. If bad spirits remain with the *ajwaka*, they can bring madness (*apoya*) to the *ajwaka*. Indeed, an *ajwaka* often releases madness from her clients into the *lum*, symbolically expelling irrationality into the depository of the *lum*. It is not surprising, then, to know that madness (*apoya*) was another characteristic attributed to the LRA because of their stay in the *lum*. Mad people, it is observed, often run to or even live in the *lum*; and so it was sometimes said that the LRA was mad. Former rebels who joined civilians at home might be stigmatized as mad not only for being haunted by the spirits of those they had killed, but also for coming to embody the madness of the space they inhabited for so long. Civilians saw rebels living in the *lum* as mad animals, putting their humanity into question.

Since the height of active combat, during which many people were killed in the *lum*, their bones left unburied, the *lum* has come to be feared as a site in which vengeance ghosts (*cen*) roam unrestrained, ready to attack those who might come across them. Women I met expressed unease at fetching firewood from the *lum*, worried that *cen* might attack them. Along with *cen*, people still fear unexploded bombs and landmines that have remained in the *lum* after the war. These are sometimes discovered in the course of clearing land for peasant farming. Reports periodically surface of these devices exploding and killing unsuspecting villagers. Most of my friends who lived in more rural villages had come across some remnants of weapons when clearing new farmland, including bullets, bayonets, and grenades. As the rebels took to the *lum*, they came to occupy elements of danger and animality preexisting in the space; at the same time, the *lum* came to be a more feared space, filled as it was by the violent weapons and ghosts of war.

The Development Imaginary and the Lum

As a space without and not for humans, *lum* also exists in a development imaginary as a backward foil for "town." In this anthropo-moral geography of development, *lum* is devoid of material or technological progress that might otherwise be seen or observed in town—electricity, roads, and concrete buildings, to name a few. More recently, however, *lum* has expanded in everyday linguistic use to refer not only to uninhabited grass, but also to rural villages far from town centers. Called *caro* in the past, these rural areas are beginning to be referred to more casually as *lum*. In town, while watching football in bars or getting repairs done at motorcycle shops, I often heard town businessmen speak of trips they had recently made or were planning to make to the *lum*—referring not, as I initially thought, to uninhabited wilderness, but to their village homes. In a region increasingly shaped by anxieties about and discourses on modernity, the village, as *lum*, has for some been reduced to a kind of spatio-moral wilderness.[10] In this usage, one that some contest as incorrect and denigrating to the village, *lum* is defined primarily against markers of modernity rather than the absence of human settlement. These markers are not mere statements of fact, but rather moral judgments that instill modernity as a requirement for humanity.

Many suggest that those who live in villages far from towns or centers are not only inferior humans, but in fact stay like animals (*gibedo lee lee*), hunting and gathering food from the forest. They have "remained behind" (*gidong cen*). Such characterization is more widely applied to the Karamojong, a tribe of northeastern Uganda that is ridiculed in Acholiland for its supposed backwardness. It is not uncommon for a student in an Acholi classroom who has difficulty learning and/or using computers and other technologies to be mocked as a Karamojong who will "stay behind" while his or her peers "move ahead." These discourses about *lum* and development almost certainly derive in part from colonial activities and ideas. One such colonial project was the introduction of the "bush school." The Church Missionary Society (CMS), which opened its first permanent post in Acholiland in 1904, created schools that they referred to variously as "village," "bush," and "sub-grade," conflating these terms in a way that discursively cast rural villages as inferior, backward, and wild in a way that Gulu businessmen replicate today. In these schools, "children from the bush" were to be educated in order to create "a more enlightened, intelligent people" who were "more law abiding and amenable to reason" in the process of "giving way to christian [*sic*] civilization."[11] This education was premised on the idea that people in the *lum* were uncivilized, irrational, and not fully human.

The supposed lack of development became a theme of co-transformation of the *lum* and the LRA. While government soldiers were said to be trained and to stay "with people" (in *gang*—specifically, in army barracks), rebels were said to be untrained and to stay in the *lum*. The opposition of a developed *gang* to an undeveloped *lum* was enhanced in the war by the opposition of a professionalized, modern national-state army to the ad hoc, trained-on-the-go rebel group whose ranks were largely abducted by force. Isolated in the *lum* and dissociated from markers of modernity, the rebels—together with the violence they perpetrated—were seen as inhuman.

LRA NOTIONS OF THE *LUM*

A largely Acholi rebel force, the LRA to some extent imagined the *lum* in similar ways to the Acholi civilian narrative. They feared evil spirits (*gemo*) in the *lum*, using special precautions like shooting bullets into the air or enacting protective rituals in the yard (a sacred site within the LRA, discussed below) to scare away these *gemo* and other spirits (*jogi*) that could attack them while traveling in the *lum*. They had to protect themselves from fierce wild animals, including lions, leopards, and snakes. They remembered times of hunger during which they survived on all kinds of wild food. They bear scars not only from gunshot wounds but also from cuts they accrued from walking in the *lum*. Many speak of the ease of life in *gang* today compared to the suffering of life in the *lum*, where their clothes and gumboots wore out, they slept in the rain, they walked enormous distances in a single day, and they constantly dealt with the possibility of enemy attacks.

But by entering into and staying in the *lum* for long periods of time, in some cases for decades, many former rebels returned to *gang* with a different anthropo-moral ontology in which the very meaning of *lum* was fundamentally remade. In this LRA understanding, the *lum* remains an ambivalent space, largely reserved for animals and full of impurity or danger. But having paradoxically become "people of the *lum*," the LRA also reinvented that space, detaching it from certain forms of animality, evil, and premodernity that otherwise define it in the Acholi civilian ontology. Engaged in "gorilla warfare," the LRA saw themselves as fierce, honorable, and tricky animals highly skilled at fighting. They transformed the *lum* into a site of life, purity, and development, challenging and in some cases dissolving the moral dichotomies that distinguished *lum* from *gang*. In doing so, they not only defied what it meant to be human in Acholi, but also disrupted some of the boundaries that civilians had made between humanity and animality.

The LRA Gorillas: Human-Animal Becomings

When the LRA first started fighting, and before they had been seen in the flesh, villagers suspected that they were wild beasts, perhaps akin to *nguu dano*, shape-shifting man-beasts known to raid livestock when night falls. Opwonya, the older brother of my friend Labwor, once told me his memories of when the LRA first began to operate in the late 1980s. At that time, many people had not actually seen the LRA for themselves. Rumors circulated that the LRA were not actually human beings, but rather very hairy creatures. Opwonya recalls that one man in their area who had hidden during an LRA incursion had seen that they were in fact human beings, and he tried to dismiss the rumor that they were animals.

Like many rebel groups before them, including Museveni's NRA, the LRA began their rebellion by taking to the *lum*—traveling, living, and fighting in this space outside the homestead or the town. "People think if you stayed in the *lum*, you're like an animal—you have four legs, you change into animals and birds, you have fur on your body," Musa, a former rebel, described to me. Civilians conceived of former rebels who had stayed in the *lum* fighting for decades as animals: "They imagine your behavior has become like that of animals. They think you eat just anything because you're a gorilla."

Like many LRA soldiers with limited or no command of English (much less Spanish), Musa heard and understood "guerrilla warfare" as "gorilla warfare." Many LRA came to understand that they were practicing "gorilla warfare," a style of fighting in which one lives in the *lum* with animals and eats, fights, and organizes oneself as that nonhuman primate might do, becoming wild or fierce like a gorilla. The space of the *lum* is central to gorilla warfare. It is, as Musa told me as we sat talking in his hut, "a place of animals and birds, not a place of people." In English, *lum* literally translates as "grass," but it is most commonly translated as "the bush"—a word freighted with significances in a (post)colonial Africa roundly equated with a bestial wild, and classically associated with animality in works such as G. W. F. Hegel's *Philosophy of History*, Joseph Conrad's *Heart of Darkness*, and perhaps the vast majority of what has been written about Africa.

Curious, I often asked my rebel friends to tell me why they thought this kind of fighting was named after, as they saw it, gorillas. "Maybe they got it from how animals organize themselves and fight," Musa ventured. Others, such as Mohammed, agreed. He remembered the way Kony talked about gorilla warfare: "[Kony said] that sometimes we will have to live like gorillas, on our own . . . without relying on anything or anyone."

My friend Labwor added his own definition of what a gorilla is, describing gorilla warfare as a sacred process of transforming from animals into humans: "[A gorilla is] someone who has already sacrificed his life and will stay the same as an animal, until he has finished his program that he has gone for, so that he becomes human." He was, he suggested, drawing this definition from a sermon Kony had given in church while they were still in the *lum* together. "[Kony] said that he who believes in me shall stay like a wild animal. And the day after tomorrow, when he's reaching the end of his life, he will change back to being a human being. And the good thing for which you are fighting, you will see [it achieved] when you have changed."

Identifying as nonhuman animals was a highly ambivalent practice for many former rebels. On the one hand, it made them, particularly in civilian eyes, appear to be backward, underdeveloped, dirty, and impure. Many recognized that civilians stigmatized them as animals and excluded them from humanity for having stayed for long periods in the *lum*; for having committed violence and killed people; and for having eaten wild foods. In this way, being excluded from the human was both an insult and a punishment. As one friend told me, "An animal is worthless. . . . [The LRA] should be compared to something else, not animals."

But on the other hand, it made them both exemplary and threatening, offering them strength and purpose as rebel fighters, in ways similar to that offered by the imagery of lions often used to characterize and glorify African leaders. Labwor, as with all names in this book, is a pseudonym, but one chosen by Labwor himself. In the Acholi language, *labwor* means "lion." "Put Labwor," he told me, when I asked him what name he wanted to appear here in place of his real name, "because I'm a lion. People should know that this guy is a *dano mager* [a wild person]." Animality in Acholi, and as conceived of among ex-LRA in particular, is not quite an unambiguously depraved condition into which one might fear falling, having been expelled from humanity.

This is in part because animality is polysemous. There are moral distinctions between animals of various types in Acholi. Some, such as the dog (*gwok*), are ridiculed and demeaned. The proverbial lament "I have become a dog" (*adoko gwok*) is used to describe the deplorable position of someone who has lost social status, wealth, and/or family, among others (see Banya 1994, 149). Others, however, such as the elephant or the lion, are seen in a different light—feared and respected (*lworre*). Indeed, sometimes former rebels would speak of themselves as different from lions and elephants not in the sense of being *less* fierce, but *more*. That the LRA were killing such fierce wild animals (*merok*) in the *lum* meant that they were *fiercer* than them. Set apart from lions and leopards, former rebels saw themselves favorably as "gorillas" engaged in "gorilla warfare."

Musa compared LRA rebels to a range of apes—baboons (*bim*), chimpanzees (*gunya*), and gorillas—primarily in terms of military organization and conduct. Reflecting the sentiment of Acholi folktales, in which monkeys are generally portrayed as wise animals, he noted that baboons are soldier-animals (*lee ma mony*). They protect each other well, taking turns guarding as they eat. When they stand, Musa reflected, they line up like soldiers. They communicate effectively, quickly spreading alerts when danger arises. *Gunya*, he noted, are also wise, and guard their young well, with some remaining awake at night to protect the others from possible attacks. They are able to see far into the darkness of night. Like the LRA, they walk anywhere in the *lum* and climb directly up hills rather than following well-trodden human footpaths. "I wasn't a wild animal [*lee tim*] when I was there in the bush, but I was using their system of living to live in the *lum*, and to defeat my enemies [*lumone*]," Musa reflected. Part of that system of living, he explained, included skillfulness in evading capture by enemy soldiers: "Animals aren't trapped easily or hunted easily— exactly like the LRA. . . . You can't find them in their base. You won't find one sleeping—they'll know [you are approaching] and go away [before you come across them] . . . And you can't trace the footprints [of the LRA], just like [you can't trace the footprints of] animals. They are very tricky." Identifying as animals in this way, the LRA were not excluding themselves from humanity in the way that civilians often did. Rather, they claimed an animal-human hybridity that contested common sense about the borders of Acholi humanity, putting the civilian category into question by living beyond humanity.

Reinventing the Lum *as a Site of Life*

The LRA were certainly in the *lum*, but this did not imply that they were constantly starving, suffering, and walking long distances through sharp, tall grass. Nor did it suggest that their lives had permanently become incompletely human or partly animal. Over time, they established bases, particularly in southern Sudan (today South Sudan), where they stayed for long periods. Like the clearing of a new compound, the establishment of bases served to make features of what had been *gang* become features of *lum*, remaking *lum* as a concept. And even when they ate wild plants to survive, they remained, stubbornly against the claims of civilians like Lacambel, fully human under the criteria of the civilian definition.

Their temporally continuous presence in the *lum* brought into question the very definition of *lum* as a place where only animals, and not people, live. For rebels like Otto, who spent more than two decades in the *lum*, the simple binary of *gang* and *lum* made little sense. Sitting in the shade of a passionfruit vine in his rural homestead, he reflected on his experience in reference to the civilian imagination of *lum*: "I knew I was at home there in what people call *lum*. And here [his ancestral land (*ngom kwaro*)] is home, too. . . . Both are home." Another rebel I knew, Acen, put it more succinctly: "*Gang* was in the *lum* [*Gang obedo i lum*]." Against the Acholi civilian analytic, *lum* had become *gang* and vice versa. The practical dis-solution of this binary was seen in the ways in which the LRA established life in the *lum* in the mold of typical rural Acholi life—building huts, farm-ing large stretches of land, having children, raising families.

One important way by which to understand the troubling of the *gang-lum* binary is through the naming of children born in the *lum* to LRA par-ents. Traditionally in Acholi, names given to newborns are highly meaning-ful, both symbolically and historically, reflecting, among other things, the conditions of life of the child's family at the time of birth; the physical con-ditions under which the child was born; or the spirits (*jogi*) said to mani-fest or be parents of the newborn (for example, a twin is given a *jok* name on account of the spiritual influence said to have effected or manifested in this unusual birth).[12] For instance, a newborn girl may be named Akec ("I am hunger") if she is born in a time of famine; another child may be named Acellam ("one is not enough") if he is an only child; another might be named Omony (for a boy) or Amony (for a girl) if born in a time of war (*mony*). Other names refer specifically to *where* the child is born. A son named Otim or a daughter named Atim refers to a child born in *tim*, or outside Acholiland; such a child might be born to Acholi parents living or working in the capital city of Kampala, for example. Similarly, a child can be given the name Olum or Alum if born in the *lum*, perhaps if the mother gives birth while going to the *lum* to collect firewood.[13]

By this standard, one might expect many children born in the *lum* to LRA parents to be named Olum or Alum. But they were not. In many cases, LRA naming conventions contravened traditional Acholi norms—some children were named after the spirits that possessed Kony (for instance Silindi or Oris); others were named after Kony himself; yet others took the names of leaders like Idi Amin, George Bush, Saddam Hussein, Riek Machar, and Salim Saleh (Museveni's brother and a former UPDF general). Additionally, *jok* names like Opiyo/Apiyo, Odoch/Adoch, or Ocen/Acen were forbidden because of their association with traditional Acholi spirituality (*tic Acoli*). Many names given to children did indeed reflect the suffering (*can*) that the LRA passed through—for example Anenocan ("I see/saw suffering"). So why was Olum or Alum not a very common name? "It's because we weren't in the *lum*, but in *gang* [in bases in Sudan]," my friend Aliya explained to me. Even though *lum* took on a broader conceptual meaning for the LRA, the naming of LRA children remained tied to the idea of *lum* as a specific, physical place of tall grass. This was also true of the names Omony or Amony; while the LRA were perpetually at war, children born to the LRA were not considered to be born "in war," and thus not meriting the name Omony or Amony unless their mothers gave birth during military operations, in the heat of battle. Whereas civilians considered LRA bases as *lum*, the rebels themselves came to understand them as *gang*, subverting the inhumanity ascribed to the space of the *lum*.

But the rebel procedure of naming in the *lum* was not the only challenge to civilian constructions of the human. In fact, when children born in the *lum* were brought back to civilian *gang*, civilians often denigrated their names as dirty and dismissed their meanings. Indeed, upon leaving the LRA, many former rebels came under pressure to change their children's names, often by their kin and/or by staff at reception centers. The parents of some children who would normally have acquired *jok* names on their birth were encouraged to rename their children according to Acholi rather than LRA conventions, often to avoid afflictions or illnesses that might befall them as spiritual punishment. Families of children who had been named after Kony's spirits feared that the spirits would afflict the children and urged their names to be changed. Children named after Kony himself would be sociopolitically pressured into using alternative names.

Some parents and children accepted these name changes, but many resisted. My friends Benjamin and Acen, who married in the *lum* and remained together after coming "home," remembered going through the World Vision reception center, where they were told to change the names of their children to give them "home names" (*nying ma gang*). The reception center staff, they recalled, said that the *lum* names would remind them of "bad things" in the *lum* and that they should be "swept away." Acen agreed with them, wanting to leave behind what she called the "*lum* mentality" (*wic me lum*) and fearing that both the child and the mother would be subjected to insults for having been in the *lum*. But Benjamin resisted this attempt to remake lived experience: "I feel bad leaving the name in the *lum*. It's good to maintain the names because such names will be used for remembering—you will remember the place you're born in. . . . If a child has been born in the *lum*, he will ask the parents the meaning of his name, and the parents will tell him that you were born in the *lum*. That is very important." Rebel attempts to articulate and remember meaningful life in the *lum* were discouraged; their previous lives were to be dismantled with new names as they transformed from violent, dirty animals into peaceful, clean people.

In addition to complicating the *gang-lum* binary by rejecting parts of the Acholi civilian narrative of *lum*, many former rebels insisted—pandering to the civilian discourse—that in spite of the differences in life with the LRA compared to life in *gang*, they too were human, just as much as people at home. Asserting that the life of people in the *lum* was indeed that of humans, Musa explained: "People think if you stayed in the bush, then they imagine you're like an animal . . . but people in the lum are people with human forms [*dano ma kom dano*], but with different rules from people here [in *gang*]. . . . People in the *lum* are just like people in *gang*, except they aren't settled in permanent houses, but temporary structures. They cook, leave, and move on."

Aliya complained that contrary to popular belief, people in the *lum* used latrine toilets. She resented it when people said of a child who defecated outside the designated shared latrine in her Gulu slum, "He must have been born in the *lum*." Similarly, eating wild foods was not a choice, but a means of survival. And being in the *lum* did not turn sane men into mad ones. In defiance of this abusive stigma and in recognition of alternative forms of being, Musa had coopted the stigmatizing label of "being mad." He insisted that he too was mad, and that he would only consider courting a woman who was ostensibly mad like him. By this, he meant a woman who was also in the *lum*, and someone who would not abuse him as a madman as other women might. Facing exclusion as the other to humanity, many rebels rejected as false the ways in which LRA life was envisioned as inhuman.

Resistance against the civilian imagination that life in the *lum* was not human life extends far beyond the fact that the basic constituents of human life—as defined in the Acholi imagination—existed in the *lum*. It was not only the forms of dwelling or the types of food in the *lum* that were (mis)imagined in ways that denied the LRA the meaningful forms of life they cultivated there. There were also more profound, indeed moral, aspects of human life that constituted the *lum* as a space belonging to the human—one that, in many ways and in the Acholi civilian analytic framework, was perhaps more human than *gang* was.

Reinventing the Lum *as a Site of the Sacred*

In cultivating certain practices, values, and beliefs seen to be morally pure in the *lum*, former rebels came to see the *lum* as more than just a site of life. It became a site of the sacred, a site that contrasted with the profanity and immorality of life in *gang*. In this disparity, the symbolic meanings of *lum* and *gang* were reversed, with the human and the good ascribed not to *gang* but to *lum*, and the animal and the bad ascribed not to *lum* but to *gang*.

"The *lum* isn't hell," Musa said, laughing at the absurdity of the suggestion once made on-air by *Dwog Cen Paco* radio host Lacambel. "People won't understand what the *lum* is if they listen to Lacambel." On one broadcast, Lacambel had said that those in the LRA who ate wild food that animals ate were not men, and if they were in fact men, they were in hell. Musa recognized that Lacambel said what he did to lure rebels home, and to fill his own pockets. But like many of my former rebel friends, Musa resisted this narrative about the *lum* as a dark and immoral place of absolute evil, devoid of humanity. Where others envisioned the *lum* as a site of suffering, hatred, sexual immorality, adultery, backwardness, and so forth, many former rebels who could make informed comparisons about life in the *lum* to life in *gang* saw the *lum* in terms that were precisely the reverse—as a site of training, love, virtuous faith, sacredness, development, and so on. Remembering and comparing life in the *lum* to life in *gang* today, they ascribed social ills and evils like laziness, drunkenness, and individualism, among others contrasted to notions of humanity, to life in *gang*.

The sacredness ascribed to the *lum* is perhaps best exemplified in the yard.[14] The yard was described to me in some detail by Musa and Otto, two friends who spent decades in the *lum* as LRA yard workers. Put simply, the yard was a holy place (*kabedo maleng*) of divination within LRA camps from which rebels negotiated, controlled, and directed the war. It was the engine of the LRA that gave strength to and cared for the rebels. Described to me in biblical terms as akin to the holy ground in the bush from which God spoke to Moses (Exodus 3), and in Acholi terms as a kind of *kac* or *abila*[15] (ancestral shrine), the yard was a place where human powers met supernatural powers in the performance of miracles, healing, and other divine activities. A physically large site within an LRA camp, bigger than the size of a normal Acholi compound, the yards moved with the LRA, and would be rebuilt in different versions across battalions. Their features were modified to fit the evolving needs of the war according to the word of the spirits possessing Kony.

The yard was where war-related problems and solutions were divined. Otto, who worked in different kinds of yards for many years, shared with me his memories of the yard. The yard was a place where, with God's intervention and divination, the war was controlled—where defeats were turned into victories; stones into bombs; and dirt into purity (via anointment). From the yard, the LRA could blunt enemy attacks; defuse enemy weapons; counteract the work of civilian militias and enemy spirit priests (*ajwagi*) employed by Museveni; and strengthen their own troops. *Cen* and *gemo* could also be dealt with by yard workers. The contents and form of the yard were guided by the word of the *tipu*.

Technicians and controllers worked in the yard. They both mediated the material and divine worlds, though the technicians tended to work within

Figure 8. Camouflage used by the LRA to anoint fighters going into battle, collected from near Aceng Hill (Got Aceng). Photo by author.

yards alone, while controllers would travel with soldiers on operations to carry out their divine work on the front lines of battle. They all slept around the yard in a circle of huts, working in shifts to oversee the holy space. Kony would stay with the people in the yard. Entrance into the holy space of the yard was restricted. Prayers were central to work in the yard, which was itself protected by taboos and ritual rules. Women were generally not allowed in at least one version of the yard (the world yard), and only brought water to the yard. Menstruating women were entirely disbarred from the yard. Yard workers were themselves made holy under strict ritual control. They did not quarrel or fight; would not eat meat for certain lengths of time; and would not mix freely with other LRA fighters. They could not have sex with women while on a spell of duty, could not eat food prepared by menstruating women, and could not come into contact with blood, especially goat's blood. These rules were held strictly for yard workers; those who disobeyed them would become impure and would be removed from the yard. In essence, for the LRA, the yard was a site of divinity in a space (the *lum*) imagined by civilians as evil and inhuman.

In the LRA imagination, then, the *lum* was by no means only a site of dangerous, evil spirits, or fierce, wild animals. It was also the divine space in which, like Moses before him, Kony received the word of God and built holy sites according to the direction of God's spirits. That this happened in the *lum* helped transform the moral imagination of that space for many rebels, particularly when they compared it to the kinds of (im)moral lives they saw on their return to civilian *gang*.

Indeed, when it came to comparing life in *gang* to life in the *lum*, former rebels largely lamented the ways in which vices such as laziness, social disunity, drunkenness, and adultery seemed to proliferate disproportionately at *gang*. Kristof Titeca (2010) and Chris Dolan (2009), among others, refer to the idea that the LRA sought to more broadly cleanse Acholi society of impurity and sin. While I did not hear this discourse directly from ex-rebels, their views on and actions within life in the *lum* compared to life at *gang* certainly reflected this. Moreover, it was not only rebels who saw *gang* life as immoral, but also people across Acholiland, especially in and around Gulu town. Many pointed to the government-NGO forced mass herding of civilians into internment camps as the origin point for this proliferation of perceived evil. Living in camps for years meant, people lamented, that children grew up lazy and unwilling to dig; that men became drunks in the absence of available work; that people slept around, sneaking to an illicit lover's hut in the tight space of the camp; and that people sought first and foremost to look after themselves rather than others in a time of involuntary scarcity.

By contrast to this recent social history of Acholi civilian life, many rebels looked back on their time in the *lum* with gratefulness for the suffering (*can*) they endured, which taught them to persevere, to work hard, to overcome. Musa was one of them. When I went to visit him one day, I found "Thank you, suffering" (*Apwoyo can*) drawn in charcoal on his front door. He explained to me that he wrote it after reflecting on the suffering he passed through in the *lum*, suffering that had taught him to work hard. Others, like Mohammed, spoke of the *lum* as a form of schooling, an education that former rebels received but that civilians did not. Stuck during the war in the camps—the sites of immorality par excellence in the Acholi imagination—

civilians were said to suffer, and often saw themselves as suffering from, a disease known as "dependency syndrome" or "give me, give me" (*miya miya*). By contrast, former rebels united with government officials in condemning the lazy expectancy of civilians to be given or handed things—as they were during the height of and in the aftermath of the war, when NGOs and humanitarian agencies supplied them with food and finance, among other things—and preferred to work hard on their own to earn what they could get. Comparing himself to his neighbors, Otto mused, "If people worked hard, 'give me, give me' [*miya miya*] would be reduced. I don't need this foolishness—I work harder. . . . They lie in the shade, smoke, and go to drink, while I work in other gardens [for wages]." He estimated that his self-perceived ability to work harder came as a result of being a soldier, put in life-and-death situations. "There's no laziness in the *lum*. . . . If you're lazy, you can die. You have to do [things at] ninety-nine speed, very fast."

Another feature of life in the *lum* that contrasted with that of life in *gang* today was that of social unity and care for one another. "In case a person has a problem in the *lum*, they are immediately helped, unlike at home," Acen explained. Her husband Benjamin agreed: "People's hearts are dark at *gang*, and they don't love each other at *gang*. . . . People love each other in the *lum* so much. They call each other brother and sister, even if they are not real brothers and sisters." Otto felt similarly, saying, "At *gang*, someone who is sick is not visited, not even by a neighbor. But in the *lum*, the sick people are kept well, medicated, and given food and clothes, with people to care for them. This was part of the unity." Individualism and selfishness were thought to characterize life in *gang* today, but social cohesiveness and unity was a feature of social life in the *lum*. Indeed, many former rebels continued to keep up with friends and relatives they made while in the *lum*. Once, on the streets of Gulu town, Aliya unexpectedly ran into the woman who served as her mother when she was abducted as a young girl into the LRA. Both were anything but traumatized by this encounter. The woman she considered her second mother was overjoyed to see Aliya again, hugging her and calling her "my daughter." Her husband, Aliya's second father and now a UPDF soldier, later gave her 50,000UGX (approximately US$20 at that time, a large amount), to help support her. Aliya remembers him fondly, saying he taught her a lot. She felt both of them loved her.

The issue of alcohol similarly divided *gang* from *lum* in the eyes of morally discerning former rebels. Alcohol was forbidden among LRA rebels, and those who imbibed illegally faced severe punishment at the hands of the LRA military police or through misfortune in battle (being killed, having one's leg blown off, or similar ill fates). At *gang*, alcohol was widely blamed for various social ills, including domestic violence, idleness and unemployment, theft, adultery, and sexual defilement (sex with a minor). Local councilors continually threatened to ban the sale of sachets, 100mL plastic packets of 40 percent ABV gin costing around 500UGX (about US20¢), which young and old men alike drank across Acholiland, sometimes from sunup to well past sunset.[16] Most former rebels who returned home began to drink alcohol, but others remained abstinent. They, in particular, spoke admiringly of the rules in the *lum* (*cik me lum*) that prohibited alcohol, and wished that such rules could be implemented at *gang* today, to curb the perceived wave of immorality brought about by drinking. They recognized that only one man—Kony—could bring these rules home, were he successful in winning the war and overthrowing Museveni's government.

Similar rules legislated for sexual morality in the *lum*, including those punishing adultery. LRA legislation restricted courtship and often assigned abducted women to men based on the proven ability of a man to keep a woman well. This regulation is thought to have restricted the transmission of HIV among LRA rebels and to have prevented widespread adultery. Those convicted of adultery were often subject to death by firing squad. While many were dissatisfied by the forced nature of marriage, both men and women who spent time in the *lum* spoke warmly of the strength of the relationships that often formed between husbands and wives (a subject we will revisit in chapter 5). Women in particular lamented the irresponsibility of men at *gang* compared to men in the *lum*. At *gang*, men might stay overnight at a town center drinking and dancing, wasting the family's food budget and courting and having sex with other women. Divorces and HIV transmission, quite uncommon in the *lum*, were, to former rebels, sad and indelible features of life at *gang*.

Even the nature of pure faith seemed to former rebels to be stronger in the *lum* than at home. On the subject of prayers in the *lum*, Benjamin reflected, "Prayers brought people together like nothing else. They prayed [in the *lum*] with a really different heart, deep hearted prayers. It's not like this at home. They have different hearts here. They don't pray, they don't fear the laws of God, but only the laws of the country." People remembered prayers in the *lum* as having more immediate meaning—and immediate gains. They might pray together for success in a particular upcoming battle—and success would come. Their prayers were *answered* in the *lum*. They felt their prayers were more pure and heartfelt in the *lum* than prayers said at home, amid a smorgasbord of churches and revival centers seemingly more interested in collecting money, singing and dancing, and/ or offering a space to show off one's fine clothes and social status than in worshipping God.

For the rebels, the *lum* was not the dirtied, immoral, and animal-like space that civilians thought it was. It was a space of social unity, hard work, sobriety, and faithfulness. These elements crystallized into a meaningful life that rebels often contrasted to the life of "dogs" that people had begun living since they were interned in the camps.

Reinventing the Lum *as a Site of Development*

Many former rebels also contested the idea that being or staying in the *lum* was a sign of backwardness or lack of development associated with living like wild animals. Lacambel constantly warned rebels via his *Dwog Cen Paco* radio broadcasts that by remaining in the *lum*, they were being "left behind" (*gidong cen*), "wasting their time" for no reason while people at *gang* "moved forward." Here, "remaining behind" has three meanings. First, rebels remained spatially behind in the *lum* as their comrades left or were captured and brought back to Acholiland. Second, rebels remained temporally behind as people at home moved ahead with imagined developmental trajectories, roughly linear in nature. Third, rebels remained materially behind, missing out on the symbolic matter of development— including laptops and motorcycles—that people in town, who had "moved ahead," were enjoying. Some former rebels, even outside the censored space of the radio airwaves, had reason to agree with Lacambel's assessment that the LRA were spurning the fruits of development by choosing to continue fighting in the *lum*. Mohammed noted that those in the *lum* did not have the money to send their children to school; did not build homes (particularly those with iron-sheet roofs, perceived as markers of status and development); and treasured foods like sorghum that those in *gang* would perceive of as free or valuable only in famine. They would see things that had become outdated (*jami ma okato*) with more importance than do those who never went to the *lum*, for instance admiring a bicycle when most at *gang* now coveted a motorbike.

While some saw truth in the idea that those in the *lum* had fallen developmentally behind those at *gang*, others felt that Lacambel was telling vicious lies over the radio. Otto was one of them. During one *Dwog Cen Paco* broadcast, a woman formerly in the LRA came on radio to call on her husband, who was still in the *lum*, to return. She said she still loved him and wanted to settle with him when he came back, and that she had not taken any other man since she herself had left the *lum*. She heard that her husband had become injured, but told him that this should not deter him from returning. There were other injured LRA, she explained, including Otto (whom she named explicitly on the air), who were back home and living well.

Otto had not listened to the broadcast himself, but when I told him about it, he felt bad and bitter. He had not seen the woman who used his name in more than four years. "How does she know I'm staying well here!?" he angrily asked. "I'm not staying well. Why is she talking like this?" he scoffed. Otto reasoned that perhaps the government was giving this woman money to lure her husband out of the *lum*. If indeed he did come out and visit Otto, he might think otherwise. "'What kind of good life was I told you were having?!'" Otto suggested he might ask him upon seeing the simple huts in his rural homestead. Recalling the conditions of his own life and those of mutual friends of ours who had returned from the LRA, he suggested that the idea that former rebels were enjoying a "good life" at home was highly deceptive.

Otto was particularly bitter with Lacambel, who tried to get him on *Dwog Cen Paco* when Otto was captured and brought back to Gulu. "He tried to drill me on how to talk on the radio—about the good things the government does, the good life we have at home, to lure back the LRA there still fighting," he recalled. "I told him right away—if you want me to say these things, just say them yourself, don't tell me what to say. I can't tell people in the *lum* that I'm living well and yet I'm not—why should I lie to them?" Feeling as though he was being coerced, Otto refused to go on the show, and claimed that those who did speak on the program had either spent very little time in the *lum* or else were bribed to say certain things. He felt unable to freely express his own thoughts through the show. Neither could he air grievances about and speak badly of the government, nor could he insist that it should be overthrown by the rebels.

Otto contested the idea that rebels would find their expectations of material modernities fulfilled if they were to leave the *lum* and return to *gang*. Like Otto, Musa complained that these expectations went unfulfilled, and that most rebels who had come back were suffering daily, digging with hoes on their small gardens in rural areas plagued by alcoholism, joblessness, and land conflicts (none of which were mentioned on *Dwog Cen Paco*). The laptops, motorcycles, and televisions that Lacambel spoke of remained distant, inaccessible dreams even once rebels had left the *lum*. But Musa also contested the idea that such material modernities were out of reach in the *lum*, suggesting that people in the *lum* had access to technologies that were thought to exist only at *gang*, and were, at that, out of the reach of poor rebels who had indeed returned to *gang*: "We had equipment there in the *lum*—phones, GPS, laptops—it's all there. . . . So Lacambel is just talking to tell people about development, without knowing that the people he is talking to already know what he's talking about." Apart from these devices, Musa noted that the LRA owned some motorbikes, trucks, and even a lorry.

Like Otto, Musa resented Lacambel for telling lies to fill his own pockets. He saw not only material development in the *lum*, but also mental development and education. People at *gang* tend to think, Musa said, that "someone there in the bush doesn't know anything. . . . They think you live on fruit and that you're not human [*pe bedo dano*]. But people in the *lum* are of different backgrounds. Some . . . have serious education." Indeed, Musa believed that those in the *lum* were more educated than people at home because of their experience. Women could cook better because they learned to make delicious food without recourse to spices and tomatoes accessible to women at *gang*. Fighters quickly learned to use complicated weapons, facing death if they could not master them. As the LRA divided into separate battalions or groups, rebels began to use satellite phones and GPS devices to arrange and meet at rendezvous points. "Even in education,

Table 2   LRA counter-ontology to the civilian imaginary dividing *gang* from *lum*

gang *(home)*	lum *(grass or bush)*
profane, immoral	sacred, moral
social disarray, ills	social unity, values
drunkenness, adultery	sobriety, sexual regulation
site of flawed development	site of education and technology
joblessness, laziness, dependency	meaningful work, self-initiated hard labor
site of enfeebled, denigrated animals (dogs)	site of fierce, honorable animals (lions, gorillas)

people in the *lum* are very bright and can do things done by educated people. I trust my own knowledge. For example, people who came from the *lum* got a short [vocational] training of three months, but do work done by people who trained for so many years. So even in education, people [in the *lum*] . . . have not remained behind [*gudong cen*]."

The only point that Musa conceded was that those in the *lum* may not have seen the construction of bigger, multistory buildings that now stand in the center of Gulu town. But he rejected the idea that these buildings signaled real "development": "I'm against these buildings. People are selling land to rich people. Where will they stay in the future? Rich people are the only ones with land, and poor people who are selling will have no place in the future." Staying in the *lum* for years did not mean that rebels missed out on development, but it did mean that they were seen as undeveloped, immoral, and inhuman in civilian eyes. In their experiences in both the *lum* and *gang*, a certain humanity born out of modernity was equally absent, or else sometimes more present in *lum* than in *gang*.

By virtue of having stayed in a wild space for so long, the LRA were even in their own discourse not fully human, but partly animal. But that did not imply that they were missing out on the elements that civilians imagined constituted humanity—namely, morality and modernity. Indeed, the rebels reformulated the distinctions between *gang* and *lum* through a counter-ontology that redrew the meanings affixed to a civilian notion of humanity (table 2).

LIFE BEYOND HUMANITY

When it comes to animality and humanity in anthropo-moral geographies, the LRA physically occupy a troubling space. Fighting gorilla warfare in the *lum*, the rebels challenged civilian common sense about the boundaries of humanity, including its proper spaces, its moral and material sensibilities, as well as its distinction from animality. They ascribed sacredness, development, and a sense of a common good to a space (*lum*) that otherwise existed outside the human; at the same time, they ascribed profanity, social disarray, and a sense of moral decay to a space (*gang*) that otherwise constituted the human. In doing so, they articulated new forms of life beyond the narrow vision that civilians came to know, in part through a colonial imaginary intensified by anxieties of development, as humanity.

The LRA terrify—not only with the threat of physical violence, but also with the threat posed to the boundaries of *lum/gang* and human/animal undergirding a contemporary Acholi ontology. Bringing into question the normative assumptions of the constituents of humanity, they lived in ways that exceeded humanity's limits. Practically, this imperiled an Acholi civilian reason and a humanitarian logic that share certain moral and spatial criteria in their visions of humanity. Indeed, in part because they threatened common sense about morality and humanity, the LRA came to be seen by civilians and humanitarians alike as irrational—mad, deluded, and illogical—and therefore somehow less than human. It is to this question of LRA reason that I turn in the next chapter.

4 Beyond Reason

MAGIC AND SCIENCE IN THE LRA

Sipping on cassava gin while lying on a plastic tarp around a fire (*wang oo*) in the middle of my friend Makamoi's compound, I found myself in an unusually rural and secluded place. Makamoi, together with several of his uncles and cousins, had recently left their wives and children living near town to return to their ancestral lands on the edge of Gulu District. This new home was about fifteen kilometers from any other homestead, accessible by a very narrow footpath that was difficult to traverse by motorbike. Though isolated from other people and institutions, without access to clean water or a nearby clinic, the men found it easier to grow crops and hunt animals on this vast land with soft, fertile soil. "Even *you* could dig there," Makamoi's wife Timkikomi joked to me, having seen how poor my farming skills were.

They had last stayed on this remote land in the early 1990s, when Makamoi was in charge of a hidden LRA sick bay in the nearby *lum*. He brought food and medicine to the wounded, including Otto, who was shot in the back and stayed with them for some time. Makamoi spent about six years with the LRA, primarily as a collaborator, in the late 1980s and early 1990s. Originally a Uganda National Liberation Army (UNLA) soldier, he joined a group of UNLA rebels known as the Uganda People's Democracy Army (UPDA), or Cilil, when Museveni took power in 1986, fighting against the NRA.[1] In the aftermath of the NRA coup, several rebel forces independently took up arms against the NRA, including Cilil, Lakwena (Alice Lakwena's Holy Spirit movement), and the LRA. Under contested circumstances, Makamoi's Cilil group joined the LRA—against their will, according to Makamoi, but voluntarily according to others.

As Makamoi remembered, Alice wanted Cilil and Joseph Kony on her side to fight together against the NRA. But Cilil commander Odong Latek refused. He had told his soldiers that he had not seen success in wars that made use of spirits, recalling that the Congolese people had fought with the guidance of spirits and failed. Alice, he thought, would similarly fail, and Latek wanted to fight with military tactics alone. However, Cilil was eventually overpowered and its members—including Latek—had to join up with Alice and Kony.[2]

A former government soldier trained in scientific-military tactics, Makamoi initially viewed the use of spirits with the same deep skepticism as did Latek. But as he started to work with the LRA, his ideas about spirits changed, moving further from the reason of science and closer to that of magic. "It was better to fight using the spirit [than with military tactics alone]," he reflected, "because the spirit protected the fighters a lot, as long as they were observing the spirit's rules." He witnessed bullets shot into but failing to penetrate the skins of people guarded by the spirit. On the other hand, he recalled soldiers who did not follow the spirit's rules and remembered that "the spirit did not delay with them [*tipu pe oruu kedgi*]," withdrawing its protection and allowing them to be killed. Many of those killed, he recalled, were accomplished UNLA commanders who were excellent military leaders, but who failed to observe the rules of the *tipu*. "They had resorted to military tactics and knowledge, and left the *tipu*'s orders. So many [of these] commanders died," Makamoi remembered. "If everyone had followed [the spirit's rules (*cik pa tipu*)] well, it would have been okay [meaning, the LRA might have overthrown the government]. But it became hard when [these UNLA commanders] didn't follow the *tipu*."

Forsaking a military science in favor of spiritual magic, Makamoi began to accept what Latek and others could not—the strength of Joseph Kony's spirit. He began to understand that the LRA had no military intelligence,[3] but rather, that they were informed of what was said and done about them—including my conversations with Makamoi, and presumably, these very words—through the *tipu*. He rejected scientific claims that Kony could not turn stones into bombs: "I saw them with my own eyes—they worked. Kony blessed a stone and it exploded. I witnessed how it broke a railway line in Alero Bwobo." He adamantly defended the powers that Kony had acquired through his spirit. "Some report it wrongly," he insisted, "saying [Kony's spirit] is not strong, and that it's a lie that Kony has a spirit. It's not true. It's real and it's strong. When Kony blessed people, people were shot at but the bullet never penetrated their bodies, even when shot at close range with the barrel of the gun on the body."

Makamoi told of the struggle between Kony and Museveni as a battle between spirits. As Makamoi saw it, Museveni had gone "underwater" to visit *jogi* that gave him the power to fight. Kony, he insisted, would fight until he reached Karuma Bridge—a bridge over the Nile River at the symbolic entrance from southern and central Uganda into northern Uganda—where he would remove something Museveni planted there. Removing this unnamed object that maintained Museveni's power would allow Kony to overthrow the government. According to Makamoi, Kony had been the first to go "underwater," where he stayed two weeks, before coming back to use the Bible to lead a rebellion.

Museveni, it is commonly said, employed various strategies to fight Kony's spirit, including bringing powerful *ajwagi* from as far away as Kenya and Tanzania to attempt to defeat it. In January 2013, I visited Awere Hill (Got Awere), a rocky outpost in Odek sub-county in southeastern Gulu District, near Joseph Kony's family home. The hill is widely known as the place where Kony first began to preach the word of God, where he prayed, and from where he was said (and continues, it is claimed) to draw magical powers, including holy water that he alone is able to find and draw. The top of the hill is a bowl-shaped plateau. Big snakes are said to inhabit the hill at night. A strange cowrie shell—an object prized by *ajwagi* for use in their work—lay under a boulder, guarded from the hot sun.

Two men, clansmen of a friend with whom I visited the hill, and who lived in the hill's shadow, spoke of a time when Museveni came with UPDF soldiers and an *ajwaka* to attempt to destroy Kony's spirit. During this time, the UPDF guarded the rock and prohibited locals from coming near it. But from afar, the two men could see what happened there. The *ajwaka* performed her work, holding sticks of burning grass on the rock, for a

Figure 9. The view from atop Awere Hill (Got Awere) in Odek, where Kony began to preach, and from where he alone is said to magically draw holy water. Photo by author.

week or two. But she could not succeed in defeating Kony's spirit. She left, and two weeks later, so too did the heavy UPDF deployment around the hill. A month or two afterward, Kony returned briefly to pray on the hill for a full day. Others, including born-again Christians, came to pray at the hill, many of them attempting to chase away the spirit from the hill. Many hills (*godi*) in Acholiland are said to be the dwellings of *jogi*,[4] and it is said that a woman *jok* occupies Got Awere. Elders from Pader, across the nearby Aswa River, were said to come and cook food for the *jok* at Got Awere.

Omony, a Catholic catechist who was a childhood friend of Kony, and with whom he used to dance *larakaraka*,[5] said that the hill had little significance until Kony began to pray on it in 1985. Omony had gone to train as a catechist near Jinja before returning to Odek to teach at a local church. When he got back, people told him that Kony had become possessed while he was away, and that he had become an *ajwaka* with the help of his older brother, also an *ajwaka*. After beginning his rebellion, however, Kony ordered the killing of all *ajwagi*, as though—Omony insisted—he were never one himself. Omony was not sure about the relationship between what he saw as Kony's *jogi* and the *jok* at Got Awere.

Makamoi eventually ended his association with the LRA. He was concerned for the safety of his family at home, and also suffered a certain loss of faith in the struggle. In particular, he was disappointed at the killings of senior LRA commanders by both the UPDF on the battlefield and Kony internally within the LRA, which left him wondering where the war was going. But he told me: "Kony's being in the *lum* makes me happy, because if not, the Acholi wouldn't be the way they are today. I pray to God that he should continue so that the Acholi can stay as they are today—for their voice to be heard, for them to be feared. If Kony weren't there, the Acholi would have become like slaves [*guci*] or else be finished."

BECOMING MAGICIAN-SCIENTISTS

Reason or rationality is a vital criterion by which one rendition of "humanity" is constructed. The idea of reason as defining Man has existed since, at least, Aristotle's articulation of Man as rational animal.[6] Reason has also configured the category of the human in anthropology, particularly Africanist anthropology. A tradition growing out of E. E. Evans-Pritchard's (1976) work on Zande witchcraft attempted to make "rational" what to the Western scientific mind remained "irrational"—and thus on some level outside of humanity. Today, much of Africanist anthropology remains in this mold, as Ruth Marshall, drawing on Talal Asad, observes. Western social scientists, she argues, approach "irrational" behavior with the idea of agency to "render such behavior rational and freely chosen," at once demystifying the Other and granting it "at last their long-denied place in the history of humanity" (2009, 32).

This form of social science has been employed in different ways by thoughtful, respected scholars studying the LRA.[7] Rejecting the dehumanizing, simplistic notion that the LRA are "bizarre," they employ reason to understand the LRA politically. While an important approach, this is not the kind of humanist social science I follow. I do not attempt to "rationalize" all that the LRA have done that seems "irrational" in order to humanize them. Instead, with Marshall, I take LRA thoughts, beliefs, and actions in their radical historical singularity—an approach that transcends the duality of rationality and irrationality, and in doing so, destabilizes a foundational measure of humanity.

In this chapter, I focus ethnographically on how LRA beliefs and practices blended magic and science, without rules, structures, or logics governing this blend. In holding a grip on both magic and science, without reconciling them, privileging one over the other, nor finding contradiction in holding them together, the LRA transcended questions of reason and rationality, and with them, humanity.

One domain in which rebels held magic and science together was through the observance and understanding of some common LRA rules and regulations, as well as the forms of punishment that occurred when they were broken. I draw attention not to the rules and punishments themselves, but rather to the ways in which former rebels narrate them. Both magicians and scientists, they were "flexible fundamentalists," tied strongly to both magic and science and attentive to the rules of logic of them both, but without an overarching logic that determined when to employ scientific reason and when to employ magical reason.

My friend Mohammed was in a unique position to observe magic and science together. As a former LRA military policeman, he was responsible for regulating and arresting those within the LRA forces who broke rules and regulations, bringing them to the Operations Room where they would be punished. He recalled, particularly while stationed in Sudan, arresting LRA rebels who: ate with and/or sold goods to Arabs without permission; entered into fierce quarrels and fights; failed to attend prayers; tried to desert; or mistreated their wives or children, among other crimes. Depending on the severity of the crime, there were different punishments. The petty criminal might be given menial labor—to uproot a tree, cut bamboo, clear an anthill, or dig a pit latrine. For more serious violations, criminals were put for weeks or even months in jail (*buc*), which often consisted of a hole dug in the ground and partially filled with water. For crimes considered most serious, including adultery or being a wizard (*lajok*), death by firing squad was not uncommon.[8]

Such policing would not normally seem so out of place in an army with rules and regulations that required enforcement. But unlike most secular armies, the LRA had rules and regulations defined by not only a military command, but also spirits (*tipu*) who both issued rules and punished those who violated these rules. The *tipu*'s punishment would often swiftly follow the crime and usually be executed in battle, where the criminal (and sometimes those around her or him as well) would lose the protection of the *tipu* and suffer injury or death. Those who had sex during times the *tipu* had prohibited it might be killed in battle. Marks on their dead bodies would reveal their transgression—they might be shot in the penis, or else the thumb might be found firmly lodged between the index and middle fingers (a vulgar sign for sexual intercourse). Those who illicitly drank alcohol would be shot in the mouth. If the *tipu* had ordered a certain number of soldiers to go to battle, and an excess number were taken, the surplus would be killed. Indeed, many soldiers recalled that commanders would sometimes send out-of-favor or unwanted soldiers to their deaths by tacking them onto units sent into battle, beyond the numerical limit specified by the *tipu*. It was in the aftermath of the punishment that both the criminal and his crime would be revealed by the *tipu*.

I was most perplexed by the ways in which these two sets of rules could exist together. Which rules would the military police issue and enforce, and which ones would the *tipu* issue and enforce? Why would there be the need for a military police if an omniscient and omnipotent *tipu* could set and enforce rules on its own?

Like Alice's Holy Spirit movement, Kony's LRA also developed what Heike Behrend refers to as "Holy Spirit Safety Precautions." Among those issued to Alice's troops included "2. Thou shalt not smoke cigarettes (1 Cor. 3, 16–20)" and "3. Thou shalt not drink alcool [*sic*] (Prov. 21,1; 23,20–21; Is. 5,11–12,20–22; Num. 6,1–4)," as well as "19. Thou shalt not eat pork or mutton or oil of the same (Ex. 12,14–18; Lev. 1,10–11; 7,11; 19,26; Lk. 8,32–33)" (Behrend 1999, 47). In discussing many of these prohibitions with former LRA soldiers, there were distinctions made between which LRA rules were issued as orders of the *tipu maleng* and which were issued as military-scientific tactics, sometimes based in bioscience.

Refraining from smoking was one rule that most of my friends saw not as an order of the *tipu*, but as a military-scientific order. One of the first times this came to my attention was when watching Steven Soderbergh's 2008 biopic *Che* with Benjamin and Labwor. Labwor was a prolific smoker, mostly of tobacco but also occasionally opium and marijuana, though he only started smoking after he returned from the LRA. From dried, crumbling tobacco leaves and scrap paper, he rolled flimsy cigarettes that he and Benjamin smoked while watching the film. The two former rebels were surprised to see Cuban revolutionaries smoking in the movie. When they were in the *lum*, they reflected, no one was allowed to smoke. I recalled to them that Che considered smoking a comfort for his troops, a way to boost morale (Guevara 2008, 54). Benjamin interjected, "Kony didn't like cigarettes because of the smell—it would break concealment and make it hard for people to hide among enemies, who would smell it and trace you." Labwor drew on similar military-tactical reasons to condemn smoking in the *lum*: "People who get used to smoking will get careless when supplies are low, going around to neighboring villages looking for cigarettes." He remembered that Kony once warned them that if soldiers smoked, they would become sidetracked and end up fighting primarily to raid cigarettes. Benjamin's wife, Acen, had a different assessment. She grew concerned during the second part of the biopic, watching Che struggle to keep up with his unit due to his frequent, severe asthmatic attacks. She lamented, "This old man [*mzee*] is getting defeated. He should have stopped smoking." Like biomedical health workers, other former rebels agreed with Acen, saying that smoking made one's body weak and unfit to fight well.

In rebel eyes, smoking was tactically and scientifically unwise, running the risk of revealing rebel hideouts while, as an addictive and harmful practice, biomedically damaging the strength and resolve of the rebel body. No one saw smoking as a "sin" or a violation of the *tipu*'s orders. Yet there was contestation over who punished smokers, and why. Some suggested that those who were caught smoking were beaten. Others said they would be killed in battle, their dead fingers found held up to their mouths in a *V*, revealing the exact transgression that led to their demise. Mohammed suggested that smoking, like illicit sex and drinking, was done in secret by disobedient rebels, and that the military police were simply unable to identify their crime of having broken a military (rather than spiritual) rule. The *tipu* alone would know that a person had smoked in secret and would punish her or him accordingly.

There were similar understandings of how and why pork and alcohol were prohibited in the LRA, and how and why transgressions of these prohibitions were punished. Pork, I was variously told, made one dizzy, weak, and lazy because of its high fat content. One could not be a reliable and watchful soldier if one ate pork. Some said it gave them diarrhea, remembering that Kony had told them pigs had worms in them and that it was medically unsafe to eat pork in the *lum* because the pigs had not been vaccinated against worms; others said that it was prohibited in "[Sudanese President Omar al-] Bashir's religion" (Islam) and that Kony said that pigs had "evil" or *cen* in them. Alcohol was similarly said to make soldiers poor fighters, weak and unfocused.[9] Fighters were warned that if they got drunk, their enemies could easily find and kill them, or that they might carelessly wander in the *lum* and encounter dangerous *jogi*. Indeed, it was sometimes said that one reason that the LRA were better fighters compared to the UPDF was that they did not drink alcohol. Refraining from alcohol was, like smoking and eating pork, almost always narrated as a practical prohibition, though it was also mentioned to me specifically as a prohibition instituted by the *tipu*. Those who confessed to drinking while in the *lum* were sometimes re-anointed (and thus re-purified).

In narrating these rules, my friends were to some extent attempting to understand or make sense of them. But that they mixed military-tactical-scientific rules with the *tipu*'s punishment, and the *tipu*'s rules with military-tactical-scientific punishment, suggested a flexibility that was neither rational nor irrational.

"A TIME FOR EVERYTHING"

A Time for Everything

> There is a time for everything,
> and a season for every activity under the heavens:
> a time to be born and a time to die,
> a time to plant and a time to uproot,

a time to kill and a time to heal,

a time to tear down and a time to build,

a time to weep and a time to laugh,

a time to mourn and a time to dance,

a time to scatter stones and a time to gather them,

a time to embrace and a time to refrain from embracing,

a time to search and a time to give up,

a time to keep and a time to throw away,

a time to tear and a time to mend,

a time to be silent and a time to speak,

a time to love and a time to hate,

a time for war and a time for peace.

(*Ecclesiastes 3:1–8; New International Version*)

Many of my inquiries about LRA beliefs with former rebel friends of mine led to maddening discussions. More specifically, these discussions maddened me, but left my friends laughing at the absurdity of my rationality. When I posed what I thought were difficult but rational questions and asked for complex, rational answers, they often—to my great frustration—referred me to the Bible, drawing on Ecclesiastes 3, the beginning of which is reproduced above. *How did the LRA recently decide to start drinking in the* lum? There is a time for everything, Musa said. *How did the LRA start to marry Congolese women when they left Uganda?* There is a time for everything, Otto said. *Why haven't the LRA won the war already?* There is a time for everything, Matayo said. *How do you look back on being abducted? Did you regret it? Did you think it was a worthwhile experience?* There is a time for everything, Gunya said. Initially, I saw this as a clever tactic by which to sidestep difficult questions. Later, I accepted that this was a common method of reasoning within a system of LRA logic. Now, understanding the ways in which the LRA held both modern-scientific and magical-prophetic time together, I attempt to release reason and irrationality altogether, taking the Bible at its word: there is indeed a time for *everything*. There is a way in which each element, carrying its own form of time, coexists easily with other elements operating according to different forms of time.

For a spiritual rebellion like the LRA, time is both a multiple and a moving target. The more precisely one knows time as magical-prophetic, the less precisely one knows time as modern-scientific, and vice versa, yet these two forms of time exist together as a multiple ontology, akin to a wave-particle. Just as wave-particle duality asked serious questions of classical mechanics, I suggest that scientific-magical duality asks serious questions of "humanity."

What does this seemingly strange world of multiple times look like? In terms of the rebellion itself, if one took a modern-scientific view of time, one would strain to explain what appeared to be an anachronistic, ill-timed war. The LRA fought using a "brutality" that, as we have seen, appeared outdated in the lens of modernity. They went without sex or eating food for certain periods of time, determined by the *tipu*. They started their war at a time that seemed obsolete to rational assessments of civilian discontent and consciousness, fighting as fish "out of water" in the late 1980s and early 1990s. Yet by 2012—at a time when discontent with Museveni led to declarations by young men that they would fight as rebels—the water seemed comfortable to swim in. They had fought, since 1987 up to the time of this writing, for a period of years that, as one NGO project seeking to end "crimes against humanity" suggests, was "enough."[10] Here, knowing time as modern-scientific offers little understanding of time as magical-prophetic.

If one, alternatively, took a magical-prophetic view of time, one would equally strain to explain a rebellion marked by periodic deadlines, swift marches, and other forms of functional time compression. The LRA declared specific dates by which they would overthrow the government— dates that came and went. They rushed quickly through the *lum*, covering as much as seventy miles on foot in one day. They kept beans soaked in jerry cans of water, ensuring that when they were cooked, they would not take long to be ready to eat. Porters sometimes even carried actively burning charcoal stoves, cooking beans as they walked, exemplifying the modern phenomenon of "fast food" in the midst of a war that was expected by some rebels to last well over a century, and certainly beyond the full lifetimes of its fighters. Indeed, it was prophesized that the majority of the LRA would return home at some point, leaving only four or five soldiers left to carry on the fight with the protection of the *tipu*. Kony would explain this prophecy with recourse to an Acholi adage, "Many mice can't make a house [*Oyoo mapol pe golo ot*]," suggesting that not everyone would be involved in its fulfillment.[11] With this prophecy in mind, Kony told soldiers to be patient. Even if staying in the *lum* was difficult, they should persevere, because their time would come to leave the front lines and go back "home" while others would stay. Given what Kony said, one might ask, in magical-prophetic terms, what the rush was to stay, to leave, or to fight?

As I attempted to concurrently "measure" modern-scientific and magical-prophetic time, it became clear that my investigations were both too late and too early. Conversations with people like Makamoi came almost twenty years after he left the LRA, his lived experience persisting as memory, but a fading one. However, with the war not yet over, and, it was prophetically suggested, possibly not ending within my own lifetime, many of my inquiries came too early. The work was impossibly timed. And I was not the only one who felt these tensions. Some of my friends also struggled to hold together what seemed to be a contradictory sense of temporal being. Gunya was one who was far more attuned to modern-scientific time than to magical-prophetic time. While with the LRA for nearly a decade, she developed a liking for the "speed" of life in the *lum*. "Speed—ninety-nine!" she laughingly exclaimed in English, remembering the quick pace of movements, decisions, and other actions among the rebels.

Rather than being captured or released from service, Gunya deserted the rebels, running away together with one of her co-wives and some others. Though generally supportive of the LRA, she was primarily concerned with her immediate well-being and that of her children. She had grown tired of fighting, which had become fierce at the time, and was concerned for her children's safety. When she overheard her co-wife whispering about plans to desert, she told her that if she tried to leave her behind, she would shoot her dead. Together, they deserted around Lira Palwo, a region in east Acholi.

When she got home, she found the pace of life slow. She pretended to be like "them" (civilians) so as not to stand out. She moderated her speed so that it did not appear strange to others, even walking at a slower tempo than she preferred, to avoid being labeled as a mad person (*lapoya*). She considered different ways of earning a living when she returned home, but she discounted many of them as being too slow. She ended up as a waitress. Digging, she said, provided cash neither regularly nor quickly, but only in chunks, around harvest time, and was too protracted a way of making money. Her land around town was not fertile, and if she went to dig in a rural village, she dismissingly claimed she would "just find *lum*" (*anongo lum keken*). She similarly discredited tailoring, in which she had some formal training. In her eyes, tailors like her friend Mohammed had no future. Mohammed had been tailoring for so many years, she observed, and yet still had not built a home with an iron-sheet roof—an important hallmark of modern status and progress among Acholi peasants and working classes. (Mohammed saw things differently—Gunya, he said, was impatient and shifted from job to job, lusting after money.) Enrolling as a beneficiary at an NGO catering to former LRA women, as many of her friends had, was similarly wasting time (*balo cawa*). It would take three or four months of training with the NGO before she could start earning money with them, and while she was prepared to work double jobs at the NGO and the restaurant, the work schedules conflicted, and she chose to continue waitressing.

As a waitress, she said, she worked very fast to prepare food and serve her customers, managing the work of four people. Other waitresses came and went, unable to keep up, but Gunya stayed, and indeed, planned to open her own restaurant. She recalled that those who returned from the LRA did not fear work, because in the *lum* they worked hard and there was little time to rest, whereas civilians at *gang* feared working and enjoyed resting. A former rebel hustling in town, she variously called her style of living "swagger" and "gangster": "I still think of the LRA, especially when I'm doing my work, and I'm working very fast. I remember that in the *lum* we also used to work very fast. If I'm working slowly, I also remember the LRA—that I'm working slowly because I'm here at home. If I were in the *lum*, I wouldn't work slowly like this."

By contrast, Matayo, among others, grasped magical-prophetic time more strongly than modern-scientific time. A born-again deacon, Matayo insisted that Kony still had a holy spirit with him and could fight another thirty or even one hundred years. He knew, magically, that God would one day return the LRA to Uganda, where they would promptly over-throw the government. While he was in the *lum*, he took fasts seriously, remembering battles that were won specifically after troops faithfully adhered to two-week-long fasts ordered by the *tipu*. He took the message of Ecclesiastes 3 quite literally, using it to explain that the *tipu* would instruct when there was a time to have sex and a time not to have sex; a time to abduct and a time not to abduct; a time to battle and a time not to battle. Referring to Joshua 10, Matayo explained how the LRA and its victory were in God's total control:

> With Kony, the time is not yet right. The children of Israel, fighting to overthrow the enemy at all costs, prayed to God and said it is time—the time has come. Kony is waiting for his time to overthrow the government, for the time God will say it is time for him to go with five people to overthrow the government. God will speak to him when it is time, and the time will be known through a sign—namely, God's word. This is the same as when the sun and moon stood still [in Joshua 10]—this was God's sign that the war was to be settled that day. . . . In the *lum*, Kony would tell his top commanders that however much you plan for the war, if God hasn't set the time for us to win, then your attempts will be futile. We will stay in the *lum* for a very long time. Maybe our children, or even our grandchildren, will be the ones to overthrow the government from the *lum*. In Joshua 10:14, it says that no one before or after Joshua could ask God to give a time for war; so that is why Kony is waiting for God to speak to him again, to signal the right time.

He lamented that many rebels left the battle, unhappy about going unpaid. They, unlike UPDF soldiers, did not receive a salary for fighting. These people, he scorned, were weak-hearted and believed in material things, not God. They did not have the true faith, the patience to wait years. Those who followed the *tipu* patiently, he noted, knew they would win the war with the holy spirit on their side.

Though Matayo retained this faith, he was released and sent home by the LRA after a service of nine years. He felt he had little left to offer the rebels after losing his leg in battle. Without thinking carefully, he once broke the *tipu*'s rules by handling a piece of UPDF clothing that had blood on it. Soon thereafter, as punishment for handling blood, the *tipu*'s protection deserted him. He stepped on a landmine and one of his legs was blown off. In a dream soon after, a spirit told him that it was "worthless" for him to continue fighting. Accordingly, he asked the LRA command to be released. His request was happily granted, as the LRA had strained to care for him after his injury. No longer physically fighting with the rebels, he only prayed for the LRA after leaving the front lines. But he continued

Figure 10. Reading Matayo's Bible under the midday sun. Photo by author.

to believe that what was prophesized would happen, so long as those remaining in the *lum* stayed faithful to the rules of the holy spirit—something Alice failed to do, he said, because she grew too impatient and set aside the rules of the spirit and God.[12] "The spirit and God has promised [that the LRA will overthrow the government], so you don't need to panic about it," he cheerfully reassured me, as I wondered with scientific reason how he knew.

Matayo worked briefly as a carpenter in Gulu town, but eventually left to settle in his rural village, where he dug in his garden and preached in his local church. He was unwilling and unable to meet the demands of modern town life, especially its compressions and continuities of time. He found it difficult to make monthly rent, and without sufficient land to farm on, had to continually buy his food instead of growing it. This meant that he had to constantly produce a cash income. By contrast, in the village he was able to live on what he grew and to generate cash through his surplus at the regular, seasonal intervals of harvest, while borrowing and loaning as needed with clan members in between harvests. Under these pressures and that of unpredictable, fluctuating prices, he found himself stressed at the end of each month in town, looking for ways of making money to pay rent. The predictability and slowness of village life suited him better than the intense rush and pressures of town life.

Distinct from Gunya and Matayo was Mohammed, who deftly held together both modern-scientific time and magical-prophetic time. On the surface, Mohammed was someone with whom I shared a similar sense of modern productive time—a certain impatience, and with it, the historically peculiar notion that time could be "wasted." He often spoke of his life decisions in terms of time and a desire to avoid wasting it. After being released by the LRA to Gulu from the front lines in 1999, having spent five years in the *lum*, he was received through a GUSCO reception center. Given the option of returning to formal education or receiving skills training as a way of reestablishing a life for himself at "home," he chose to train as a tailor.

Had he chosen schooling, he would have returned to primary school, third grade, at the age of twenty. "I felt it would waste my time [*balo karena*] to go to school because of my poverty [*can*]. To start earning money fast to alleviate the *can*, I decided on skills training. If I went to primary school, it would take long and I would wait long before starting to earn money." He saw others enter formal education, spending years schooling at secondary school and even the university level, without any guarantee of gainful employment upon completion. That would not be an efficient use of his time. Instead, he became a respected tailor with large, steady contracts to fashion uniforms for primary-school children. As his tailoring work was seasonal in nature, there were times when he was short of contract work. He did not waste this time, either. In these periods, he got discounted rides from town back to his rural village from his friend, a motorcycle taxi (*boda boda*) worker who was also a former LRA rebel. There, he dug in his large, fertile garden, growing cassava, *simsim* (sesame), and other crops that he later took back to town to sell. He refused to participate in collective digging (*aleya*), saying it was a waste of time since he could dig faster than others. He would, he maintained, be able to dig more efficiently on his own. "I tailor in the dry season and dig in the rainy season. . . . So that's also partly why I decided to do tailoring—it has a separate season from digging," he explained.

But while he was personally attached to modern-scientific time in his quotidian life, he also retained an attachment to magical-prophetic time. He believed that Kony was and remained truly filled with a holy spirit, and was not—as others scornfully claimed—a deceitful *ajwaka* in disguise. But his belief could not stop him from moving on with his own life. "I couldn't wait for the *tipu*," he reflected. "I didn't want to waste my time there, but I knew the 'good time' [*kare maber*] for the *tipu* was far away." He chose to shape part of his own subjectivity according to modern-scientific time and another part according to magical-prophetic time. He noted that if Kony came back and overthrew the government tomorrow, he would grab a gun from the UPDF barracks in Gulu and join in the fight as it proceeded south toward the capital. He held both times together— each true in their respective logic, but evoked according to different contingencies. As he focused on modern-scientific time, the magical-prophetic time of Kony's overthrow seemed more uncertain and distant. Similarly, as he thought of the overthrow and imagined reassuming the role of an armed rebel, his efficient productivity as a tailor and farmer was thrown aside.

THEY COULD NOT STAND THE *AJWAGI*, BUT IMITATED THEM

> There is no question about it, the Acholi are a fine race, and
> will make splendid soldiers of Jesus Christ when once [sic]
> they have done with their old heathen customs.
>
> A. B. Lloyd, annual CMS letter from Patigo, November 13, 1907

Implicit in the notion of reason is a question of truth or authenticity. How can a reasonable person believe that which is false or fraudulent, or reject that which is true or authentic? In these questions, what is methodologically central to the process of reason is an ascertainment of truth. Debates surrounding Joseph Kony's spirits can be seen as these kinds of attempts to ascertain truth, and in the process, to discern the reasonable from the unreasonable. Was Kony a mere trickster, someone who duped gullible villagers by disguising bombs as stones? Was he an *ajwaka* in disguise, possessed by a powerful, violent *jok* that made him fight and kill? Was he a messenger (*lakwena*) of a Christian God, possessed by holy spirits that sought to do away with "old heathen customs" by killing witch doctors (*ajwagi*), witches (*lujogi*), and ancestral shrines (*abila*)? These questions were of intense concern to Acholi civilians as well as to former rebels, each of them staking claims to truth by how they interpreted Kony's perform-ances, variously as tricks, magic, or miracles. In the midst of these debates, it seemed as though the fight over truth was essentially about who was rational and who was irrational.

Yet rather than examining these debates as questions of truth and rea-son, I want to draw attention to the importance of mimesis in LRA ideol-ogy and practice. Mimesis was the basis on which these debates took place, as LRA practice mirrored Christian and, especially, traditional Acholi spiritual practice, sometimes making it difficult to distinguish LRA practice from its others. This focus on mimesis, I suggest, moves beyond questions of reason in the sense of truth. It shows how, in the midst of countless copies of countless originals, truth and falsehood, rationality and irrationality, coexisted precisely through the power of mimicry.

Those debating over Kony's spirit took one of several positions. Some, particularly among the educated middle and upper classes of Acholi civil-ians, insisted that Kony was nothing more than an illiterate trickster who deceived people with clever hoaxes. In this narrative, Kony began to win favor with Acholi peasants through prayers, which peasants enjoyed. He then deceived people into believing that he was capable of performing miracles. He mixed petrol and water, and shocked people when the "water" turned to fire. He boiled insects and animals and used them as medicine, medicine that worked through the placebo effect. He wrapped grenades in foil obtained from the insides of cigarette cartons, making peasants believe that he could make "stones" explode.

These stories were fairly rare, and sometimes less actually held beliefs than performances of class and status, and by extension aspirations toward or anxieties about modernity. Through these performances, one rejected the spirit world entirely in affirming the absolute truth of science. But it was an open secret among all that Kony was possessed by some kind of spirit(s). Most Acholi civilians and some disaffected former rebels identified that spirit as a *jok*, making Kony a spirit priest (*ajwaka*) in the tradition of Acholi religion (*tic Acoli*). While he claimed to be a man of (a Christian) God possessed by holy spirits, this was a mere facade, hiding a form of traditional spirit now considered by Christian doctrine to be satanic. Born-again Christians condemning Kony designated him as a devil disguising himself as the angel of light. Like Alice and Severino Lukoya before him, Kony was said to be possessed by a "bad spirit" (*tipu marac*), a *jok* that only claimed to be a holy spirit (*tipu maleng*). This particular *jok* of Kony's, according to this narrative, was powerful, made people fear it, and attempted to destroy all *abila* of other *jogi*, treating these *jogi* as competitive threats. It was indeed capable of turning stones into bombs, a practice more associated with the powers of *jok* than those of *tipu maleng*. It was a fighting *jok* (*jok lweny*) that turned Alice and Kony into warriors rather than normal *ajwagi*. If it were truly a *tipu maleng*, it would not do "bad things" like killing and destroying.

But the majority of my friends who spent long periods of time as LRA rebels suggested that Kony had not a *jok/jogi*, but one or more *tipu maleng*. They remembered the way the *tipu* predicted the future, warning of war, disease, and other problems the rebels would face. The spirit prescribed both medicine and preventive measures that, if followed, ensured health and success for the rebels in battle. It had this good side, but also a bad side—bringing messages of death, of who would die in battle—messages that would, rebels said, bring Kony great sadness, but about which he could do nothing. The ambivalent nature of the spirit shook the faith of rebels not in the *tipu* itself, but only in its intentions. Mohammed reflected, "People aren't sure what the *tipu* is up to. Kony said the *tipu* would change after some time, but he [Kony] doesn't know when that time will be. . . . So he himself isn't sure about this *tipu*. . . . There's a lot of uncertainty." God was somehow speaking though Kony, who was His prophet, but His message was sometimes unclear and other times difficult to accept.

What was particularly remarkable about the narrative descriptions and memories of Kony's *tipu* was the ways in which it was almost always constructed against the archetype of the *jok*. Rebels described in detail how Kony left behind what missionary A. B. Lloyd, in the epigraph to this section, termed "old heathen customs," with the LRA literally becoming

AN LRA BATTLE SONG

It was sung, according to various accounts, on the front lines of battle as well as in celebration following successful battles. After his gun jammed in the midst of battle, one commander was said to have sung this song to clear the jam before being able to continue firing.

Lalar, Lalar larowa	The Savior, the Savior saves us
Pe tye gin ma loyo Rubanga Wonwa	There is nothing that defeats our God the Father
Aleluya	Hallelujah
Pe tye gin ma loyo Rubanga	There is nothing that defeats God
Lalar, Lalar larowa	The Savior, the Savior saves us
Pe tye gin ma loyo Rubanga Wonwa	There is nothing that defeats our God the Father
Aleluya	Hallelujah
Pe tye gin ma loyo Rubanga	There is nothing that defeats God
Wacako wot, wacako ki nying rwot	Even starting to walk, we start in the name of the Lord
Pe tye gin ma loyo Rubanga Wonwa	There is nothing that defeats our God the Father
Aleluya	Hallelujah
Pe tye gin ma loyo Rubanga	There is nothing that defeats God
Mac wacelo ki nying Rwot	We fire bullets in the name of the Lord
Pe tye gin ma loyo Rubanga Wonwa	There is nothing that defeats our God the Father
Aleluya	Hallelujah
Pe tye gin ma loyo Rubanga	There is nothing that defeats God
Wa nek, waneko ki nying Rwot	Even killing, we kill in the name of the Lord
Pe tye gin ma loyo Rubanga Wonwa	There is nothing that defeats our God the Father
Aleluya	Hallelujah
Pe tye gin ma loyo Rubanga	There is nothing that defeats God

Ciro too, waciro ki nying Rwot	Withstanding death, we withstand in the name of the Lord
Pe tye gin ma loyo Rubanga Wonwa	There is nothing that defeats our God the Father
Aleluya	Hallelujah
Pe tye gin ma loyo Rubanga	There is nothing that defeats God

something not far from the "splendid soldiers of Jesus Christ" of whom Lloyd metaphorically spoke. As my friends attempted to describe Kony's powers and spirits, they went to great pains to distinguish them from those of *ajwagi* and *jogi*, pointing out defining distinctions. They took care to draw these distinctions not only because there was little historical precedent from which to directly understand the *tipu maleng*, nor only because they felt compelled to push back against a hegemonic civilian discourse that (mis)identified the *tipu maleng* as a *jok marac*. But also, they drew distinctions because the form and content of Kony's beliefs, practices, and possessions closely mimicked those of an *ajwaka*. The *ajwaka* and her *jok* was the Alter by which Kony and his *tipu* was defined.

The LRA could not stand the *ajwagi*, but imitated them—from place, to language, to practice. As described above, Kony found a spiritual home at Awere Hill, where he would pray and gather holy water. As hills (*godi*) are widely known to be the homes of *jogi*, it was speculated by skeptics that Kony was possessed by a *jok* there and only pretended that it was a *tipu maleng*. Benjamin, who believed that Kony got his *jok* from the hill, recalled Ecclesiastes 3, saying that the time for a holy spirit coming to the people had already come and gone with Jesus Christ, and therefore Kony's spirit was satanic. Believers in the *tipu maleng*, like Otto, dispelled this idea, adding in Christian details to Kony's activity at Awere to distinguish Kony's *tipu maleng* from *jok*. "People went to pray from [Awere Hill] to increase the strength of the LRA. . . . But also, this is where a white pigeon dove came and landed on Kony's shoulder, like it did to Jesus." Matayo saw the dove as an angel, a sign of Kony's holiness.

In language, rebels drew upon careful linguistic distinctions to differentiate Kony's *tipu* possession from *jok* possession. Foremost among these was the very word used to describe "possession"—*ido*. While commonly used to describe possession by a *jok*, *ido* was not used by rebels who believed in the *tipu* to describe Kony's possession. In place of *ido*, Matayo and others said that Kony was "filled" or "loaded" with the spirit (*opong ki cwiny*). Similarly, referring to practices of making offerings or sacrifices, rebels referred to the LRA performing Christian offerings (*tyer*) but not the sacrifices (*tum*) made for spirits in *tic Acoli*.[13] This minor linguistic distinction was vital in marking Kony apart from an *ajwaka*, particularly when other distinctions were more subtle, or sometimes nonexistent. The very term *ajwaka*, for example, was also used by Protestants to refer to servants of God (*ajwagi pa Lubanga*), or priests.[14] In a similar way, Otto sometimes referred to the yard as *abila pa Kony*, repurposing the terms of *tic Acoli* for holy Christian use, and in doing so, echoing early missionary practices that attempted to translate existing concepts from *tic Acoli* into Christian terms to ease the task of evangelization.[15] Given the way in which some of these words were burdened with multiple and often nonoverlapping meanings, terms were easily confused, and sometimes the wrong one slipped out. Once, during an intense conversation with Otto comparing and contrasting Kony's spirit to the *jok* of an *ajwaka*, my friend Jimmy caught himself talking about Kony's *jok* before correcting himself to say *tipu*. Otto waved away his apology. "It's OK. The Acoli call it that," he shrugged.

There was some debate as to the physical manner in which Kony was possessed that became a method by which to distinguish whether he was possessed by a *jok* or a *tipu maleng*. My *ajwaka* friend, Akello Sabina, suggested that Kony could not be possessed by a *jok* because *jogi* tend to stay in one place for a long time, without traveling as Kony had done throughout the war. Benjamin, among others, insisted that he had seen *jogi* possess people before he joined the LRA, and when he saw Kony's possessions, he found them indistinguishable from *jok* possessions. He concluded that Kony was possessed by a *jok*. But those claiming that the spirit was a *tipu maleng* pointed to differences in the way the spirit was embodied to distinguish it from *jok*. *Ajwagi* generally have to actively call spirits, often using music or rattling sounds, in order to communicate with them, and work with individual clients who come to see them one by one; by contrast, Kony's *tipu* seemed to abruptly and spontaneously possess him and talk through him with many others present, and without his active participation. Unlike *ajwagi*, Kony did not shake or tremble during his possessions, but only his eyes transformed through the process. His possessions did not occur behind curtains (where, Otto suggested, the *ajwaka* could be "faking things"), but mostly in front of others, including commanders who transcribed what the spirits said; and what was said was not spoken in inaudible hushes, but clearly and distinctly. Kony's instruments also differed from those of the *ajwaka*. Whereas an *ajwaka* would shake a calabash (*awal*) in the midst of possession, Kony would only use an *awal* in the yard, to carry blessed water. When he was loaded with the spirit, he wore a white cassock and held a rosary, dipping his fingers into a glass of blessed water before making the sign of the cross.[16] Unlike *ajwagi*, and indeed, unlike pastors or preachers from churches of varied denominations and types, Kony's *tipu* did not ask for money or other compensation, like goats—wealth that made *ajwagi* and pastors relatively well-to-do in their communities, and subject to scorn from some who claimed that they were more interested in riches than in the "truth" of their work.

As a way of emphasizing the distinction of their copy from the original, the LRA exercised great violence against *ajwagi*, practices of *tic Acoli*, and other magical practices. The LRA were well-known for killing *ajwagi*, burning *abila*, and destroying other practices and people related to *jok*. While some rumored that Kony was an *ajwaka* who consulted with others, most know that Kony attacked them and destroyed *abila*, driving many from rural villages into the refuge of Gulu town. For the LRA, these practices constituted evils that had to be destroyed. Otto recalled, "We burned all things, the working tools of *ajwagi* and of *jok*. I burned so many drums, calabashes, and cowrie shells. If Kony didn't have a strong spirit to protect me ... [the *ajwagi*] could have attacked and killed me, but they didn't." These practices mimed those of Christian evangelicals who spoke of the *abila* as a demonic material practice that kept one in "captivity." They performed forms of material violence similar to those performed by the LRA, collecting fetishes of various forms, including charms, shrines, and clothes, and burning them in large drums during revival campaigns.

Similarly, those within the LRA who were caught night-dancing[17] or suspected of being wizards (*lujogi*) were arrested and sometimes released, but often killed. Labwor recalled, "Kony had no mercy for *lujogi*—he even ordered his soldiers to kill his own wife who was a *lajok*, along with the children, who he said were going to become *lujogi*." *Lujogi* were detected by either their family line or their actions and were killed, some speculated, on the order of the *tipu*, who refused to allow the use or worship of any other spirit.

Practices against *ajwagi*, *lujogi*, and *abila* were only part of a broader attack on and distinction from *tic Acoli*. Musa once made this point quite clear to me, saying, "We do God's work [*tic pa Rubanga*; Christianity], not *tic Acoli*. We didn't rely on traditions." As part of this distinction, the LRA also abandoned the practice of *nying moi*, *kwero merok*, and the giving of *jok* names to newborn children. Otto insisted that were a problem to arise that would otherwise suggest the need to *kwero merok*, the LRA simply conducted prayers to solve the problem. "This is because *kwero merok* is a bit of a *jok* issue [*lok jok-jok*]," he reflected. "*Kwero merok* involves *kwer* given to the *jok*, but in the *lum*, people didn't do anything related to *jok*. We were religious and followed God." Similarly, there were no *jok* names given to children born with unusual marks or in unusual ways that would otherwise be given according to Acholi custom. "If you produce twins in the *lum*, there is no *kwer*," Otto continued. Accordingly, twins would not be given the names Opiyo (the first-born twin) or Ocen (the second-born twin).[18]

As part of the otherization of *jok*, the LRA also employed certain measures to protect themselves from *jogi* they might have encountered in the *lum*. Smearing the body with oil was said to disarm the power of a *jok*, protecting especially children from it. Anointing new rebels was in part to protect them from *jogi*. Of course, the strength of Kony's *tipu* was also said, together with a strong faith in God, to defeat *jogi*. Matayo noted, "The *tipu* captures *jok* [*tipu mako jok*]," and recalled that those who had weak faiths in God were more susceptible to being attacked by *jogi*. It was for them, Matayo suggested, that strict rules about drinking, among others, were made—to prevent them from being possessed by *jogi* who preyed on their weak faiths.

The distinctions between LRA practice and *tic Acoli*, through narrative, violence, and other means, were made precisely because they looked very similar from the outside. Otto, who was a spiritual technician, admitted, "It's true—there are a lot of similarities with the *ajwaka*. . . . The controllers were like *ajwagi* of God [*Rubanga*]. The fact that you used *awal*—we were *ajwagi*, but we were *ajwagi* of God [*Rubanga*]."

While the LRA mimed practices of *ajwagi*, claiming to be true messengers of God, they simultaneously mimed Islamic values, Catholic priests, and born-again preachers. They adopted Islamic practices, such as not working on Fridays—a mime they were said to have developed in conjunction with their military cooperation with Sudanese Arabs (Dolan 2009, 86). They prayed Christian prayers, read from the Bible, adopted Catholic materialities such as rosaries and sanctification, and sang Protestant and evangelical hymns. Generally, Christian priests denounced Kony and the LRA as deceptive liars, especially when the LRA attacked churches and missions. In turn, the LRA often denounced them as corrupt, greedy materialists, lacking true faith in God and only becoming religious in order to make money.

This multiple mimesis, a copying of several originals, enhanced the collective power of the LRA by compiling the mystique of each original into an unrecognizable singularity that, in the midst of the failure of the originals to transcend postcolonial binds, offered new hope. This was no mere bricolage. Rather, it was a complex mimicry that combined both truth and falsehood, mimicking the false original and claiming the copy as truth, while retaining the power of the false original. It was in this way that one of my friends, who spent a brief time in the *lum* with the LRA, suggested that Kony practiced both Christianity and *tic Acoli*, and had both *jok* and *tipu maleng*.

The LRA's violent mimicry, I argue, was a form of what Michael Taussig (1993), drawing on Max Horkheimer and Theodor Adorno, has described as an "organized control of mimesis," a mimetic repression that Nazi fascists used in exterminating Jews. For Adorno and Horkheimer, repressing mimesis was a way of eliminating the threats to one's existence posed by internal elements. For Nazis engaged in notions of pure reason and civilization, repressed impurity was projected onto Jews, who suffered the violence against the forbidden within the Nazi. To be clear, I am not implying that the LRA were violent fascists on the level or scale of Nazis. There was, however, a certain coincidence of the moment of fascist anti-Semitism with that of Ugandan postcoloniality—a peculiarly modern time in which a past "savagery" of *tic Acoli* was to be left behind; a colonial present of Christian practice failed to offer liberation; and prophesized futures remained uncertain. Internally in both moments, anxieties about civilization appeared simultaneously with horror of the primitive, projected by Nazis and the LRA onto Jews and *ajwagi* respectively, who were "charged with practicing forbidden magic and bloody rituals" (Horkheimer and Adorno 2002, 153). In practicing postcolonial "mimetic excess," the LRA lived "subjunctively as neither subject nor object of history but as both, at one and the same time" (Taussig 1993, 255). As both subject and object, both original and copy, following both *jok* and *tipu*, holding both the true and the false, Kony and the LRA—through the post-dualist practice of mimesis—exceeded debates over rationality based on pure divisions between magic and science.[19]

CHAMELEON MILLENARIANS

> [Kony] is a strange man, but sometimes says things
> that *make sense.*
>
> Ugandan minister Betty Bigombe, quoted in "Bigombe:
> The Woman Who Dared Kony," emphasis added

Why were the LRA fighting? Among scholars, international observers, and civilians, this is perhaps the most debated question surrounding the LRA. It is also the one most often posed within the unhelpful and value-laden plane of rational discourse. Human rights activists and moralizing humanist scholars decry violence committed "for no reason" (Ehrenreich 1998, 82) and say that the LRA leadership has "poorly articulated" its vision of an alternative society (Van Acker 2004, 336), expending "little effort in presenting a coherent and rational face to the world, or even to their Acholi brethren" (Blattman and Annan 2010, 154–55). Some argue that while committing such violence, the LRA made "rational decisions"—including the use of terror as a "strategy of choice"—that demanded punitive ICC intervention (Allen 2006, 44). Political scientists often attempt to analyze LRA beliefs and practices to show how they serve "rational and functional purposes" (Titeca 2010, 61) in rebel operations, or to contextualize their violence in terms of its political structure and a morphing political agenda (Branch 2005). Some scholars, attentive to rebel manifestos, stress LRA political claims and causes, in part to dispel the idea that the LRA fight for "bizarre and mysterious reasons" (Finnström 2010, 74). Finally, despite their strong opposition to the Museveni regime, many Acholi civilians potentially sympathetic to the LRA sometimes found themselves unable to support a force killing their own people (see Finnström 2008, 118) or waging a war that they felt had little chance of succeeding (see Gersony 1997, 59). From a rational perspective, the LRA fight was one that simply could not be won, and therefore made little sense.

Rather than entering into a historical or contextual analysis of the roots of the war, or trying to either dispel or prove the hypothesis that the LRA war was "irrational" or "bizarre," I attend to the ways in which rebels narrated and understood both a "political" and "religious" raison d'être of the rebellion, separate but together. I argue that rebels in practice distinguished political and spiritual-religious reasons for fighting, a distinction that reflected the contexts in which the rebels lived and were asked to give accounts of themselves. As with scientific and magical time, they did not hold political and spiritual causes for fighting congruently together. There was comparatively little mixing of spiritual and political symbols as in ostensibly similar forces like Zimbabwe's ZANLA rebels (Lan 1985, xvii–xix). The spiritual logic and the political logic maintained separate worlds, without an overarching scheme by which to organize them. Under the scrutiny of modern reason, the LRA became "bizarre" because they simultaneously had cause (in political form) and no cause (in religious form). They fought for something and they fought for nothing. Drawing on the work of Harri Englund (2002), and taking seriously Musa's suggestion to me that former rebels are like "chameleons," I argue that the rebels were "chameleon millenarians"—figures characteristic of postcolonial protest in which dynamic, diachronic, multiple, and coexistent identities inhabit a world itself dynamic, diachronic, multiple, and coexistent. Sometimes, the LRA were soldiers of God; other times, they were human-rights defenders of the Acholi people; still other times, they were slaves to a divine will that was uncertain and unknowable. They changed their colors through time according to a shifting, fragmented world, displaying a flexibility that in part explains the endurance of their struggle. More precisely, LRA ideology is chameleonic and multiple because it confronts multiple, dynamic forms of governance in the postcolony.

Otto's understandings of the LRA cause offer a typical illustration of the dynamism and multiplicity of this chameleon millenarianism.

A spiritual technician who spent around two decades in the *lum*, Otto was no stranger to the LRA's dynamism, spirituality, or politics. At the beginning of our conversations together, in late 2012, Otto—like many of my friends—posed rational-concrete answers to the rational-concrete question: Why were the LRA fighting? He spoke of overthrowing Museveni's government, suggesting that Museveni had rigged elections, continuing to hold onto power even after he had "lost" the ballot box. He recalled the violence that Museveni and the NRA had inflicted on the Acholi in the immediate aftermath of his coup in 1986, and spoke of rumored plans that Museveni was going to unite Rwanda and Uganda, giving away Acholi land to the Banyankole, whom the Acholi would be forced to serve as slaves.[20] Kony, he said, would offer Uganda something different—an end to tribalism, a minimum wage for the poor to live on, moral codes on dress, the outlawing of prostitution, adequately staffed and supplied health centers. Indeed, this was the form of narrative that emerged when the LRA had to present itself to a liberal international community, as at the Kacoke Madit in London in 1997.[21] In his document on behalf of the LRM/A, James Obita listed five "aims and objective [*sic*] of the LRM/A":

a) To remove dictatorship and stop the oppression of our people.

b) To fight for the immediate restoration of competitive multi-party democracy in Uganda.

c) To see and [*sic*] end to gross violation of human rights and dignity of Ugandans.

d) To ensure the restoration of peace and security in Uganda.

e) To ensure unity, sovereignty and economic prosperity beneficial to all Ugandans.

f) To bring to an end to [*sic*] the repressive policy of deliberate marginalization of groups of people who may not agree with the NRA ideology. (Obita 1997, 4–5)

Speaking to largely leftist, secular audiences, rebels provided rational, logical arguments for the LRA struggle, often couched in terms of human rights abuses, a lack of democracy and prosperity, and uneven development. This "political" discourse was in part an exercise in translation, of making the struggle legible to others through a modern language of "goals" and "aims." Otto noted the importance of "letting foreign countries understand what you are fighting for, so that they are able to help you, not only logistically, but through manpower, too." But it was also part of a self-identity that articulated the deep-seated discontent and protest against Museveni's regime in the practical terms of everyday life—the lack of livable wages, visibly uneven development, lack of medication at the local health center. For Otto, Uganda had become irreparably corrupt, and the only way out was war, via the LRA. When particularly frustrated with corruption, Otto said, he would often think that he had to return to the *lum*. He was a political and politicized rebel.

This was only one identity of the rebel, distinguished from the spiritual one. As Otto, Musa, and I sat to watch *Che* one day together, Otto drew similarities between the Cuban rebellion and the LRA. He compared Batista to Museveni, noting similar oppression of political opponents, and saw that the Cuban people, like the Acholi, were suffering under tyrannical rule. But he was struck by the lack of visible religion in the Cuban struggle. Unlike the Cubans, he said, the LRA would require a go-ahead from the spirit to go to battle, and would pray before going into battle. "Just surrender everything in the heart of God. God knows the outcome of the war. . . . I know God is still with Kony," Otto insisted. In this way, he was a spiritual rebel, following the word of God as given through His messenger, Kony, who would save people from the evils of the world. The millenarian terms of this prophecy foresaw an overthrow of Museveni's government, but did not give specific political content to that moment. God had chosen them to be His fighters, who faithfully obeyed Him, but the content and achievements of the war lay beyond their hands in His.

The *tipu* did not speak of uneven development or inadequately maintained health centers, of human rights violations or multiparty democracy. Nor did the listed aims or objectives of the LRA include obedience to the received word of God through his prophet, Joseph Kony.[22] They were domains compartmentalized, articulating multiple selves in the multiplicity of spaces of the postcolony, spaces ruled by God, spirits, the nation-state, the international community, discourses of humanity and human rights, and so forth. As rebels navigated these spaces and their respective discourses, they—like chameleons—changed colors to fit the given space.

Sometimes, Otto understood the LRA fight in secular, political terms as a Ugandan citizen. Other times, he understood it in spiritual-religious terms as a subject of the *tipu*. But often, letting himself fully enter the world of the *tipu*, he understood it precisely by not understanding it, inhabiting a space of intense uncertainty and unknowability. "I can't tell exactly the reasons for the war," he reflected sometime after we first met, "and I'm not the only one. Many people don't understand, even the likes of [former commander Brigadier Kenneth] Banya. They don't know exactly why Kony was fighting." This might have seemed a remarkable thing to hear from a seasoned, informed rebel who spent two decades fighting in the *lum*. But while apparently puzzling, it was by no means contradictory for Otto to identify political and spiritual reasons for fighting while simultaneously not knowing why the LRA were fighting. From within the space of the ultimate unknowability of the divine, no one but God's *tipu* could really know the purpose of the war.

The LRA world was fragmented into multiple cosmologies, all with their own, often nonoverlapping logics and discourses. This nonoverlapping multiplicity was neither original nor unique. In fact, it mirrored a postcolonial regime that experienced its raison d'être in similar fragments. Even as Museveni and his NRM outlined development schemes and ten-point plans that identified "ideological disorientation" as a stumbling block to prosperity, they existed similarly as chameleons. They drew variously on evangelical cosmology, Fanonian, socialist, and neoliberal discourses, in addition to (it was rumored) witchcraft and spirits to confront the realities and challenges of postcolonial rule.

I am not arguing, as many do, that the chameleon character of LRA millenarianism was duplicitous or ingenuous.[23] Nor am I suggesting that the chameleon is a kind of *bricoleur*, struggling to get what he or she can through a shotgun approach to the enactment of a different world. Rather, it is the demands of the world itself, a world fragmented and compartmentalized into multiple cosmological frames, that allowed rebels to identify sometimes political reasons, sometimes spiritual-religious reasons, and sometimes no or unknown reasons as to why they were fighting. That there was no rational, clearly articulated vision by the rebels, scholars, or other commentators of why the LRA were fighting should not necessarily be seen as a failure of the rebels to make their voices heard, nor as a sign of their "irrationality." Rather, the absence of a clear vision indicates the failure of the concept of "reason" to fully encapsulate the multiple complexity of a postcolonial mire in which politics, religion, spirituality, and rights coexist disjointedly. The LRA recognized—and attempted to heal—this fragmented postcolony with a disjointed approach to a disjointed problem. To inhabit the full meaning and texture of these LRA life-worlds, one must move beyond conventional notions of "reason."

BEYOND REASON, BEYOND HUMANITY

The LRA inhabited what might appear to be contradictory logics simultaneously, holding together faith and science; modern time and prophetic time; *tipu* and *jok*; political, religious, and no raison d'être for war—or more simply, rationality and irrationality. In doing so, they answered some old yet persistent questions of cultural relativism. Clifford Geertz's (1984) commentary on the relativism debates suggests that what was at stake in these debates was essentially "reason" and "humanity." From the positions of relativism and anti-relativism, we could, for example, accept LRA practices of mutilation on the grounds of reason, or alternatively reject them—also on the grounds of reason. Relativistically accepting these practices would imply a humanism in the mold of an underlying sameness, in which there are different ways of being human. Anti-relativistically rejecting these practices would imply a humanism in the mold of a fundamental human nature.

Through their practices, the LRA implicitly rejected both relativist and anti-relativist claims made about humanity. They did not ask to be reduced to the Same, as relativists might. They saw themselves standing above both science (as practiced by the UNLA or the UPDF) and magic (as practiced by *ajwagi*). Nor did they assign moral primacy to either magic or science as anti-relativists might, but employed them both. And with their practice of holding magic and science together, they were both magicians and scientists, *bricoleurs* and engineers.[24] They occupied classifications of both rational-science and irrational-magic, as outlined in table 3.

Table 3   Rational-scientific and irrational-magical ways in which the LRA thought
and practiced

Holding these logics together, they transcended them

rational-scientific	*irrational-magical*
logic	faith
military tactics	spiritual tactics
modern time	prophetic time
truth, as in the holy spirit and its messenger	deception, as in a *jok* and its *ajwaka*
fighting with a political raison d'être	fighting with a religious raison d'être

To practice a social science that repurposes LRA practices as reasonable, and thus humanizes them, operates a moral logic that remains trapped
within the binds of (ir)rationality as a further attack on unreason. Taking
LRA practices in their singularity forces us to displace reason and
humanity as concepts by which to understand them. Transcending rationality and irrationality as a Cartesian duality, we disrupt humanity insofar
as Man is defined as *animal rationale*.

Interlude

Do [the reception center staff] see them as rebels, or do they see them as human beings?

World Vision rehabilitation center staff member, personal interview in 2013, emphasis added

The first half of this book explored the experiences, memories, logics, and being of rebels fighting in the *lum*. It showed the ways in which LRA violence became inhuman in the eyes of modernity; how rebels transcended human-animal binaries through life in the *lum*; and how they combined magic and science to go beyond the problem of rationality. The remaining chapters focus on different forms and practices of life after fighting—what was commonly referred to as the "return" or "reintegration." From kinship to love to politics, rebels reconfigured existing frameworks by which to understand these concepts, both in their singularity and in their relation to the concept of humanity.

Prior to returning "home," many rebels were processed by and spent probationary time in "reception centers" such as World Vision or Gulu Support the Children Organisation (GUSCO), and/or in the custody of the UPDF.[1] Like salvation, the return was fetishized as a transition from darkness to light, hopelessness to hope, worthlessness to value, captivity to freedom, *lum* to *gang*, trauma to health, emaciation to fullness, irrationality to reason, violence to peace, destruction to production, pollution to cleanliness, and indeed, inhumanity to humanity.[2] In conversations with employers, medical workers, reception center employees, and other

> The CRG [Child Reference Group] perceived "low-risk" children as being:
>
> Children who were abducted, but were not forced to commit atrocities, who were not forced to have children; *they have a more human than an animal mind.*
>
> Gulu Support the Children Organisation (2002, 15), emphasis added

civilians, and during broadcasts of local radio programs, "reintegration" was spoken of as a set of required transformations and treatments of rebels that would rid them of their "bush mentality,"[3] teach them "what is life,"[4] and "let them be human beings" (*wek gubed dano*).[5]

Violent, fierce, animal-like rebels were to be transformed into peaceful, gentle human beings through both formal and informal means. Returning rebels were seen as potential robbers and killers, threatening the stability of community life and places of employment with their "harshness" (*gero*). Compared with civilians, they were thought to be less compliant with the law, tended to have shorter tempers, and could not be fully trusted. Many could be "reformed," though some were hopeless. "You can't tame them," one hotel manager professed regarding the most "difficult." Some were accused by reception center workers of being haunted by *cen*, effectively stigmatizing them as violent, unjust killers. They were told to leave behind and forget their lives, harshness, and killings in the *lum*. In the confines of the reception center, returning rebels were surveilled and screened for signs of violent behavior, such as reacting angrily to being kicked in a football match. "Those who are reformed will be reintegrated with the public. Those who are very stubborn are put in the army so that they don't come terrorize villagers," one medical worker working with ex-rebels told me.

Indeed, experienced reception center officials admitted that the vocational skills training commonly given to ex-rebels (tailoring, carpentry, and so forth) was not primarily meant to provide useful life skills or means of earning wages. Rather, it was a form of "therapy," meant to "help change their minds" and to "keep them busy" so that they would not return to the

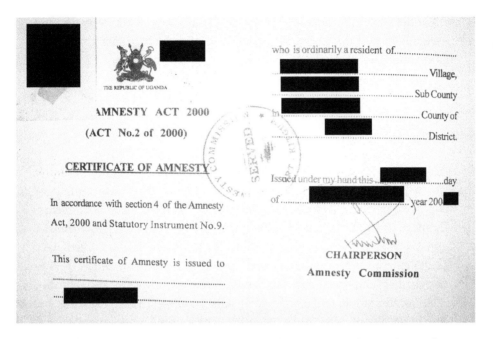

THE REPUBLIC OF UGANDA

AMNESTY ACT 2000

(ACT No.2 of 2000)

CERTIFICATE OF AMNESTY

In accordance with section 4 of the Amnesty

Act, 2000 and Statutory Instrument No.9.

This certificate of Amnesty is issued to

....

....

who is ordinarily a resident of............................

.... Village,

.... Sub County

in... County of

.... District.

Issued under my hand this......................day

of.. year 200▮

CHAIRPERSON

Amnesty Commission

Figure 11. A typical amnesty certificate issued to former LRA rebels according to the Amnesty Act of 2000. Photo by author.

lum. To give a better sense of the ways in which the processes of reintegration were conceptualized, I scatter selections from primary-source reception center policies, reports, and interviews throughout this interlude.

In both theory and practice, the actual processes of reintegration took place quite differently from what civilians imagined and desired. Drawing on history and ethnography, I offer a "re-turn," both a response to and a change of direction from the way that the reintegration of rebels was conceptualized and experienced; and a "dis-integration," a dissolution of the moral binaries through which reintegration was conceptualized.[6] In the case of the LRA, "reintegration" was not attempted as a process by which people were brought together in ways that carefully considered the uniqueness of their experiences and being. Rather, it was an attempted process closer to a "re-subjectification," a disciplinary attempt— as the epigraph suggests—to make new subjects ("humans") and destroy old ones ("rebels"). As with prisoners and slaves, the subjectivity of the rebel was to be exorcised as a moral imperative. There was nothing meaningful that the rebel was presumed to offer civilians, nor any significant way in which civilian subjectivities might be productively reshaped by "reintegration."

A BRIEF HISTORY OF "REINTEGRATION"

"Reintegration" was by no means a new concept to the region. In fact, it was a process that had been envisioned during the establishment of colonial-era Church Missionary Society (CMS) freed slave settlements, the post–World War II return of King's African Rifles soldiers (*askari*), and prisoner reentry programs. The CMS ran Frere Town, a freed slave settlement near Mombasa, Kenya, operating in the late 1800s. It was designed to "help freed slaves back onto their feet" with education, health, religion, sanitation, and employment skills training (Everill 2013, 30–31). Providing "loving care" and a "peaceful, happy home," the settlement was ostensibly part of the British campaign to put down what Reverend A. B. Fisher, who served in Acholiland, called the "inhuman trade" (ca. 1890–92, 134, 140).

Similarly, the return of thousands of *askari* or servicemen following the end of World War II posed problems of how to "fit" soldiers for civilian life (see Killingray 2010; Parsons 1999). Optimistic reports by missionaries and colonial officials suggested that these soldiers were changed people, returning to their tribes as disciplined, trained, and civilized harbingers of progress.[7] By contrast, on-the-ground reports from the Upper Nile suggested that many *askari* returned unhappily to low standards of living, suspicious of missionaries preaching tolerance and patience for improved conditions of life.[8] Missionaries in turn worried about the indiscipline of returning soldiers, few of whom attended church and many of whom preferred to spend their leisure time drinking.[9] More recently, attention to the rehabilitation of Ugandan prisoners has led to the development of agricultural and vocational skills training and education for prisoners,[10] programs also offered to returning rebels. Like reintegration discourses, stories of prisoner reform are often narrated as ones of "transformation, rehabilitation and hope" (Araali 2013, 4), buttressed by claims that

> These children have been exposed to psychocologically [*sic*] wounding
> events *beyond the normal boundaries of human experience* and as a result
> evidence stress reactions. They need immediate psychosocial support to
> enable them to return to as normal a family life as possible in the circum-
> stances so they can commence the process of recovery.
> GUSCO and Red Barnet (1998–2001, 3), emphasis added

Ugandan prison recidivism rates are among the world's lowest (Mudoola 2014).

Whether prisoners, freed slaves, or returning soldiers, polluting subjects out-of-place were thought to need cleansing, lest they idle unemployed, (re)foment rebellion, be left behind by a civilizing Christian
modernity, or re-offend as criminals. In no way was it expected that slaves
could have meaningful experiences, or that prisoners could offer something constructive to society that they had gleaned out of prison. Rebels
were treated similarly.

"WE AREN'T MAD"

The process of "reintegration" saw civilians attempt to turn rebels into
patients—sometimes willing but often unwilling ones—and subject them
to specific treatment regimens. Envisioning reintegration as a passage
from inhumanity to humanity, they often posited the process as one of
"repairing [rebels'] heads" (*roco wii-gi*).[11] Some rebels accepted this imaginary, resigning themselves to the treatment process and getting on with
post-reintegration life.

But many rebels refused to accept the idea that they were sick, resisting
what they felt was unnecessary and involuntary treatment. Labwor was
particularly upset at passing through the reception center, which he likened to both an asylum and a prison: "We said we didn't understand why
they kept us at the reception center. 'We aren't mad,' we told them. 'You're
keeping us in prison.'" He and his friend Otto were especially upset
that husbands and wives were divided into separate reception centers.

> Those who took long in captivity have *unstable mind* [*sic*].
> Lakot (2003), GUSCO internal document, emphasis added

> Movement outside the gate is strictly on permission by the social worker
> on duty. . . . Unnecessary movement at night is not allowed.
> Gulu Support the Children Organisation (GUSCO) (n.d.C, 9)

After their capture, he and Otto were sent to World Vision, while their
wives were sent to GUSCO—a painful separation that deeply saddened
Labwor.[12]

Gunya spent time in prison herself after leaving the front lines, following an arrest for a minor assault. She remembered prison life as harder
than life at World Vision, with worse food and harder work regimes. She
also felt she was treated with greater suspicion than other prisoners for
having been a rebel. "The prison wardens were strict on me," she said. "I
wasn't taken outside to work [as a prisoner-laborer] because the wardens
were told I was a rebel, and they had to be very careful with me. They
feared that if I were taken outside, I would remove a gun from the prison
warden and run back with it to the *lum*."

But while life in prison was hard, she found that the restrictions on her
freedom there were comparable to those in the reception center. Like
Labwor, she resented them.[13] She recalled a strike that the rebels at the
center staged, complaining that they were being detained against their
will and demanding to be released home. "The staff at the reception center
refused, saying we can only be released when we finished the time we were
meant to stay at the reception center," Gunya said. Counselors were sent to
talk to them to "cool them down." "We refused to listen to the counselors,
saying we wanted the manager," she recalled, as the rebels demanded to be
heard as imprisoned subjects rather than mad objects. "Some [rebels]
who came from far away . . . said they were ready to walk on foot to go
back home when they are released, because we were used to walking
long distances in the *lum*. After this, [the manager] started releasing

people . . . and they shortened the time people were staying at the reception center." Seeking freedom from the prison of the reception center, Gunya disagreed with those who saw life in the *lum* as a "captivity," as it was commonly seen within civilian circles. "For me, I can't say life in the *lum* is like the life of a slave [*opii*]," she asserted. "Maybe when I was still a recruit, I might have thought like that, but after some time, my thoughts changed. I didn't see life in the *lum* as a slave's life. Life in the *lum* was easier than life in prison."

THE EFFECTIVENESS OF SYMBOLS: THE RITUAL BURNING OF OLD CLOTHES

As discussed briefly in chapter 3, rebels often had their clothes taken away by staff and ritually burned upon their arrival at a reception center.[14] As the policy detailed below explains, this ritual—as implemented at the GUSCO reception center—was part of the treatment regimen meant to bring the diseased rebel out of the sick "past life" and into the "new one," burning to ashes old clothes that symbolized life, experiences, and memories with the rebels. Gunya, whose own clothes were burned, remembers what she was told about this ceremony: "They said the clothes were like dirt from the *lum* [*cilo me lum*], so they wanted it to remain there. Since we were home, with no guns, [they said] we should get rid of dirt in the *lum* and become new people." The burning of these looted clothes was also meant to "protect" rebels from facing stigma or persecution from those civilians who might recognize the stolen goods as having once been their own.

Ostensibly these measures were taken for the benefit of the "children," as former rebels were called. But the burning and other similar cleansing rituals were, some of my friends suggested, more often performed for the benefit of civilians.[15] Gunya and others explained that they did not really see their clothes as "dirt." Indeed, I heard stories of how rebels gave up torn or older clothes to be burned in the ceremony, but hid nicer clothes from staff inside pillowcases, saving them and later sneaking them out of the centers when they were released. "I felt it wasn't really dirt," Gunya reflected on the clothing. "But [the reception center staff] feared the

---

RITUAL BURNING OF THE OLD
CLOTHES AND PROPERTIES

This ritual is done after the children have been received at the center, and the social worker has to explain to the newly arrived children, the meaning and importance of the ritual. Meaning:

 i)   It symbolizes the complete change from the past life to the new one
 ii) Burning away the past ways of life
 iii) Burning away the past memories
 iv) It is also for security reason, i.e., in case the cloth was looted from someone; this could expose the child to problem

Reproduced from Gulu Support the Children Organisation
(GUSCO) (n.d.C, 9)

Some come [to the reception center] with their real clothing that they came with from the bush. And it's not washed, *it's very dirty*, you know?

Guidance counselor, World Vision Children of War Rehabilitation Center, personal interview, 2013, emphasis added

---

frightfulness of the rebels [*lik pa adui*]. They didn't like to see how we looked—ugly [*rac*] with dreadlocks. They didn't want to see it—that's why they shaved [our heads]." Mohammed echoed this sentiment, suggesting that clothes were burned less for the benefit of the former rebels and more for the security and peace of mind of their former civilian owners. "They didn't want [civilians] to know you were in Lakwena and had stolen their clothes," he explained.

THE SEARCH FOR PURITY: TEACHING HYGIENE

An important part of everyday life within reception centers like GUSCO and World Vision was instruction on hygiene. Reception center workers guided and sometimes supervised returnees on how to maintain personal hygiene,[16] including how to bathe, how to use soap, and how to use latrine toilets. It was an unnecessary education, often insulting to rebels. "They thought we just walked in the *lum* [spent all our time in the wilderness]," Mohammed sighed. He and others resisted the idea that rebels were literally dirty and polluted, in need of cleaning and education on hygiene after living in the *lum*. "There was no need to teach people how to use [the toilet]. We had latrines in the *lum*, for each coy [company]. People didn't [defecate in] the *lum* anyhow except on operations."[17]

This fact did not prevent civilians from imagining rebels as dirtied subjects capable of defecating anywhere. Aliya bitterly recalled that whenever feces were found outside the shared toilet in her Gulu slum, residents would clamor that it must have been a "child from the *lum*" who had done it. On the contrary, according to many of my friends, the LRA kept hygienic practices better than civilians did. Mohammed felt civilians were lazy when it came to digging pit latrines. "At *gang*, people have the tools they need—a hoe, spade, digging tools, et cetera," he observed, "yet they might not have dug a pit latrine. But in the *lum*, with meager tools, the pit latrine was well dug." Indeed, while on the way to my friend Matayo's house one morning in a rural village, a large pile of human feces greeted me on the footpath. Matayo blamed it on a drunk who stopped to defecate on his way home the night before. Matayo himself had only recently begun digging his own pit latrine. His work was in part quickened by the impending visit of sub-county health inspectors who would, he said, fine him for not having one. He recalled that some people learned about high standards of cleanliness in the *lum* and kept those standards even after they left the front lines to stay in *gang*. He sheepishly admitted that others forgot these lessons, and their standards regressed.

LRA practices of hygiene and cleanliness were not limited to the use of pit latrines. Aliya remembered that different LRA battalions meeting in the *lum* did not embrace or shake each other's hands without some kind of cleansing—a practice not only spiritual but also hygienic, preventing the spread of infection in case someone had handled diseased blood in battle.[18] In settled camps, rebels swept compounds, kept pits for burning trash, and constructed drying racks made of elephant grass on which they kept washed utensils out of the polluting reach of domesticated animals. Commanders, fearing that they might be poisoned, sometimes demanded immaculate cleaning of utensils and saucepans (including their under-neaths, where residues of burnt coal built up). Some women were dele-gated to inspect the quality of the cleaning and mete out punishment if it did not meet a sufficient standard. Rebels were careful about food hygiene, refusing leftovers sometimes offered by Arabs for fear they had been left out overnight and spoiled. Bathing basins were not shared to avoid spread-ing communicable diseases like scabies and diarrhea.[19] People learned to dress smartly, washing their clothes well and even using iron sheets to press them. Some rebels, especially those living in Gulu slums, found huts in the *lum* clean and well smeared, kept in better conditions than those in town. Aliya was particularly nostalgic of the way in which menstruating women did not sleep in the same beds with their men in the LRA, com-pared to what she saw as dirty menstruation practices at *gang*:

> One day, I was going to buy bread from the market, and the seller was a menstruating woman. I was going to buy bread, but she got off her stool, and I saw marks of blood on the stool. She was menstruating. It disgusted me [*emphasizing her disgust by her tone of voice*], and I refused to buy the bread. We were taught to bathe before starting to do anything from the *lum*, but it seems she didn't bathe in the morning.

She lamented that people at *gang* did not meet the hygienic standards of those in the *lum*, condemning their dirtiness compared to the cleanliness of the rebels.

WHO'S HEALING WHOM?

> The final paradox of the search for purity is that it is an attempt to force experience into logical categories of non-contradiction. But experience is not amenable and those who make the attempt find themselves led into contradiction.
> Mary Douglas, 1966

Some rebels not only resisted the transformative treatment offered at the reception centers by denying the various diseases ascribed to them, but even identified their civilian "doctors" as the truly "sick" ones. "This is weakness of mind [*goro wic*] of the [staff] that are in the reception center," Mohammed remarked on the ways in which he and other rebels were taught how to use soap, how to use toilets, and how to be social with other people—as if these experiences were alien to their lives in the *lum*. "Sometimes, there is no need to say a domesticated pig is sharper than a wild one. A domesticated one can do a lot of bad too, more than a wild boar—like eating feces and destroying cassava," he philosophized, questioning the moral and pathological order dividing civilized civilians from wild rebels.

Aliya similarly rejected the idea that rebels needed treatment, ascribing to reception center workers a misrecognition based on a diseased understanding of *lum*. "People from here pretend they are free because they are not in the *lum*," she suggested. "But they are suffering at home. . . . I feel I was free in the *lum*, while here [at *gang*] your husband mistreats you and you don't eat well. There, you boarded vehicles to take you to hospital, and your work is just to breastfeed your kids. Life was better off there than at home today." For her, civilians were the ones truly suffering, not rebels like her. It was the space of *gang* that was diseased, not the *lum*. To her, the process of "reintegration" was one in which rebels were acclimatized to the suffering of *gang* following a meaningful life in the *lum*.

The transformative disciplining of rebel appearances and minds was an attempted form of healing made by and for the civilian unconscious. It reasserted the image of the rebel as absolute Otherness capable of conversion, an imagined change thought to provide a form of self-security and safety for the civilian who harbored anger and resentment at the rebels. Many civilians felt that the rebels received undue care and assistance, particularly during the time of the camps. There were jealous complaints that ex-LRA should not benefit from World Food Programme rations if they were already collecting supplies from reception centers. Aliya remembered that civilians sometimes lied, claiming that they had been in the *lum*, in order to receive benefits reserved specifically for ex-LRA. "We didn't care to stop them," she reflected, "because we felt they were also suffering at the same level of those people who were abducted." Other times, however, rebels were angered by being used for the benefit of others. RV remembered that Kony told them, "Many people will be satisfied in your

> *What is gratifying* . . . are the testimonies of transformation from the children of how while in the bush they were living in darkness, but that after receiving counseling and physical treatment, they are living in the light.
> Anukur (n.d.), emphasis added

name." Indeed, different groups, NGOs, and people—not all of them with pure intentions—solicited and extracted money through interventions, programs, and other schemes designed, at least nominally, for the care of former LRA rebels.[20]

This was not the only way in which civilians projected their sicknesses onto rebels, and their imagined cures through a discipline and control of them. My friends vividly and often angrily remembered conversations that they overheard among some staff that revealed other projections. They remembered how staff: celebrated the return of (for instance) a child who had robbed or looted them, feeling relief that they could now rest easy; claimed that a returned rebel and his family would no longer "gain wealth" from being in the *lum*, feeling more secure that others would suffer with them financially instead of getting rich; and sought to protect themselves and other civilians from the killers, robbers, beggars, and wild people they imagined former rebels were or might become. Benjamin was furious when a World Vision staff member once told him and his fellow ex-rebels that they had done "enough" and should now "enjoy" their wealth: "[The idea] that we got rich—none of us were paid, it wasn't true. It angered me a lot."

Through the ritual transformation of a dreadlocked, mad rebel wearing "dirty" looted clothes into a shaved, clean, and sane human being, civilians violently tried to destroy the Other as an attempt to give life and sanctity to their own fragile, threatened self-identity. Such a self-prescribed "cure" did little to help civilians transcend their binary logics. Indeed, the "reintegration" process merely reinforced existing binaries of *lum* and *gang*, madness and reason, animal and human, cementing rather than exceeding an opposition between inhumanity and humanity. Purifying the "dirt" of rebel experience by humanizing rebels, civilians thought they were the healers tidying up the logical categories of non-contradictory social life. But in doing so, they blinded themselves to the alternative form of healing offered by dirt in its capacity to reveal the disease inherent to the pure notion of humanity—namely, the delimiting of strict moral boundaries of what was considered legitimate forms of life. Falling outside these boundaries, the meaningful experiences that rebels brought back from the front lines threatened to disintegrate the binaries hardened into the concept of humanity.

The next two chapters examine rebel experiences of love, kinship, and politics that were burned or washed away in the "humanizing" process of reintegration.

5 Rebel Kinship beyond Humanity

LOVE AND BELONGING IN THE WAR

In the eyes of most of the humanitarian West—including the International Criminal Court (ICC)—many LRA practices constitute crimes against humanity.[1] Among the charges of crimes against humanity that the ICC has leveled at LRA commanders are forced conscription of soldiers, forced marriages within the rebel ranks, and unusual acts of killing. Characterized as inhuman, these acts are thought to constitute a seriously violent evil beyond the pale of humanity.

Although many of these acts were indeed violent, this did not imply that meaningful and valued relationships did not form through these so-called crimes. Simply understanding these crimes as "against humanity" fails to appreciate the breadth of rebel kinship that flourished in and through the violence of the war—forms of meaningful and often nonviolent social life that were lived beyond the moral limits prescribed by humanity. This chapter explores forms of social connection forged rather than dissolved through violence, shifting who related to each other and how in unexpected ways. It begins with the story of Amito, a woman forcibly abducted and married into the LRA who unpredictably developed close ties to her husband and his family, creating love out of violence. It then examines the forms of militant kinship that formed out of forced conscription, a kinship that sometimes coalesced into a sense that the LRA had become a clan of its own.

VIOLENT LOVE: THE PROBLEM OF INHERITING AMITO

> Who shall fight for love?
>
> A pregnant woman, cradling her distended tummy, asks her unborn baby, in a line from Acholi playwright Judith Adong's production *Silent Voices* (performed at the National Theatre, Kampala, in July 2012). The play reproduced a humanitarian narrative about civilians caught between the violence of the UPDF and the LRA. It ended with a song imploring the audience: *Don't let innocence die! Save love, save the future!*

Amito was forcibly abducted by the LRA from her village home in northern Acholiland in the late 1990s, near the border with what is now South Sudan. She was about eleven or twelve years old. She became a babysitter (*ting ting*) for Onen, an LRA officer who was keeping five wives, the most senior of whom was Gunya. At first, Amito looked after Gunya's children. Within a short time, she became Onen's sixth wife. She gave birth to Ojara, her first child with Onen, at the age of fourteen. She wanted to escape and did not want to stay with Onen, who took her as his wife by force.

When Amito first narrated this story to me, she was emotional and tearful. Her narrative followed the arc of the story often told about women in the LRA, according to which young girls were kidnapped and made sexual slaves of male rebels. By legal definition, she was abducted, defiled, and raped—entering a "forced marriage." As two human rights scholars of marriages between LRA men and women adamantly declare, "Forced marriage as it was practiced by the LRA is a crime against humanity" (Carlson and Mazurana 2008, 64).[2] Even scholarly accounts that attempt to disrupt this narrative by questioning the image of the passive female victim of war or by contextualizing abduction of women within Acholi marriage customs emphasize that such marriages were forced, referring to women in these arrangements as "wives," in ersatz quotes.[3]

These moral labels offer very little understanding of the complexity of Amito's experience as Onen's wife (a term that in her case cannot justifiably be qualified with ersatz quotes). As she continued her story, she began to remember her co-wives (*nyeggi*)—who they were, where they came from, and what their relationships were like with each other and with Onen. Amito's facial expressions and story line changed dramatically. She was Onen's most beloved wife. Everyone told her that Onen loved her the most. Her *nyeggi* became filled with jealousy (*nyeko*) of her, performing a language in which the word used to signify "jealousy" is also used to signify "co-wife." Amito worried that they were plotting to kill her while Onen was away, to throw her body into the *lum* and blame her death on the Lotuko people.[4] Amito told Onen about these plans, and he began to protect her from his other co-wives. He also called together his co-wives and asked them to explain what had happened, warning them that jealousy was illegal among LRA co-wives. Indeed, many of my friends reflected that jealousy was well regulated and that co-wives lived together more harmoniously as rebels in the LRA than as civilians. Fights between jealous co-wives in the *lum* were dangerous because they could bring injury or death to the husband in battle. Onen's own finger was injured because of a fight between Gunya and one of her co-wives.

Once, Amito recalled wistfully, she suffered a bad injury. Government troops had tossed bombs at the rebels, and one of them exploded near her, felling her on the battlefield and rendering her unable to move due to the severity of her wounds. The rebels ran away, and she was abandoned. But Onen had not forgotten her. He searched for her for three days before finding her and carrying her back to the LRA defense, where he put warm water on her wound. He struggled for a month to procure medicine for her and cared for her wounds until they healed. While others around her were killed or died, Amito had Onen, who took excellent care of her. After she delivered Ojara, she saw Onen's love for her grow. He sought to find a way to return Ojara to Amito's mother, Min Amito, to keep him safe.

On closer inspection, the relationship between Amito and Onen was hardly a "crime against humanity." He was, as the quote opening this section asks, precisely the one fighting for love. Yet his love for Amito was considered incompatible with humanity insomuch as it was forged in circumstances outside of either his or Amito's choosing.

After about six years with Onen, Amito left the LRA. She was separated in the course of a battle and captured by the UPDF before being sent to the World Vision reception center. Though she was happy with Onen, she found life in the *lum* hard and was secretly longing to leave the front lines. She did not know how to ask Onen to send her home, though, as he wanted her to stay with him there. While staying at the reception center, she was delighted to reunite with her mother. She was bitter and angry to learn, however, that while she was with the LRA, the rebels had killed her father, ambushing a vehicle he was traveling in and shooting him dead.

Members of Onen's family also came to see her in the reception center—an act of social recognition that might be unexpected for a "crime against humanity." Hearing that one of Onen's wives had returned, Mohammed, Onen's first cousin and a former LRA military policeman, showed up. So too did two of Onen's brothers. When Amito finished her required time at the center and prepared to leave, Mohammed helped her carry her things to her mother's place in town.

At first, she decided to spend some time with her mother. She was unsure of what the future held for her and Onen, but she planned to wait for him to return, too, without a desire to get another man. She noticed that many of her friends she had left behind when she went to the *lum* had died of HIV/AIDS, and she was grateful that she had been abducted so as to have escaped their fate. In time, people around her began to ask why she was waiting for this man who was still in the *lum*. They questioned how long she would wait for him to come back. Some advised her to continue to wait for him. Others, including staff at the World Vision reception center, advised her to forget him. In fact, they insisted that Onen had abducted her forcefully and told her that she should pray that he would die. Amito found this "rather stupid talk" (*lok ming ming*); her mother, Min Amito, called it "really bad" (*rac tutwal*). Instead, she prayed daily that he—the father of her son, the husband who took care of her, and someone whom she could not let go of—would come home safely. Onen was also abducted against his will, she retorted to the staff. She angrily asked them if praying for someone's death was consistent with the evangelical teachings of World Vision. Though others found her relationship with Onen morally unacceptable given the violence in which it was forged, Amito deeply valued it and longed for him.

Kinship in Question: The Conflict over Inheriting Amito

Soon enough, Amito decided she wanted to go visit Onen's family at their rural home in Palik.[5] So she, Min Amito, and Ojara journeyed from town to visit them. They were happy to see her and welcomed her and their son, Ojara, who increasingly bore a striking resemblance to his father. Amito wanted to stay with them there, and so did Onen's family. They respected her and told her that if Onen were to come back, they would be married. This would be her home, and there would be land for Ojara to dig on, they assured her. Though entitled to ask for illicit sex payment for keeping Ojara (*latin luk*), Min Amito and Amito had not yet done so, a claim respectfully reserved. This was hardly a typical relationship between the family of someone who was "raped" and "forcibly married" and the family of the "rapist."

Amito wanted to stay in Palik, but she wondered who would take care of her there as she waited for Onen. She did not have to wait long to find an answer. She soon perceived that Mohammed was indirectly courting her, starting by being very supportive of her and Ojara. Mohammed bought Ojara clothes, books, and shoes, and began paying for his school fees. Mohammed and Amito had only known each other as acquaintances in the *lum*. Onen had introduced Mohammed to Amito as his clan brother, the son of his father's brother. But Amito and Mohammed were in different battalions and did not get to know each other well until they both returned from the front lines. Mohammed, Amito recalls, started courting her from afar, like a cat trying to get food sitting on a table, sneaking steadily closer and closer. He was a bit shy and fearful, and not at all direct in his courtship, she remembered.

Once, he took Amito on a motorcycle taxi (*boda boda*) from town to Palik to harvest some crops. On that trip, Amito witnessed a growing conflict between Onen's family and Mohammed's family. She wanted to stay in Palik with Mohammed's family, but Onen's family was furious about this. Sensing that an intra-clan dispute was about to erupt with her at the center, Amito broke off her nascent relationship with Mohammed. At the heart of this conflict between the families was a contestation over kinship, wealth, and social death manifesting in a dispute over widow inheritance. By conventional kinship rules, Mohammed had little right to inherit Amito. It was only through the militant kinship that he had forged with Onen in the *lum* that he staked his claim against those of Onen's brothers.

Widow Inheritance in Acholiland

Widow inheritance (*lako dako*) was until recently a common feature of customary Acholi social life.[6] As my friend, the elder Ogweno Lakor, and others described it, *lako dako* occurred when a woman's husband died and the late husband's brother took over as the woman's new husband. The woman was allowed to choose which of the brothers she wanted to marry, with whom she would begin staying following a cleansing ceremony involving the ritual use of a chicken (*buku gweno*).[7] The chosen brother could not refuse to take care of her and her children. Often, the chosen brother was close to her family and helpful to them while her husband was still alive. A brother produced from the same mother was considered most eligible, though brothers from the same father but different mothers were also considered. More distantly related clan brothers could be chosen, Ogweno Lakor said, on the condition that there was precedence in the family for such a practice. If there was not, the clan brother would be treated as an outsider and obligated to marry the woman with cash, paid not to the widow's family, but to the deceased husband's family.[8]

By contrast, inheritance by brothers from the same mother or father paid nothing, assuming the wife had been formally married to her first husband. Inheritance by the closest male friend of the deceased was almost unheard of; such an inheritance would also require payment to the deceased husband's family, and would, Ogweno Lakor warned, cause great enmity between the friend and the deceased's brothers. Given how integral the wife and her children were considered to the family, to whom they customarily belonged after marriage and part of whose wealth they constituted, the brothers might even seek to kill the friend for inheriting their wife. By taking their wife, such a man would be mocking and insulting the clan, as though it had no remaining men to care for a wife.

Conflict also arose if the process of inheriting a wife took place while the first husband was still alive. According to some, including Ogweno Lakor, inheriting the wife of a man still alive but perhaps working abroad or living far away was a serious offense. The only way for a husband's brother to help

the wife in this situation, he insisted, was to keep the children, dig her garden, buy clothes for them, and the like—but by no means should the
brother have sexual intercourse with the wife, as it was presumed that the
husband would someday return. There were, however, situations in which
a husband was presumed or thought to have died when in fact he had not.[9]
In these cases—not uncommon during World War II and the LRA war—a
soldier or rebel returning home might find that his wife had been inherited
by his brother, with whom she may have produced more clan children. In
this case, elders returned the wife to the original husband after a cleansing
ceremony, and the brother was told to never go back to the inherited wife
ever again. If he did not heed this advice, conflict would arise between him
and his brother, the original husband.

Mohammed's Attempt to Inherit Amito

Mohammed's suspected attempt to inherit Amito was contested precisely
over many of these customs. Onen's immediate brothers, it seemed, wanted
to inherit Amito, and together with their mother Min Onen, were unhappy
that Mohammed—a more distant brother—was trying to court her. Min
Amito heard rumors that Min Onen had tried to curse Mohammed for
attempting to inherit Amito.

At first, Min Onen denied these rumors, saying that she would be happy
if Mohammed inherited Amito. She lamented that her own sons (Onen's
brothers) were not responsible enough to take care of Amito, nor were
they capable of dealing with the jealousy (*nyeko*) that their own wives
would have toward Amito if she were to become a co-wife to them. Min
Onen, together with her son Obwola (Onen's brother), suggested that
Mohammed was helping Amito and Ojara because of how caring Onen
was to him in the *lum*. Onen helped to facilitate Mohammed's return from
the front lines, after all, she recalled. But she later adamantly proclaimed
that her own sons should be the ones to inherit Amito. Only if all her sons
had died, she insisted, would the clan brother Mohammed be allowed to
inherit Amito. A prominent chief of Ker Kwaro Acholi[10] confirmed Min
Onen's assessment when this case was presented to him in anonymized
terms—the brothers, not the clan brother (Mohammed), should inherit
the wife.

On the surface, it appeared that customary kinship rules clearly excluded Mohammed from inheriting Amito ahead of Onen's brothers. But these rules were fundamentally challenged by new forms of rebel kinship and brotherhood developed in the *lum* with the LRA and under conditions of intense violence. Gunya, for whom—together with her and Onen's child—Mohammed also cared, agreed that Onen and Mohammed were not immediate brothers, but said that they were close friends who were like brothers. She argued that because they had stayed closely together in the *lum*, and because Mohammed had cared for Onen's wives there as though he were Onen's real brother, he himself was the *true* brother (*omin Onen ki kome*). She remembered that like a true brother, he welcomed Onen's new wives into their home in the *lum*, joking, talking, and playing with them as they adjusted to their new family. He helped develop Gunya and Onen's relationship, facilitating their courtship and earning her respect as a responsible brother to Onen. He took better care of Onen's children than Onen's biological brothers did, she reflected. She suggested that if Onen were to come out of the *lum*, he would be angered by the way in which his brothers had neglected his wives and children. Because of both the time he spent with Onen in the *lum* and the way in which he took responsibility for Onen's wives and children, Mohammed had effectively confronted existing rules of kinship and staked his claim as more than a mere clan brother to Onen—and therefore the first choice to inherit Amito, as illustrated in figure 12.

Mohammed also felt he had a special bond with and special directions from Onen, based on their time together in the LRA. Before Amito had become Onen's wife, Onen had suggested to Mohammed that he court Amito. Mohammed refused, saying he did not want to keep a wife in the *lum* because of the control the Movement asserted over married couples.[11] But he and Onen grew close fighting together in the *lum*. Their brotherhood remained strong and was melodically commemorated in the form of Mohammed's ringtone. Whenever his phone rang, it blasted out the sound of a sequence of rapid machine gunfire. He explained how he chose his ringtone:

> There was a time when [Onen and I] came for operations here [in Uganda], and when we reached a field which was well cleared, a gunship reached and found us there on the bare field. I was with Onen and he was shouting,

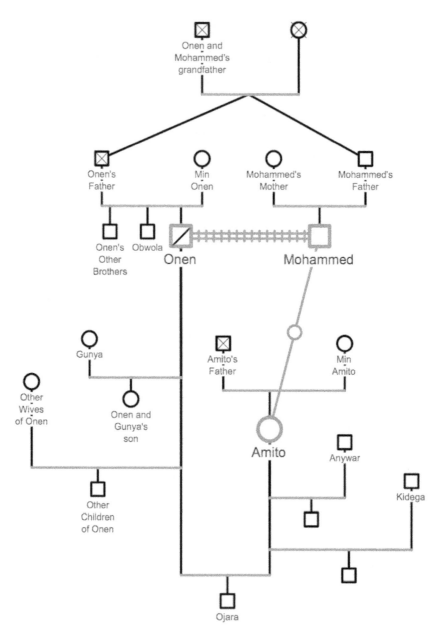

Figure 12. Family genealogy with a focus on relationships of Onen, Mohammed, and Amito. Note the transgressive relationships between Onen and Mohammed as "true" brothers (marked by railroad track) and between Mohammed and Amito as potential husband and wife (marked by circle on line). Figures marked with X are deceased. Onen is marked with a slash, representing the precarity of his social life a result of living in the *lum*.

"Today, this gunship is going to kill me and my brother. God help us." The gunship came and started firing at us. We all went down but Onen still got up and ran to check whether I was alive. So, when [the phone rings] I start thinking about how the gunship came and shot at us but we didn't die, and again remember how Onen and I used to make fun of this, because we would laugh at each other about how we panicked and the way he was shouting. So, [the ringtone is] for remembering what happened to us.

While he may have made a new claim of rebel brotherhood to Onen, Mohammed also posed a threat to Onen's existence with his suspected courtship of Amito. Min Amito stressed that Onen was still alive in the *lum*, and so any talk of inheritance was premature. Indeed, the family received updates every now and again about Onen's status, often from rebels recently returned from the front lines. Min Onen insisted that inheriting a wife whose husband was still alive would curse the husband to an untimely death, inflicted wherever he was. This is why, she suggested, some women were particularly keen to avoid having sex with other men while their husbands were away (for instance at war)—it was thought that such illicit sex (*lukiro*) would lead to the husband's death.

Mohammed's courting of Amito thus touched on the difficult subject of Onen's very life. There was an enduring uncertainty as to whether Onen would ever return alive from the *lum*, having spent more than two decades with the LRA. The question of who would inherit Amito had not only begun to push Onen into a zone of social death, but physically threatened his very life. Onen's family suggested that Mohammed, in surreptitiously aiding Amito so that he could inherit her when Onen died, was wishing death upon Onen.

As a relatively successful man making money in town, Mohammed also attracted the jealousy of his clan brothers with his pursuit of Amito. While some of Onen's brothers also worked in town, they had their own families to care for and were struggling for money. Mohammed was seen to be both unattached and relatively richer, in addition to being among the more responsible men in his clan. Mohammed was not the only one imagined to have wealth and status in this situation. Were Onen to come back from the *lum*, Gunya pointed out, he would become a moneyed big man, most likely converted to work for the government or UPDF in some capacity. (Of course, were the LRA to win the war, his status would be even higher.) Gunya suggested that were Onen to return to see how poorly his immediate brothers had treated his wives and children, he would angrily refuse them patronage.

Mohammed himself acknowledged that Onen's family began to suspect him of trying to inherit Amito. He continually denied these claims, insisting that he only helped Amito and Ojara because no one else was doing so. He also agreed that no one should inherit Amito as long as Onen was still alive. Indeed, he recalled that he and Onen lived well together in the *lum*, and he believed that Onen wanted him to continue to help Amito while Onen remained in the *lum*. He felt that Onen's immediate family was unable to help Amito, and that they erroneously thought that this meant that he should not help her either. But, having incurred their wrath, he began to pull back and became more reserved when it came to helping Amito and Onen's other wives.

Before Mohammed had returned from the front lines, Onen instructed him that his clan should take care of his children who had returned from the LRA, even if he died. Mohammed refused to renege on the responsibility he felt Onen had given him. After Mohammed returned from the LRA, and from time to time, he and Onen communicated on the phone. When Amito returned home, Onen called Mohammed and asked him to go see her. He wanted Mohammed to let his other wives know that he did not expect them to wait for him to return, that they should feel free to find other men if they liked. But he had different plans with Amito, whom he promised he would marry when he returned. Indeed, Mohammed recalled, when Onen occasionally called into the radio show *Dwog Cen Paco*, he always greeted Amito first, sometimes even asking the host Lacambel to go to Amito and Min Amito's home so that he could directly talk to them—but not Gunya nor any of his other wives.

Amito's Nostalgia for Onen Grows

When Amito came back from the *lum*, she often sought out Mohammed for life advice, including wisdom on what she should do about her husband. Mohammed told Amito that she was free to find another man if she wanted. But he told her that once she got another man, he would inform the new husband that this woman [Amito] with whom he would be staying was "our wife" (*dako-wa*), and that when her husband [Onen] returned, the husband might take her away.

Both Amito and Min Amito knew of Onen's plans to marry Amito. So when Amito got another man in town, Anywar, Min Amito was shocked and unhappy. She called Mohammed to let him know what was going on and to share her displeasure. Min Amito did not like Anywar: he did not respect her; he refused to take care of Ojara, who he made clear was not his child and therefore not his responsibility; and he was not earning money to support the family, leaving Amito to pay for food and rent by herself. As their relationship deteriorated, Amito's family grew worried about her and brought her back together with her second child to Min Amito's home, ending their relationship.

Min Amito wanted Amito to wait for Onen. But after a year or two, Amito found another husband, a *boda boda* rider named Kidega, with whom she was staying at the time I met her. Kidega was, as far as Min Amito could see, an equally poor husband to Amito. He too refused to have any of Amito's other children stay with him, and so Ojara and his half-brother remained at Min Amito's home. When Amito's family sent Kidega a letter assessing the fine that he owed for unsanctioned elopement (*luk*) with their daughter, and came to see him to claim it, he did not give them a single coin—not even to help pay for transportation from their rural village to town. Min Amito felt he was very disrespectful, wanting only Amito and not her kids or family. Unlike Onen's family, his family did not seem serious about caring for Amito as their own daughter.

Min Amito had become frustrated. She never wanted Amito to take another husband in the first place. Now, Amito had been through one difficult marriage and was unhappy in her second. Moreover, Amito was pregnant again, with her third child. Min Amito wanted her daughter to wait for Onen, and in the meantime to either come home and stay with her or go to Palik and stay with Onen's family. She would have been happy if Mohammed inherited her daughter, but understood the internal family conflict that prevented that from happening. Instead, she waited for Onen—a better, more mature man than either Anywar or Kidega, someone who would provide for her daughter and love her. She recounted a time when Onen saved Amito from drowning in a strong river current while in the *lum*, himself nearly drowning in the process. She reiterated her desire for Amito to return to Onen. Even though he took Amito as his wife without courting her, he was a responsible man, she reflected. She knew that people would stigmatize her, saying that her son-in-law was a rebel (Lakwena), but she did not care. She had already given Ojara to Mohammed for him to see his father's land, even though *luk* had not yet been paid—a sign of her tremendous respect for Onen.

Amito was torn over what to do. She wanted to accept Mohammed's courtship and stay with him, but could not. She also wanted to wait for Onen, but was becoming more and more impatient. How long should she wait, she wondered? She knew that she wanted to produce a total of four children, but with Onen still in the *lum* eight years after she had returned, she had grown anxious. She also found staying alone difficult, feeling as though she needed a husband to help care for her and her family. She wanted him to come back alive, and she still dearly loved him. If he returned, she would go to him, leaving behind her current husband, Kidega. Indeed, she prayed that Onen would come back so that she could be together again with him.

At the time of this writing, Onen was still in the *lum* with the LRA, more than a decade after Amito's return. Whether Onen would leave the *lum* remained as uncertain as ever. Min Amito longed for him to return from the front lines, inferring from her daughter that he was a good, respectful, and mature man who was and would be a much better husband than either of the two men Amito had found at *gang*. He cared for Amito and their son, Ojara, and loved them both very much. She was not sure what Anywar or Kidega would do if Onen were to come back, but she was sure that she wanted her daughter to reunite with Onen. Over time, however, she began to lose hope of his return. When I last spoke with her in 2017, she lamented to me that though Kidega remained a poor husband and son-in-law, they had to live in the present and not think too much about the past.

Forged in violence, their relationship endured, held together by strings of love and networks of kinship stewed in rebellion, and holding strong in the face of competing civilian loves and kinships. It was through violence that they had proved their love for each other; through the rebel brotherhood that Mohammed had staked his claim as Onen's true brother and thus challenged existing kinship rules about Amito's inheritance; and through violence that Amito and her mother grew nostalgic for Onen in his absence. If Amito and Onen's marriage was indeed a "crime against humanity," it was not a crime that they or their families cared to recognize.

MILITANT KINSHIPS: BROTHERHOOD AND SISTERHOOD IN THE LRA CLAN

> I feel as if I've left my clan *[kaka]* and am staying far away in
> a foreign land *[rok]*, not in my clan. . . . I still find life hard.
> If I were to decide again, I would choose to stay with my clan
> [the LRA].
>
> Makamoi, reflecting on the kinship he had within the LRA and had lost
> since leaving the rebels

Just as some like Amito longed for their "forced marriage" partners from the *lum*, others who had come back from the front lines spoke glowingly of the forms of mutual being they shared with fellow rebels with whom they had been forcibly conscripted. Musa, who had returned in the early 2010s, was particularly nostalgic about the sense of brotherhood and sisterhood that rebels cherished in the *lum*: "Since I've returned, there has been nothing good with people at home. . . . People don't help each other. If, for example, a fire destroys all the sorghum, even your real brothers won't help give you food to eat." By contrast, Musa and many others noted, people in the *lum* were united. "In the *lum*, people helped each other a lot, there was a lot of sharing—of food, sugar—it was all shared to the last bit, even if it was scarce," he recalled. "This doesn't happen at home—people only care for their own kids. . . . There's a lot of jealousy among people, people aren't united, and they work on their own."

Articulating a sense of mutuality that is not uncommon within military groups,[12] Musa spoke of his fellow rebels as his *real* brothers and sisters:

> The LRA are more than my family at home. . . . The relation was really strong, stronger than my real [biological] brothers. I might have helped some person in battle who was on the verge of death, protecting them from death—something that my real [clan] brother won't do. Even at home, if I was on the verge of death, he wouldn't do it, but [instead] run away and leave his own brother. But in the *lum*, people helped each other to the final

Figure 13. "My brother, change your mind. Let's unite" (*Omera lok tami. Waripe.*), inscription on the outside of Musa's hut, directed toward his biological clan brothers. He explained that in writing it, he wanted to "repair people's heads" (*roco wii dano*), reversing the discourse of the rehabilitation centers that attempted to "repair" the heads of rebels. Photo by author.

> moment. So today, so many [who knew me from the *lum*] come to see me, and want me to visit them in their homes. But you're not invited in the same way from your family who live elsewhere. So the bond in the family relations in the *lum* is stronger than it is here.

Musa's anger at his clan kin, and nostalgia for his LRA kin, was in part fueled by their denial of his claims to land. But such nostalgia was not romantically unmeasured. Musa had deserted the LRA after suspecting other rebels of concocting a plot to have him killed. His attachment to LRA kin was made all the more remarkable by the mistrust this plot stirred in him.

Musa claimed new kinship ties with his former LRA comrades, as though they were a clan of their own (as Makamoi alludes to in the epigraph of this section). But he insisted that he gained more than just concrete social relations while a rebel—he gained the capacity of sociality itself: "[With the LRA, I learned how to] stay with people. Socializing together with people of different areas—we stayed with people there from different areas and walks of life, as brothers. . . . I also learned to live together with [different] tribes, making me know how to socialize with people."

Like Musa, others maintained relations with fellow rebels who had returned from the front lines, even as physical distances often kept them apart. "The relationships [*wadi*] in the *lum* are stronger than the ones here [biological kinship]," Gunya declared. Within town, whenever Aliya met with or ran into another former rebel woman, she greeted her as a sister (*lamego*), a practice she explained as a result of the LRA spirit of togetherness (*cwiny me bedo karacel*). She recalled how people in the *lum* supported one another as though they were blood family, and that many of these networks of support were maintained after their return from the front lines. In her own family in the *lum*, when her husband was not around, his brothers would help their family with what they needed, providing them with cooking oil and other supplies. At *gang*, she lamented, a husband's brother refused to help. People had lost their sense of helping one another, she mourned, working only as individuals. She saw this as an effect of the war—people had become poor and kept what little they had within their families, unable to maintain larger patronage networks.

This unity among former LRA was partly an effect of rules and regulations that, many noted, controlled problems that were frequently troublesome at *gang*, including adultery and jealousy (*nyeko*) among co-wives. It was also a transformation of belonging that included a break from one's clan kin as part of the process of becoming rebels. While they were in the *lum*, Gunya explained, they "didn't know" their relatives at *gang*. "People at *gang* know that even if you are a relative to an *adwii*, you shouldn't get close to him," she said, meaning that rebels did not always hesitate to injure or kill their clan kin if they had to. Labwor spoke of his gun as his mother and his father, the weapon often eclipsing the ties to his clan kin. Otto similarly referred to his gun as his mother, his wife, his everything— because with it, he was able to provide for himself and others through its force, robbing food and supplies, among other bad behaviors (*bwami*).

As these new relations of rebel kinship were established among men and women who had been conscripted against their will, blood itself came to embody these ties and mark them off as different kinds of biological kinship. Gunya once complained to me that her son would often run into the *lum* near their home on the outskirts of Gulu town whenever he was criticized or disciplined. She joked that dealing with children who were born in the *lum* was very hard. She said that her son had bush blood (*remo me lum*) or rebel blood (*remo pa adwii*). At first, I thought she was speaking metaphorically, but she explained, "People in the *lum* have a different blood from people at home." She recalled that when their son was young, she took him to the hospital to have an operation on his left knee, from which, she claimed, they removed "bullet acid." She wondered if the bullet wounds that she and her son's father suffered in the *lum* had been transmitted to their child. "The blood of the parents is the one that makes the blood of the child. Both of his parents were *adwii*, and now he is too. He has *adwii* blood—that is why he runs to the *lum*," she concluded. Indeed, she suggested that he might one day become a fighter himself, as either a rebel or an army soldier. "The child takes to the idea of fighting as the parent did," she explained of the inheritance of a martial character. Not only had rebel kinship come to challenge clan kinship, establishing new patterns of mutual care, but it had slowly become one of its very forms. Importantly, this was not a kinship of brothers and sisters who had signed up to fight together with a shared vision and common goal. Rather, it was a kinship that emerged from a so-called crime against humanity—the forced and often random conscription of soldiers who, by and large, had no intention to fight.

REBEL KINSHIP BEYOND HUMANITY

In and through so-called crimes against humanity such as forced marriage, forced conscription, and inhumane acts against civilians, the LRA redrew relational boundaries to create what we could broadly categorize as rebel kinship. Rebels became husbands, wives, brothers, sisters, and children, caring for one another.[13] As a form of mutual belonging, rebel kinship challenged and often overtook conventional relations—as exemplified in Mohammed's becoming Onen's brother as the expense of his birth brothers.

These relationships suggest that violence is not exclusively something destructive that must be coped with or survived, but can also be creative, producing new forms of mutual belonging.[14] Like the violence of heroin addiction in the Española Valley in New Mexico described by Angela Garcia (2010), the violence of the LRA war destroyed certain relationships but also constituted others. When the causative violence is characterized by an international humanitarian audience as "against humanity," however, it becomes very difficult to understand the meaning within or produced out of the violence. This is not to say that the violence itself was moral; rather, it is to recognize that understanding the violence and its consequences through the moral framework of humanity limits an understanding of life itself. Exceeding certain confines of the good, these forms of rebel kinship thrive beyond humanity.

To be "against humanity" here means opening new moral spaces beyond the limits set by this concept. It means taking seriously the complex kinds of social relations and reformulations of kinship that emerge under practices often dismissed and labeled "against humanity" simply because they occur in forms of violence that Western humanitarians consider unacceptably immoral. It means, essentially, acknowledging forms of social life that are created beyond humanity.

6 Rebels and Charity Cases

POLITICS, ETHICS, AND THE CONCEPT OF HUMANITY

"I'm not a civilian! I'm a soldier!" Otto exclaimed, correcting a friend who had assumed that once he had left the front lines, he was no longer a rebel. Unlike many rebels who defected or otherwise returned willingly from the LRA, Otto had been captured by the UPDF and brought home from the war against his will after more than twenty years with the rebels. "I had no desire to leave and come home," he explained. "I grew up there and have spent more time there in the *lum* than I've been at home. My life was there in the *lum*. I didn't think of returning home, but only of when we were going to succeed. But I had no longings to come home." His plans with the rebels were disrupted one day in the early 2000s, when he was staying in an LRA camp in Sudan. Otto's friend Labwor had gone to some fields to harvest food, taking his wife Adong and Otto's wife Amony with him. Otto remained behind with his own kids and one of Labwor's. A UPDF unit surprised them, capturing Labwor, Adong, and Amony. Three days later, Otto was also captured, and they were all taken back to Uganda.

Otto never thought he would return this way. "I thought we would either succeed one day or else I'd die in the struggle," he reflected one afternoon inside his hut, where we sat eating lunch, regaining our energy after a tiring morning of hilling potatoes in his fields. Like many veterans,

he enjoyed reminiscing about victories in battle. He boasted of facing a
UPDF unit led by a feared commander, one who was known to relentlessly
chase after rebels. Camped in the *lum*, the rebels learned from an informer
that this commander had heard of their presence in the area and was coming with his soldiers to attack them. Otto helped set up an ambush on the
UPDF as they walked through an area of burned grass (*lyek*), killing, Otto
remembered, at least thirty soldiers. The LRA continued firing at their
backs as the remaining UPDF soldiers retreated. Under the cover of night,
the rebels removed supplies and weapons from the dead bodies of the
UPDF soldiers. The UPDF commander, Otto later learned, narrowly survived the ambush, and came away with a strong fear of Otto, who earned
a reputation as a fierce fighter.

"A true rebel has to be caught and can't just come back voluntarily," he
declared, insisting that those rebels who had defected were not fighters,
but mere porters who carried supplies, and that it was they alone who
claimed that Kony would be captured or would lose the war. At the time of
his capture, Otto had not been actively fighting. His role in the LRA had
been drastically altered after he lost one of his legs. In the late 1990s, he
was selected to go to a battle after having initially been picked only on
standby. He immediately feared he would get injured and had a premoni-
tion that he would be going to Khartoum. Demoralized, he walked slowly
on the front lines, staying slightly behind his fellow rebels as they
advanced. In the midst of the battle against a group of Dinkas, he ran up
and over an anthill, stepping down onto a landmine, which exploded and
blew off his leg. He screamed for help and was carried on the back of a
colleague as the LRA retreated to a base at Jebelen. There, he was taken to
a crowded hospital for treatment, before being transported first to Juba
and then to Khartoum, where he rehabilitated for seven months before
returning to Juba. In Juba, he reunited with the commander who had
placed him into that fateful battle, disobeying the *tipu*'s orders and thereby
putting Otto's life on the line. Otto was furious with him.

On his return to the LRA, he was decommissioned from fighting. He
dug in LRA gardens and prayed with the rest of the rebels, but did not fight
at the front lines. He felt awful about being forced to remain behind while
others went to battle. He knew that the LRA did not look well upon the
disabled, as they could not be sent to fight and took away able fighters to be

Figure 14. Otto's prosthetic leg; he asked me to take this picture and include it in this text with the following description: "War is what brought this. People are now using prosthetic legs. This is a peg leg on its own." Photo by author.

their assigned caretakers, guards for the sick bays where the disabled stayed. "You're spoiling their work [*itye ka balo tic-gi*]," he lamented of himself and other injured rebels. But he noted that, provided with food and clothing, they were taken much better care of in the *lum* than at home.

Otto found life harder than expected after he was returned to Acholiland. "Back then, I thought that what [the reception center staff] told us was true—that we would come home and stay freely without any problem. But it's not true. Things have not changed. We aren't staying freely." By the time I met him, he had settled in his rural home, where he spent his days tilling his fields by hand. He remained deeply dissatisfied with the conditions of life he faced. Complaining of rampant corruption across Uganda, he lamented that people only thought of themselves and was pessimistic about possible futures: "There is no way forward. We tried for more than twenty years but without success, and people who were supposed to join hands with us [civilians] didn't. What else can people do? Change the leader. Elections are good but the person in power has guns and refuses to leave power—so there is nothing to do." He had become resigned to his condition. "If it's there, it's there, if it's not, it's not [*Ka tye, ci tye. Ka pe, ci pe*]," he rued, rehearsing part of the lyrics of a well-known song by Oweka John on the hopelessness of living in camps during the war. There was of course the possibility of returning to the *lum*, as some other fighters had done. I queried Otto if he too had ever thought about returning to the LRA. "No, because I'm disabled," he answered in disappointment. "I thought of it, but I can't—because I'm disabled. Otherwise I would find a way of going, but there's no way. I'm staying like a woman now."

Reduced to a subordinate standing in life, he felt somewhat nihilistic about the possibility of social change. But he remained adamant that the LRA struggle to overthrow the NRM government, even if unlikely, was the most desirable of all options, and indeed the only way out. He wanted others to join the LRA war, if they could. Museveni should be overthrown, but he was stronghearted like former Libyan ruler Muammar Gaddafi—pictures of whom often adorned wall calendars sold in and around Gulu town—and was most likely to die like him, clinging onto power.

Otto maintained a strong belief in Kony and his *tipu*. He dismissed those who claimed that the *tipu* had stopped working or left Kony: "The tipu is *there*. It knows of plans being made against the LRA. It's a lie that it isn't there." Just as the *tipu* had not left Kony, Otto's convictions about the LRA did not desert him after he was captured. "My being at home doesn't mean I don't believe in the LRA. I believe. I grew up there and lived most of my life there. It's part of me. How can I not believe? I believe. . . . I know God is still with Kony." He explained the prophecy that he heard from the *tipu*: "The *tipu* said this when we were there: that there will be a time when you'll leave and go home, but you'll still believe in me. Just surrender everything to the heart of God. God knows the outcome of the war. And different people will come to ask you—tell them everything—the truth. No lies, no secrets. This is what is happening. It's all true. I've left it in the hands of God." He held onto hope because Kony was still there in the *lum*: "Anything can happen—he can still overthrow the government." Indeed, he envisioned that the LRA would still be in the *lum* another twenty-two years into the future.

Otto was deeply antagonistic toward Museveni and the NRM government. He angrily remembered the violence committed by the NRA shortly after its coup in and around his village home. A group of the NRA under the command of Kakooza Mutale, he remembered, had defecated in the mouths of dead cattle, and in villagers' stocks of maize and millet flour. "They sodomized our fathers in front of us, and slept with [raped] our mothers in front of us," he howled. These acts fueled his desire to fight back. "I wouldn't have come back if I weren't captured in battle," he lamented.

Once, while he was fishing through his wallet to find information on his SIM card, which he wanted my help to reactivate, I caught a glimpse of an ID card. He had taken a picture wearing a yellow shirt—a color strongly associated with the NRM. In rural areas of Acholiland, practically the only yellow shirts people had were those freely given out by NRM officials during election time, many of them bearing a glowing picture of the president with the slogan "Museveni Forever" (*M7 Pakalast*). I joked that I did not know he had voted for Museveni. "It's not Museveni's shirt, it just resembles it. I would *never* wear Museveni's shirt," he insisted. Otto's own voting practices sat somewhere between boycott and opposition. He claimed to now refuse to vote, insisting that years of voting would not change anything. In the 2011 elections he voted for Kizza Besigye, Museveni's former personal physician and onetime NRM colleague, who led the Forum for Democratic Change (FDC), the leading opposition party. Otto supported the idea of creating a Nile State, a self-governed autonomous country separate from southern Uganda. A Nile State, he felt, would prevent Museveni from using the region for his own interests—including accumulating land and extracting oil—and would keep money and development in the north.

Otto was clear about the kinds of political changes that the LRA would bring about if they overthrew the government. Wealth would be redistributed to help the poor. The fruits of development—including better-quality health care and education—would be brought to rural villages, and a minimum wage established for hired laborers. All the tribes of Uganda would be united under a harmonious state. Sexual immorality, including the wearing of miniskirts and the proliferation of prostitution, would be curtailed. Museveni's alleged plan to unite Uganda and Rwanda into "Rwaganda," a state under which the Acholi would become subservient cattle keepers for Museveni's people, would also be stopped.

Given his identity with the rebels, it came as a great surprise for me to learn that Otto had worked for Invisible Children, the San Diego–based NGO that lobbies for American military intervention against the LRA, and that (in)famously produced the "Kony 2012" viral video, which at the time of this writing has been viewed more than 101 million times on YouTube.[1] At first, he had joined them seeking to continue primary school education, but he ended up making bracelets for them for a few years in Gulu town. He loved his work. It paid very well, around two hundred thousand shillings a month. Though he did have his disagreements with the staff, sometimes upsetting them with his "straight talk" that corrected lies about the LRA or resisted epithets used against rebels, he got along well with them and held nothing against them. "They helped me a lot," he gratefully explained. He spoke nostalgically of the organization. He did not look on them badly, and he was greatly disappointed when his contract with them ended, forcing him to return to the daily drudgery of digging with a hoe on his rural village field, cultivating pigeon peas and sorghum. If Invisible Children were to call him up, he would immediately return to work with the organization. He was also willing, he noted, to join the UPDF's center at Mubende for soldiers with casualties. "I wouldn't be going to battle, but money would flow," he imagined.

Otto was one of many of my friends who had spent years in the LRA and continued to hold strongly antigovernment views, but had nonetheless joined on their return home various organizations or groups that explicitly positioned themselves against the LRA. Among these groups were the UPDF, which sent ex-rebels to the front lines to fight the forces of which they had once been part, and humanitarian NGOs like Invisible Children that treated them as apolitical children,[2] victims of abduction and forced violence who were robbed of their "humanity" and were in need of rehabilitation, love, and care. How could an ex-rebel like Otto, captured in war and forcibly returned home, join an NGO like Invisible Children? How did former rebels supportive of a war to overthrow the Ugandan government simultaneously adopt ethical subjectivities that appeared to eschew politics in ways seemingly inconsistent with LRA interests?

This chapter examines the apparent paradox of how former LRA lived as both rebels and charity cases. In the framework of a global post-Marxist turn from politics to ethics, from rebellion to humanitarianism as a means toward social change, how can we understand the transformation of militant former rebels into victimized charity cases? How can their narratives and experiences speak to anthropological concerns regarding the ways in which ethical regimes of humanitarianism are thought to deny the political, and with it, humanity itself?[3]

POLITICS, ETHICS, AND REBELLION TODAY:
THE PARADOX OF THE HUMANITARIANIZED REBEL

In the aftermath of 1968, we have witnessed a politics left behind for an ethics, a swinging of a dialectic between the political and the ethical toward the latter.[4] Encompassed in this broader change is the putative birth of the hegemonic form of humanitarian action we see today—one in which "victims" of "conflict" are "cared for" in the moral name of human rights or trauma, rather than struggled alongside with in the political name of revolution. Broadly replacing a politics of justice with an ethics of compassion, this turn privileged the "truth" of "humanity" over the ideological commitments to Marxist revolutions, a turn best exemplified by Bernard Kouchner and others who founded Doctors Without Borders (MSF)—former Marxists turned humanitarians, former modernists turned postmodernists (see Rieff 2002, 105).

In this turn, the political content of actors as rebels or militants was thought to have been evacuated and replaced by moral content, re-creating these actors as suffering victims. Violent Palestinian martyrs, for example, were re-subjectified as vulnerable sufferers.[5] This is often seen as a turn to the right, to the kind of conservative or bourgeois socialism described by Marx and Engels (1848) in which a politics of justice is replaced by a politics of life. This turn is perhaps best exemplified by Kouchner's gradual transition from Marxist to government minister.

Scholars following these trends often take up the critique of "humanity" put forward by political theorist Carl Schmitt. For Schmitt ([1932] 1996), to be human is to be political—namely, to maintain a distinction between friends and enemies. Within this logic, if LRA rebels are recast as victims (as they often are by humanitarian regimes, as we will see below), they risk removal from the realm of the political, and thereby from humanity itself. In other words, to invoke humanity—a concept that abolishes the friend-enemy distinction—is to dehumanize. By extension, the "humanitarianized rebel" appears at first glance as a contradiction. "Humanitarianization" implies the depoliticization of a subject; on the other hand, the "rebel" is a subject defined precisely by its politicization. A "humanitarianized rebel" thus implies a subject both politicized and depoliticized, both political and moral, combining logics and identities often directly at odds when traced through a history of the rise of Western humanitarianism and human rights.

How, then, can we begin to make sense of the way in which former LRA rebels saw themselves as both depoliticized victims and politicized agents—in other words, as both charity cases and rebels? How did humanitarianized rebels make sense of this apparent contradiction? How was someone like Otto able to work for Invisible Children while maintaining his belief in and support for the LRA? This chapter offers a glimpse into how rebels speak and act in the trenches of discourses of victimhood and militancy, identifying as both helpless victims and politicized militants. In doing so, it challenges the idea that "victimhood" denies actors their political agency and thereby strips them of their humanity.

A rigid Marxist analysis of northern Ugandan class, land, and labor might dismiss humanitarianized rebels as ideologically naive, insufficiently politicized or conscientized to refuse to work with anti-rebel groups such as Invisible Children. This might, in turn, easily be rationalized within the conditions of land ownership in northern Uganda, largely communal and without significantly high barriers to access.[6] In other words, the conditions were not ripe for rebellion; peasants had too much at stake to risk it all in a war.

This is not an incorrect analysis, as Otto reflects below. But it is an incomplete analysis, because it relies on a universal notion of politics and ethics that does not hold for the LRA. That is to say: rather than being ideologically disoriented and insufficiently politicized, the rebels were in fact quite attuned to the workings of postcolonial politics. Rather than being disempowered by a turn to ethics, they were invigorated by both the material gains and spiritual promises of this ethics. Wandering in the wilderness, the LRA operated according to different forms of politics and ethics than Schmitt imagined, transcending a specific notion of humanity.

WATCHING *CHE* IN RURAL ACHOLILAND

"Most of these soldiers aren't very sharp," Otto critiqued, as he watched a group of inexperienced Cuban recruits assembling for training under the command of Che Guevara. We were viewing Steven Soderbergh's 2008 biopic *Che* on my laptop, which sat balanced on a winnowing basket atop a pile of recently harvested sorghum inside Otto's hut. Musa had joined us to see the first part, which chronicled the victory of the 26th of July Movement over the Fulgencio Batista regime in the Cuban Revolution, during which Fidel Castro took power as prime minister. Otto had not seen Musa in years, since the time when they were both together in the *lum*. "You've grown up!" he exclaimed, remembering Musa as a young boy in the LRA and marveling at how he had become a tall and strong man.

I had introduced the film as the story of the overthrow of a dictator in a country where there had been severe poverty. Otto and Musa watched keenly, often making comparisons between the Cuban rebels' tactics and styles of fighting and their own. They derided the way in which the rebels fired their B10 rifles and the close distance they kept while marching, a strategy that would make a landmine explosion more deadly. They did, however, admire their use of ropes to ford rivers, which they recalled having done themselves. The Nile was an exception, they remembered, a river they had to cross using small boats. Beyond these military-scientific observations, they drew several parallels between the Cuban and the LRA rebellions.[7] Watching the opening historical footage of Batista's police beating protesting citizens, Otto recalled the way in which Besigye had suffered at the hands of police on the streets of Kampala during various protests. He likened Museveni's government to Batista's, noting that Museveni's government was also very oppressive.

Otto marveled at the growing ranks of the Cuban rebel group, and in particular the support and strength they garnered from civilians. If civilians had supported the LRA like that, the LRA would have won the war already, he mused. The Cuban revolutionaries must have been educated, he ventured, and Castro must have had a lot of knowledge, with a serious education. He wondered if it was difficult for Kony to convince Acholi civilians to join the LRA because he did not communicate his plans very well to people, whereas the Cuban rebels did. Kony did not study much, Otto bemoaned, and perhaps that was why he did not know how to communicate his message very well to people.

He likened Che's morale-boosting speeches and tactical instructions to Kony's. Kony also warned his soldiers not to beat civilians or loot their properties, he recalled. Some of Kony's commanders did not heed his instructions, however. Watching as some of Che's recruits defected and began to masquerade as rebels, asking for food and eventually raping a young peasant girl, Otto remembered that similar things happened within the LRA ranks. Some rebels who found conditions in the *lum* too hard defected and formed gangs known as *boo kec*, parading as LRA rebels while looting beer, money, and meat for themselves.[8] Some of these gangs were arrested, taken back to the LRA, and their leaders killed. Otto approved the order of death by firing squad for the Cuban miscreants: "They deserve to die because they spoiled the name of the movement."

Otto was struck by the way in which Cubans were suffering, forced to rent their own land and taking only a small portion of their own harvests: "This was a real rebellion." He ventured that if the same conditions had been present in Acholiland, many people would have joined the LRA voluntarily. But the conditions were not as bad as those in Cuba, he decided. Musa agreed, noting that the Ugandan government worked hard to get civilians on their side, and was wise in convincing people to back them instead of the LRA. He lamented that Museveni was now controlling the Ugandan economy to feed his own interests—including helping rich people from the south come to buy land in the north. "We will become squatters without land," Musa predicted sadly, at a time when the Madhvani

Company was in talks with the government to establish a sugarcane plantation on forty thousand hectares of "idle" land in Amuru, in West Acholi (Owich 2014).

Otto was surprised to see religion absent from the Cuban struggle. "The LRA prayed before every operation, getting the go-ahead from the spirit to fight," he noted by contrast. Both he and Musa spent time working in yards, LRA holy shrines, as a technician and a controller respectively. Otto, knowing that Musa had come back from the *lum* relatively recently, was curious about the latest news regarding the *tipu maleng*. Musa noted that it did not come to talk in front of people anymore, but came to Kony via dreams. It was still powerful, though, Musa decided, noting that Kony still anointed people by dipping them into water, and that the *tipu* had helped a barren woman conceive and give birth.

While the Cuban Revolution followed a familiar narrative and definition of the political, the LRA struggle was quite different. Redefining the political was, as we will see, what made it possible for former rebels to live as both rebels and charity cases.

WANDERING IN THE WILDERNESS, OR PATHS OF POSTCOLONIAL POLITICS

The Search for Liberation

In this section, I pose the story of Joseph Kony as the biblical Moses wandering in the wilderness as an instantiation of the search for liberation in or beyond postcolonial politics. Many of my friends saw Kony as akin to Moses, a comparison that they heard in the *lum*, articulated especially by the late chief LRA catechist Abonga Papa.[9] In this narrative, the LRA struggle was similar to that of Moses. The LRA had taken up the lives of the Israelites, who traveled from Egypt to the promised land in the bush under the guidance of their prophet Moses. Kony was the LRA's prophet and miracle maker, who, like Moses, had wandered into the wilderness to lead his people to the promised land. The yards that the LRA constructed in the *lum* were likened to the burning bush (Exodus 3), a holy place not to be entered wearing sandals nor any other kind of shoes. That the next rather than the current generation of LRA rebels were said to be the ones to retake Uganda aligned with Moses's conviction that only the next generation would take over the land of Canaan.

Considering Kony as a Moses-like prophet, we might understand him and the LRA to be in the midst of (at the time of this writing) their years of wandering in the wilderness. The curse of wandering manifests as the problem of the postcolonial situation, a malaise sometimes referred to as Afro-pessimism but which Achille Mbembe more aptly calls "radical uncertainty" (2002, 636). After the broken promises of pan-Africanism and independence, and in the midst of the growing emptiness of Museveni's socialist rhetoric (which contradicts his neoliberal practices), a modernist drive toward an envisioned future has descended into nihilism about the very possibility of a future. As Otto put it with a shrug, "There is no way forward."

To the extent that politics had become a postcolonial wandering, the LRA had become political actors par excellence. Indeed, following Karen Fields (1985), we might see LRA millenarianism not as distinct from or symbolic of political movement, but as politics proper. That is to say, much as they were derided for having no political agenda or not clearly articulating their "goals,"[10] they were acutely attuned to the realities of postcolonial politics. Rather than attempting to salvage a traditional politics in their rebellion,[11] or condemning the apparent lack of a traditional politics,[12] I argue that they embodied politics as a dynamic category, adapted to its limits and forms in the present historical conjuncture. When the postcolonial future remained uncertain, ideologies could not be fully or conventionally articulated (except as uncertainty), and therefore ideological stances like "sacrifice" remained alien to most rebels.

Drawing on Faisal Devji (2008), I suggest that like "terrorists," the LRA are at the forefront of crafting a politics in a global society with no proper institutions yet to its name. In this conjuncture—at once postmodern and postcolonial—a new actor of history is sought to replace the proletariat, and is often found by terrorists and humanitarians in the figure of "humanity." For the LRA, these actors are the chosen ones—the four or five "slaves of God" who will one day in the future return to Uganda to overthrow the government. But now is a time of wandering. The categories of "politics" and "ethics" themselves are in flux. In this moment, it is difficult to concretely identify an "ideology" or a "practice" of a particular form of politics. Where the future remains unknown, the actions of the present cannot be ideologically certain or informed, except as an ideology of uncertainty—an ideology for which a belief in the guidance of divine spirits is apt.

Politics as Deception, or Why the LRA Avoid Politics

> The armed conflict in northern Uganda has been overlooked and misunderstood for the past 18 years. It is a tragic struggle for power involving children, who are used as pawns for military and political purposes. They are abused; they are manipulated; and by most, they are pitied, then ignored. In spite of good intentions and laws against child abuse, these children have no protection for their security and basic rights.
> World Vision, *Pawns of Politics: Children, Conflict and Peace in Northern Uganda*, 2004

"It's not true, what's being read," Labwor told me, as I narrated the above passage to him, wondering what he thought of how most standard NGO reports characterized LRA rebels as pitiable and politically naive child soldiers. "When I'm abducted and taken to the *lum*, I don't see any politics needed to make me fight there. I already wanted to become a soldier before I went [to the *lum*], because I saw bad things happening at home."

It was not the reaction I had expected. Knowing Labwor's strongly antigovernment views, I had assumed he would have refused the idea that he was simply a manipulated child pawn, identifying instead as a political subject. But he rejected "politics" outright, treating it with disdain, while simultaneously identifying a just cause to fight. Like many of my friends, Labwor recognized "politics" as synonymous with "deception" or "tricks," sometimes referred to as "working on people's heads" (*tic ki wii dano*).[13] My friends used "politics" (untranslated from the English in Acholi) to specify the way that the government treated LRA soldiers during peace talks—trying to trick the rebels, without a genuine desire to reach an agreement. "[The LRA] don't use politics," one friend told me, explaining that they spoke the truth, without lying or fooling people.[14] In this sense, Kony—informed of future events by prophetic *tipu*—was immune to politics, incapable of being tricked. By contrast, Gunya felt that in the *lum* she had learned "politics"—a form of trick playing that made her more skillful and smarter at home, allowing her to do things like giving her amnesty certificate to her sister to use to enroll in tailoring school.

Here, "politics" and the "political" did not quite refer to an art of government or opinion about how society could be changed for the better. This is not, of course, to say that rebels lacked "politics" in the latter sense,[15] even as some rebels claimed that the LRA "don't use politics." Indeed, my friends commonly articulated "political" demands such as the need for better health care or schools. However, we cannot simply dismiss the rebels' use of the "political" as a peripheral distortion of or departure from an essential meaning. Rather, in their use, they were redefining "politics" itself in conversation with how they had experienced it in their own lives. In many ways, the art of government in Uganda was indeed full of tricks—promises not kept, money embezzled, carefully worded lies.[16]

If the LRA had left behind "politics" for "ethics," it was not because they had abandoned rebellion for humanitarianism and development as a methodology for social change, as Western liberals had. Rather, it was because they operated under a different understanding of "politics," one that had in their experience forestalled rather than promoted social change. They also operated according to a different understanding of "ethics." In this context, it was the transcendence of the divine that offered the possibility of a different future. But since such a future was inherently unknowable, the rebels were left to wander in the wilderness, patiently or impatiently awaiting the deliverance of this future.

Ethics as Divine, or Reframing Human Ideologies amidst God's Plans

It may have seemed contradictory for someone as committed to the LRA as Otto to join Invisible Children or another organization opposed to the LRA, such as the UPDF. Indeed, such apparently divided loyalties were precisely what Museveni referred to in his critique of postcolonial bottlenecks to development across Africa—namely, an "ideological disorientation" that involved the discordance of a subject's speech and/or action from (NRM) party beliefs or systems. As Museveni put it, "In Africa, you find a lot of ideological bankruptcy by groups that push the line of sectarianism by tribe and religion. These groups fail to accurately define the interest of the People and push pseudo interests instead" (2014). Following a roughly socialist rhetoric, Museveni implied that such practices were incoherent and politically uninformed, forms of false consciousness preventing forward progress in an imagined teleology of development.

In Acholi, this form of practice often elicited the cautionary proverb, "Two roads confused the hyena" (*Yoo aryo oroco lalur*). It could be heard in churches, warning their congregations not to practice both satanic *tic Acoli* and holy Christianity. It was also used by Kony, who chastised his commanders for giving their soldiers orders that contradicted his own, and who supposedly killed LRA officers like Otti Lagony for double-dealing, working for both the LRA and the UPDF.

But such cautions did not stop Otto and others from joining Invisible Children or the UPDF. "I worked with Invisible just to get money to help me," Otto explained. "But this doesn't mean I have changed my inner feelings." This was not an incidental or unusual practice. In past parliamentary elections pitting NRM candidate Betty Bigombe against the Democratic Party's Norbert Mao, the NRM distributed free supplies and goods to people in Gulu in an attempt to win votes for Bigombe. A popular slogan grew in response to this campaign that encouraged voters to take what the NRM gave them without giving them their vote: "Eat Bigombe, vote for Mao!" (*Cam Atuku, bol ki Mao!*).[17] Others working for the NRM, brought from rural areas to campaign for Museveni in town, would humorously chant, "It seems like there are no votes for this cattle raider!" (*Kwir pa lakwo dyangi nen calo peke, ba!*).[18] These NRM "supporters" were more interested in free rides to town than in actively campaigning for the party. A friend claimed that even if Bigombe were to bring a health clinic, a borehole, a school, and other facilities to her rural village, she would still vote for Mao, because he spoke the truth and was not working with Museveni as Bigombe was.

This was not simply pragmatic double-dealing. Not just happy to join an NGO, Otto even reflected positively on the possibility of Kony's death. I was shocked to hear him say that he would be happy if Kony were to be killed, and asked him to explain how he could wish such a thing on someone he saw as God's messenger. He responded: "Jesus was a servant of God brought to Earth to save people, and he was killed by his own people. When he was killed, it was to save people [*laro dano*]. Maybe if Kony were also killed, God has seen his work has ended there, and someone else needs to take over. Kony said it [himself]—if he dies, someone else will take over his work." Part of what seemed like a contradiction between ideology and practice could be explained by the primacy of divine intervention. "Nothing can spoil the fight of the LRA," Labwor reminded me. "For us as flesh [*del*], we can do and decide what we want, but the *tipu* might reject it and give another idea." In other words, "disoriented" rebels joining NGOs or the UPDF to make money for themselves had no effect on the outcome of the LRA war, which was governed by and in the realm of the divine. "There is no harm that they can cause," Labwor said dismissively of Invisible Children and the UPDF. "Their plans can't ever be successful. They won't succeed."

The outcome of the LRA struggle may not have been affected by the work of NGOs or armies. But that did not mean that one's individual relationship to the struggle and the divine was not affected by one's relationship with these NGOs or armies. Whether or not joining these LRA enemies brought a kind of divine punishment on such LRA "defectors" was contested. Labwor, who refused to join the UPDF ("not even for one million shillings a month," he claimed), insisted that those who did were throwing away the rules of the *tipu*, becoming Museveni's puppets (*Rwot, ineka ki nyero*, literally "Chief, you're killing me with laughter!," referring to the sycophantic response a puppet might have to a chief's bad joke). Their hearts changed, filled with a lust for money, and the *tipu* left them unprotected. "They don't sacrifice themselves," Labwor critiqued, citing the case of Onen Kamdulu, a former LRA commander who surrendered, joined the UPDF, and was later convicted of armed robbery and sent to a maximum-security prison at Luzira. "They easily change when something painful comes to them—they can't sacrifice. They're now the enemies [*lumone*] of the LRA. If I find them in battle, I will kill them. I don't leave him just because he was once with us [former LRA]," Labwor said, as though he were still an actively fighting rebel.

Gunya saw things a bit differently. Gunya had in fact joined the UPDF, becoming a reservist after returning home. She occasionally marched in military parades. Since the father of one of her children, Onen, was still in the *lum* with the LRA, she had in theory become Onen's enemy, I pointed out. She laughed. Ever mischievous, she in fact felt good about taking a UPDF salary. "I get money and live on it, because they have to pay me for working. I'm using their money but I have a different heart," she explained. "When things turn around, they will say, 'Oh shit, why did we pay her?!'" Like Labwor and others, she found NGO and military efforts to destroy the LRA, including the $5 million bounty for Kony offered by US President Barack Obama, fruitless. "I think no matter how much they plan against Kony, this thing [destroying the LRA] won't happen. I've never seen anyone as wise as Kony in Uganda. If he wasn't [wise], he couldn't have survived in the *lum* for so long . . . because if something is planned against Kony . . . it won't happen, the *tipu maleng* will give directions on how to avoid it." But against Labwor's views, Gunya claimed to be able to separate her heart (for the LRA) from her work (against the LRA): "However much you work with these organizations, your heart won't change because in the bush, you did anointing and other things that have an impact on you for your mind not to change. For me, why do you think I believe in them after this long? . . . I believe strongly because we have been anointed." She had become a believer, and her belief could not be reversed.

As long as they were wandering, waiting for the *tipu*, rebels ultimately found NGO and UPDF salaries personally defiling at worst, and helpful to their own livelihoods at best. In the end, though, neither NGOs nor the UPDF could begin to touch the sanctity of a divine plan. Taking UPDF or NGO money was not, therefore, necessarily harmful to the LRA struggle; they were, more often than not, simply irrelevant, insignificant actions and plans of people that stood little chance of disrupting the as-yet-unknown divine plans of a *tipu*. This was a form of ethics distinct from both liberal bourgeois ethics (which judge present actions through the lens of past precedent) and Marxist revolutionary ethics (which judge present actions through the lens of future outcomes) (Merleau-Ponty 2000). A divine ethics largely ceded the power of judgment to God, changing not sociopolitical realities (controlled by the divine), but at most, only one's own subjective relation to the divine. Moreover, it was an ethics rooted not in the abstraction of humanity (as in humanitarianism, one form of a post-political, postmodern ethics), but rather in the suprahuman divine.

EMBRACING VICTIMHOOD, BECOMING
HUMANITARIANIZED: FROM THE LRA TO THE NGO

"They have politics in them," Otto warned me, of some of the former rebels
I spoke with who were employed by a Christian NGO I will call Eternal
Salvation. Many ex-LRA devised creative and sometimes deceptive ways
of turning the symbolic capital they held as former rebels into profit
within humanitarian economies.[19] Within these humanitarian economies,
former LRA rebels were not portrayed as politicized, willing soldiers.
Rather, they were subjectified as victims whose innocence was taken from
them as they were horrifically abducted into a murderous and mad cult.
NGOs like Eternal Salvation were there to "reform" them. As Eternal
Salvation's coordinating manager told me, "We are transforming them as
they came out of the bush. We work with them to be whole on the inside
again. . . . They were robbed of their childhood, of school, of their parents,
and now they are beginning to live again." Later, showing off the grounds
of the NGO to white visitors, she proclaimed, "We believe they have been
empowered and their dignity restored."

In humanitarian economies in northern Uganda, these "victims" might
have expected to have their children taken to school, sponsored by a white
person or an NGO; they might have attended community meetings called
by NGOs, taking home "allowances" of five to ten thousand shillings per
meeting; some, like one of Otto's former wives, were even helped to emi-
grate out of Uganda, or else taken on trips to places like London to lobby
before governmental and nongovernmental funding agencies for more aid.

The first time I met Labwor, he tried to convince me that his then-wife,
Alimocan, had also been in the LRA. I talked to her about her "time in the
lum," listening to stories of her suffering unsheltered from rain and surviv-
ing by eating wild *boo* leaves. Something did not add up. Her stories
seemed too caricatured to be true, and I grew suspicious of what she might
be hiding and why. Once, Labwor's brother Opwonya sat down with me
while Labwor was still working in his garden and divulged that Alimocan
had never been in the *lum*. Labwor was captured together with Adong
(whom I would later meet), not Alimocan. Alimocan was a civilian woman
who had been selling bananas around the Gulu bus park when Labwor
courted her. She was Labwor's third wife after Adong, who had left him

after suffering incessant abuse from Labwor's mother, Amayo. Labwor told Opwonya that when we first met, he thought there might be some "help" involved in my project. Labwor convinced Alimocan to pretend that she had also been in the *lum* so that I "should feel pity." Opwonya told Labwor that it was not good to deceive me like this, and Labwor regretted having done so, but he could never admit to me what he had done. When he finally did acknowledge that Alimocan had not been in the *lum*, he suggested that she was the one who had deceived him. He revised his story to suggest that he had met Alimocan at home, and she told him that she had also been in the *lum*, in a different battalion from his own. "If Alimocan deceived me, then it's true that I deceived you," Labwor apologized, trying to save face.

When Otto later came to visit Labwor, my colleague Jimmy jokingly suggested to Alimocan that she must know this visitor, inviting her to come talk to him. "Ah, you're just disturbing me," she mumbled, shying away in shame. Otto was dismayed that we had let Alimocan deceive us. "You should have asked who abducted you, in whose home you stayed, and where at that time people were staying exactly. She won't be able to tell such details," he advised. Otto also later privately admonished Labwor for lying.

Because of the huge influx of humanitarian workers during and after the war, many former rebels commonly assumed that I too was an NGO worker and was providing some kind of assistance, even if I "claimed" to be a student. Over the course of some months, as they gained a greater understanding of the nature of my work, they came to see me as their student and their expectations of gaining financially from my work abated, but this did not stop their friends and neighbors from assuming that I was a source of capital that they too could try to access. One late afternoon, I found myself waiting outside Gunya's hut in a crowded Gulu slum, waiting with Jimmy for her to return from work, as we often did. As I sat atop my motorcycle, under the shade of a mango tree, a woman caught my attention, speaking loudly to her friends as they sat outside their own huts nearby. Her friends were asking her why she did not attend their recent microfinance association meeting. She confidently touted that she had so many NGOs to attend, she was confused about where to go. She had, she claimed, been to War Child, Good Samaritan, and even *Dwog Cen Paco* (amusingly, not an NGO but a radio program). She got up and passed by us. Jimmy stopped her and asked if she had been abducted by the LRA. She said that she had, and had spent four years in the *lum* with Gilver battalion. Gunya had helped her in the *lum* and facilitated her defection and return home in 2009, she asserted—but 2009 was well after Gunya had left the LRA. Jimmy and I were amused. When Gunya got home from work, we asked her about this woman. "She's a liar," Gunya laughed dismissively. "I didn't know her in the *lum*. Maybe she was abducted and stayed there for a few days, but I didn't see her in the *lum*."

Crafting Victimhood Self-Narratives: A Different Kind of Humanitarian Ethics

I could not really fault Labwor or Gunya's neighbor for their "politics." They had embraced humanitarian subjectivities as a hustle, a way of getting money by any means.[20] Though this was a politics in the sense of deception rather than of governance, it too was an art, one of crafting one's own subjectivity, a different kind of humanitarian ethics from the one usually associated with notions of altruism or moralizing principles like "do no harm."[21] I asked my friends who had negotiated wage-paying positions as beneficiaries of Eternal Salvation to share more details about the styles and techniques of this craft. Their self-fashioning constituted a type of "value addition" (to use Museveni's language of economic development) to the existing symbolic capital they held within humanitarian affect economies—namely, the experience of having been abducted by the LRA.[22] "Everyone is in business," as my friend RV put it. Indeed, the rise of a humanitarian economy around the war had become a business for not only mobile sovereigns, but also local actors. "They use the war to make money—it's like a business," Otto remarked. An unemployed friend who was laid off by a humanitarian NGO once joked to me that he wished the war would return, so that he could find employment in what had become a dying humanitarian job market.

"Those who claim they were wives to Kony were often taken to Kampala for meetings and given sitting allowances," said my friend Aber. "So that is why many people deceive others that they were with commanders in the *lum*." Like RV, Aber had worked for several years for Eternal Salvation, earning money by making dolls that were later sold to tourists and others

Figure 15. Some of the dolls Aber produced for Eternal
Salvation. RV, who also worked at this NGO, noted that the dolls
were made for about 1000UGX (about US$0.40) but sold for
60,000UGX (about US$24). She and others complained that a
greater percentage of the profits should go to the makers, instead
of ending up in the NGO staff's pockets. Photo by author.

in the Global North (often online) at a high profit. As with others whose
names appear as pseudonyms in this book, "Aber" chose her pseudonym
herself, recycling a fake name she had used to register for aid from the
Northern Uganda Social Action Fund (NUSAF), a World Bank–supported
development project. "It's not known by people," she reassured me.

Having seen commanders and their wives receiving special interests and benefits from the government and other programs,[23] rebels who had no or low ranks learned to try to embellish their roles in the *lum* as a means of accessing cash, goods, respect, and other benefits offered to those of rank. Falsely identifying as one of Kony's wives (of whom there were rumored to be around sixty) or the wives of other top-ranking commanders was one useful strategy for women. Aliya recalled that she had at some point been recruited to serve in a group of ex-LRA women mobilized to go to villages and talk to other women who had returned from the *lum*. Among their group was a woman named Aciro. Aciro had been a wife of Vincent Otti, a senior LRA commander killed in 2007, thought to have been executed on Kony's orders. Aciro, Aliya, and other ex-LRA women went to a village in Kitgum in East Acholi to talk to former LRA women. As the women introduced themselves, one of them claimed that she was Aciro, Otti's wife. The real Aciro laughed. Aliya's group told the woman to stop deceiving them— the woman whose name you are using, they said, is right here. Ashamed, the woman went quiet and retracted her claim to be Aciro. She had tried, but failed, to claim kinship with a high-ranking commander in the hopes of receiving cash, goods, and/or other benefits. By contrast, RV said, someone claiming to be the wife of Otto (a low-ranking officer) wouldn't be taken anywhere. "Not even to a lowly guesthouse in Gulu," she laughed.

Often, access to programs that aided in resettlement required that rebels spend a certain length of time in the *lum*—often around five years— to be eligible to receive funding. Someone who spent a matter of weeks in the *lum* would thus not be eligible to receive such benefits.[24] Some of those who would have otherwise been excluded lied, saying that they spent, for example, seven years with the LRA when they perhaps only spent a month, in order to reach the baseline requirement. According to Aliya, the Amnesty Commission gave 230,000UGX to someone who had spent five years in the *lum*, but only 40,000UGX to people who spent less than five years with the LRA.[25] In order to get 190,000UGX more, Aliya said, people lied and said that they spent six to seven years in the *lum*. This kind of requirement, she remembered, was true for not only the Amnesty Act, but also other scholarships and sponsorships. Claiming to have been in the LRA for a longer time than one actually was proved vital to accessing benefits.

Feigning conversion to Pentecostalism was another respected technique, given that a large amount of humanitarian funds channeled toward former rebels trafficked through evangelical NGOs. Aber and her friend Laduka both acted publicly as though they were born-again Christians. When I first met Laduka at her hut in a Gulu slum, she insisted that we solemnly pray before sitting down to eat and chat. She later laughed heartily when I suggested that perhaps she had just been pretending. "You have to pretend to be born-again in order to benefit at Eternal Salvation," she explained, still giggling. She feared that if she revealed herself as a pretender, she would be kicked out of the NGO, losing her job. Those who appeared to be devout evangelicals, she said, were always paid promptly and treated with more lenience than those who "wanted to convert" but had not yet done so.

Aliya, who had also recently joined Eternal Salvation, remembered that the NGO staff asked her for the names of her children when she first registered. As her children had Muslim names, she was forced to explain that it was their father who was Muslim, and that she was no longer together with him. They did not deny her a spot as a beneficiary at the NGO, but did warn her that if she joined, she needed to learn the Bible, which they would study every Wednesday. She obliged and soon became familiar with certain biblical verses and chapters.[26] "I pray everywhere," she said one day, meeting me after she and her son had returned from prayers at a mosque. "With Muslims on Fridays; at Eternal Salvation on Wednesdays; and here [at the Pentecostal church in her Gulu slum] on Sundays." And the spirit's priest (*ajwaka*) on Mondays? I jokingly suggested. She chuckled. I asked her what religion she considered her own. "I'm now bornagain with all my heart," she said, unconvincingly, then self-consciously added: "People from Eternal Salvation come to follow up to see that I'm praying." From her face, it was clear that she did not want to admit even to me that she was also still Muslim, such was her fear of losing her job at the NGO.

Access to health care was sometimes similarly regulated according to a biological regime of war truths. Aliya explained that a certain medical program was tasked with dealing with injuries that were suffered in the *lum*. The organization would provide humanitarian aid for bullet wounds and other such wartime injuries. However, corruption was said to be rampant in the program, and there were so many requests for treatment that the organization selected former rebels who had spent a long time in the *lum* to verify whether or not injuries and scars were in fact suffered there. These ex-rebels were to separate biological truth from biological lies, based on their experience of seeing and knowing the kinds of injuries inflicted on themselves and their colleagues. Implicit in this kind of truth production was the idea that experienced rebels could very easily verify someone's claim that they had been in the *lum*—in much the same way that Otto had urged me to question Alimocan.

Attempting to evoke pity through suffering narratives was yet another technique that seemed to increase the value of one's symbolic capital. Among the attempted strategies of evoking pity used by some women was to claim that they had been raped by LRA rebels, occasionally by multiple men. According to RV, "You sometimes find that this woman is just faking her stories, that she's never been abducted. I know that the LRA didn't rape—they only gave women to specific people, though they did so regardless of age. You can be given to an old man [*mzee*] and struggle with him there. It's very painful to hear these kinds of stories told. The LRA didn't share women—that's a big lie." Indeed, I often asked my friends what misconceptions or lies were told about the LRA that they wanted me to correct in my work. The majority of them—men and women alike—immediately responded as RV did, wanting to dispel the idea that the LRA raped. "I don't know why," RV offered as she tried to think of why women said that they were raped by the LRA. "But maybe it's because they want jobs with NGOs."

Victimhood as Exploitation

Much as rebels sought to add value to their own symbolic capital, they were wary of and became upset when others extracted surplus from their symbolic capital within a compassion economy.[27] Because she felt that the NGO staff would be lobbying for funds and earning money using her name, Gunya was particularly resistant to joining an NGO. A friend and fellow former rebel had tried to convince Gunya to register with Eternal Salvation. Gunya declined, explaining: "She advised me to register with these organizations that help women who returned from the *lum*, but

I refused. I didn't want the world to get rich with my name. I cancelled my name completely with Eternal Salvation. I don't want the world to get rich with my blood. I've suffered enough. . . . Why should I make people rich with my name?" The resentment that Gunya and others held toward those who, as Kony prophetically predicted, got rich using the name of the LRA was not merely a critique of NGO staff as capitalists who claimed to "earn" their salaries by organizing the machinery and labor force of the humanitarian factory. It was often also a critique of unfair and/or unpaid wages due to NGO staff and other "middlemen" siphoning off money that donors sent to aid ex-rebels. Gunya complained: "Others who manage the organization or link the ex-LRA to donors will take advantage and take money. They'll say, 'Oh, the money wasn't sent [by the donor] this month,' but [in fact] the donors had already sent it [and it was eaten by staff]."

Staff, too, ex-rebels observed, employed the kinds of "politics" that ex-rebels themselves used. When I read Musa the same World Vision Uganda (2004) report that I read to Labwor, he dismissed it. "This must have been written by a woman who doesn't know how war goes," he said, "and who divorced her husband and is lacking money to live well. . . . She wrote it so that it appears big and they use the article to lobby, to maintain her job and salary." Regarding the same report, Benjamin said that World Vision wanted to "exaggerate the help they gave . . . to get rewards for what they did." Reflecting further on the World Vision statement, he disagreed that the war was such a bad thing after all:

> It wasn't very bad, because it helped so many people, especially at home. People became rich because of the war, business came because of foreigners who came to help, and employment with foreigners—it improved life status, and these people got extra money and help that was supposed to help ex-LRA. They used [the ex-LRA's] name and ate the money, and got rich. This is why some ex-LRA get frustrated—the money is supposed to help them, but it is being eaten.

Lobbying for funds in the name of ex-rebels, many organizations would have to show results or outputs, often in the form of nebulous "workshops," to keep the money coming in from donors. Other times, the narratives of ex-rebels themselves, called upon to speak to white visitors (and potential donors), were just as important. Aber resented the ways in which she was forced by Eternal Salvation to exaggerate and sometimes even lie in stories to white visitors, as her realities were re-crafted to elicit donations for the NGO: "You're forced to say things that aren't true, or to exaggerate the help they give you. I don't like it. They say, 'You tell them you're getting enough money,' but you're not." But she could not speak honestly, for fear of losing her job: "It's not what I'd like to say. But there's no way to get out of it, no way I can leave [Eternal Salvation]—I have to stay there. Because I would be the one to come home and suffer [if I were to disobey and be kicked out]."

Indeed, their interactions with white visitors were carefully staged and disciplined. Certain women would be called to come tell their stories to visitors, but women were not to speak with the whites without permission. Aber remembered witnessing what happened when one spoke out of turn: "A new intake talked to some white person [*muno*], and I thought, 'Oh, this woman doesn't know this place yet.' Sure enough, she was called to the office, and I think she got warned, 'The next time you do it, you'll be expelled.'" Aber was particularly suspicious because she had previously been with a different NGO, where a staff member had swindled money that was meant expressly for her. She explained:

> I was with [a different NGO] and a white man came and started supporting me, saying he wants to be able to talk with me well [in English] and that the first thing was to teach me English. He advised me to get a teacher and a man called John coordinated this, for an adult literacy class. This man sent money via John and I paid [my school fees], but the second [semester], I didn't see the money. John told me to use the money I was working for to pay myself at school, and he swindled the money. It got difficult for me and I left, but that man might still be sending money up to now, with John chewing the money.

NGOs were not the only ones to exploit the symbolic capital of ex-rebels. Sometimes, high-ranking former LRA commanders who had defected found ways to exploit lower-ranking rebels in different kinds of work schemes, including one at Labora Farm, for their own gain (see Perrot 2012). In this humanitarian economy, low- or no-ranking rebel-workers found themselves exploited and/or coerced not only by the capitalist NGO staff, but also by their fellow workers, who sold them out to become part of humanitarian or development management.

Becoming Pitied Subjects

Much as accessing humanitarian aid through the symbolic capital of the suffering "victim" was a game or a hustle for many of my friends within a compassion economy that involved a certain amount of "politics," this did not mean that they did not find meaning or truth in the raw material that they had acquired, by luck or misfortune. That is to say, many of them saw themselves worthy of pity [*kica*] as people who had suffered for having been abducted and taken to fight.[28] "I *am* a person with problems [*lapeko*]," Otto stressed. "These problems wouldn't have been there if I hadn't been taken away [by the LRA]. If I had stayed at home, I wouldn't be a *lapeko*. I was forced to be a *lapeko*." Gunya felt similarly: "[Ex-rebels] *should* be pitied. Being a rebel isn't easy [*bedo adwii pe yot*]." I showed her a political cartoon depicting common civilian notions of the "child soldier." The image showed a presumably African child carrying a rifle, having just shot the head of a teddy bear wearing a T-shirt reading "childhood." I read her (in translated Acholi) the cartoon's caption: "The first victim of a child soldier . . . [is] childhood." Should people treat her, I asked, as a child without a political opinion? "You feel good for [them] treating you as a child. Someone who forgives you likes you, so you like them," she answered.

Initially, I saw this as a conundrum. As Didier Fassin and Richard Rechtman explain, the "victim" has arisen relatively recently as a new social figure, morally judged by the discourse of trauma. In Palestine and across Latin America, the language of "trauma" has had the effect of transforming oppressed fighters into resilient, traumatized victims, debrided of other social, political, and historical realities and meanings (2009, 160). In Acholiland, the language of victimhood had arrived aboard the mobile humanitarian sovereign,[29] where it was readily adopted by international and local NGOs.

How then, I wondered, could such hardened rebels as Otto and Gunya simultaneously see themselves as worthy of pity for having fought? Should they not have been resisting through a language of stoic oppression and self-sacrifice, rather than accepting one of childlike self-pity? How and why did they identify as both victims and rebels?[30]

An important starting point to address this apparent contradiction is to understand that the contemporary idea of the "victim"—in particular its potential to depoliticize—does not translate easily into Acholi. The translation I often used was "a person whose body is befallen by suffering" (*dano ma can opoto i kome*). On *Dwog Cen Paco*, Lacambel translated "victims" as "people who stayed with problems" (*jo ma gubedo ki peko*).[31] Others simply used "a person with problems" (*lapeko*). Here, "pity" was not opposed to "politics," but rather to a perceived mistreatment or vengeful attitude toward former rebels for having killed fellow Acholi. In this way, my friends were often grateful to be pitied, since it was an alternative to being scorned. Labwor explained to me how some of his relatives pretended to pity him, only to turn against him later: "They came to the reception center and told me, 'Thank God for your return,' but when I returned home, they turned around and said a different thing—'I don't know why he's returned, better he had been killed there.'" Labwor did not need pity for himself, since he identified as a soldier trying to save his people. But he could not reject the pity that he was shown, knowing that doing so would lead civilians to speak badly of him as someone who enjoyed killing. "I let them [pity me]. There's nothing I can do," he shrugged.[32]

Indeed, some ex-rebels clung to their identities as pitiable subjects as a way of eluding stigma or hatred from neighbors and kin on their return. "Some came back and were rejected by their parents and had a hard time starting up their lives," RV reminded me, when I questioned if dedicated rebels returning from the *lum* could really be seen as "victims." Many women, in particular, came home unmarried, unemployed, and with children "from the *lum*," and faced being ostracized and mistreated in different ways. Most rebels were simply surprised when people treated them with kindness. When Benjamin returned and visited a small trading center near his home, people came and welcomed him back. "I hadn't been pitied like that before," he reflected. "I didn't think they would have pity like this on someone who returned from the *lum*. It was strange to see."

Accepting the "mercy" (*kica*) that they were shown was sometimes a precondition for political safety, for de facto amnesty. "People who are still rebellious can change to start fighting again anytime," Gunya warned me of what the UPDF thought of someone who had not yet accepted the *kica* shown to him or her. And if you rejected amnesty, as a statement of resistance and show of support for the LRA? "That's good," Gunya agreed, "but since you reject it, if any problem comes to you from society . . . no one will protect you. They'll say, 'Let him be killed,' and they won't save you." In this sense, accepting and seeing themselves as victims allowed many ex-rebels rights to justice and other forms of legal and social protection that they needed to continue to live securely. Matayo suggested that he could never say how he felt about the rebellion to others—that is, "I have been fighting the government to free you"—because most civilians looked on the LRA vindictively for having killed their friends and family.

Claiming victimhood was not only a utilitarian act designed to ease a major life transition or escape the scrutiny of civilian neighbors. It also became, for some, a deeply ingrained, if compartmentalized, aspect of their subjectivity, particularly after having been subjected to regimes of humanitarian discourse for many years. My friend RV had spent about fifteen years in the *lum*, where her husband was a senior commander. She had had a child that Kony had named after one of the holy spirits that spoke through him. After she returned from the front lines, she tried to join Invisible Children, where Otto was, but was unable to get a job there. She complained that nepotistic staff members chose their own kin to take what she felt should have been her position. Instead she joined Eternal Salvation, graduating from the training course for beneficiaries and rising up the ranks to earn a job as a staff member, serving as a recruiter of, counselor to, and role model for new beneficiaries. By the time we met, she had spent more than four years at the NGO.

At first, like Labwor and many others, RV was guarded in speaking to me, unsure of my intentions. She seemed to very easily reproduce humanitarian discourses of "formerly abducted persons" in the form in which Eternal Salvation and other humanitarian regimes taught ex-rebels to narrate their stories, which they were often called upon to share with white foreign visitors. This form was chronological and redemptive, and told: how they were abducted; how they were taken to the *lum*; how they stayed in the *lum*; how they were received by their family when they returned; how they were received and kept at the reception center; how they joined Eternal Salvation; and—most importantly—how Eternal Salvation had helped them. They were coached to speak about how they did not feel useful when they came back from the *lum*, but now found themselves useful thanks to Eternal Salvation's intervention. I assumed this was an act that she would, in time, drop as she let down her guard and got to know me better.

I was not entirely wrong. Over time, RV revealed to me the ways in which Eternal Salvation and others extracting their symbolic capital would censor their stories. Sometimes she would participate in television programs that would ask her about her experiences in the *lum* with the LRA. Watching the final cut, she would find that much of her critique of the government had been cut—perhaps, she speculated, a result of intentional mistranslation. Stories of government violence against rebels were among the excluded critiques. For example, RV recalled once seeing pictures from a captured UPDF camera of killed LRA women, their abdomens dissected down to their vaginas. Some of the women had been pregnant. The dead fetuses had been cut out of their bodies and laid out alongside them. RV remembered that she and other women were upset at how their interviews had been censored in ways that covered up such government violence, about which she felt she was never allowed to speak. She felt similarly about the stories she and others were asked to tell white visitors. She noted that one could not speak of, as Otto had to me, a desire to go back to the *lum* and continue fighting, for fear of the government learning of this desire and taking punitive action against her.

At times, RV spoke candidly and warmly of Kony and the LRA. Around March 2013, when Séléka rebels overthrew the Central African Republic (CAR) government, she received a call from a former rebel friend, then working in Juba. He shared rumors that had been circulating in South Sudan that Kony had joined the new government of the CAR, after assisting the rebels in their coup. The new government had expelled external forces, he claimed, because they feared that they might recognize and take Kony away if they saw him in the capital. She speculated that, if true, Kony could reorganize his forces with the help of the new CAR regime, before coming back to Uganda "in style" (spoken in English). She glowed happily at this possibility. At the same time, she worried about the $5 million reward that US President Barack Obama had offered for information leading to Kony's arrest, fearing that he might be betrayed by the CAR government or others who might be giving him safe haven. She feared Kony could face the same fate as the late Osama bin Laden.

Although RV's initial demonization of Kony and the LRA gave way to more affection, it did not—to my surprise—stay that way. Her politics seemed to be of two minds. On any given day, I was not sure which

RV I would encounter—the one who seemed a mouthpiece for Eternal
Salvation, or the pious rebel loyal to Kony and the LRA. One day, she
would speak of Kony's spirits with grateful affection, claiming that they
prevented the Acholi people from being exterminated in the aftermath of
Museveni's coup; the next, she would speak of how much relief (*kwer
cwiny*) she felt in Eternal Salvation, of how they had helped her realize her
self-worth at a time when she had given up on life, blaming Kony for wasting her time and wishing arrest or death upon him. Another time she
would speak spiritedly of how life in Uganda would change were the
Moses-like figure of Kony to overthrow the "satanic" government of
Museveni, describing an end to corruption and the flourishing of religion
and morality; soon after, she decried rebellion, calling Kony a "false
prophet" and LRA abductions a "plague" (*two gemo*), and insisted that
social change should occur only through elections.

   She wanted to believe in Kony, but her belief wavered. Others, for
instance Otto, maintained his strong belief in Kony concurrently with his
identity as a *lapeko*, understanding his predicament as one of God's making, a divine design that left him a chosen slave. Leaving behind certain
historical and political valences in its translation into Acholi, "victimhood"
became a condition under which not only ex-rebels, but also the majority
of people in Acholiland, qualified. For some it was merely a discourse of
safety or a way to access capital; for others it also spoke to a certain truth
about their lives, one that could coexist with militancy. Being a "victim"
did not preclude ex-LRA from being active fighters or resisters. Indeed, it
was precisely suffering and problems that led many young men to boast to
me of being ready to go to the *lum* to join the LRA or another group of
rebels, and that led former LRA like Otto to wonder whether they would
have been better off were they still in the *lum*.

BEYOND BARE LIFE: FLEXIBILITY IN
UNSTABLE TIMES

In theory, as Didier Fassin and others argue, the category of "victim" has
become part of an ethical way of eliding politics post-1968. From the outside, this kind of move seems to depoliticize and pacify the subjectivities

of rebels, who, denied their political agency, would be reduced to a kind of bare life. Stripped of their politics, they would—in the Schmittean sense— also be stripped of humanity itself.

However, in the case of ex-LRA rebels, this argument overestimates the subjectifying power of humanitarian regimes and discourses, including "victimhood," to denude people of their political claims. It ignores the complex ways in which ex-rebels themselves speak and act in the trenches of such regimes and discourses. And perhaps most importantly, it fixes the meanings of the "political" and the "ethical" in ways that do not necessarily coincide with how they are deployed among "victims" themselves.

The LRA did not follow usual notions of "politics," which to them more often connoted trickery than the making of enemies. Where they did create enemies like the UPDF, it was not uncommon for rebels to later join them—not out of a lack of political commitment, but because of the way in which the enemy (and with it, the political itself) had already been structured and negated by the divine. At the same time, to embody the figure of the victim was not a passive descent into bare life. By contrast, it was often an active, agential hustle.

I do not argue that rebels "retain" their "humanity" in the face of a humanitarian attempt to pacify their politics through an ethics. Rather, I point to the way in which "humanity" as a concept is historically constructed in a particular configuration where the "ethical" opposes the "political." While politics and ethics struggle dialectically in a postmodernity of human rights and humanitarianism, they mean very different things and dialogue in very different ways in a postcolony like Acholiland.[33] When "politics" is an art of deception or a way of inhabiting uncertainty, and "ethics" is a self-surrender to the divine, the tension between the purported subjects of these fields—the rebel and the charity case—falls away. Both rebels and charity cases, former LRA illuminate how, in a global society in uncertain flux, "humanity" in the postcolony prematurely fixes the "political" and the "ethical," when they are in fact dynamic and multiple. In dealing with radical uncertainty, we would do well to learn from the LRA's flexibility, treating "humanity" as a passing placeholder for a politico-ethics-yet-to-come rather than a bourgeois sanctity toward which we aspire, and which we often feel compelled to prevent from being pillaged.

7 Conclusion

BEYOND HUMANITY, OR, HOW DO WE HEAL?

This book began by suggesting the need to scrutinize the concept of humanity and the claims it makes. Throughout the chapters, I demonstrated ways in which the experiences, narratives, and identities of former LRA rebels resist or deconstruct the concept of humanity, in its various iterations and against its various Others. In the course of the LRA war, and as both a "Western" concept introduced (colonially and postcolonially) through notions of development, human rights, and humanitarianism, and as an "Acholi" concept, humanity became a moral analytic of interpretation and action, with a range of functions and effects. As chapter 2 showed, the concept of humanity became a way to make moral distinctions between "good" and "bad" violence in a way that dismissed the violence of rebellion. This was in part because of humanity's genealogical roots in modernity and its corresponding configurations of technology, reason, time, and kinship structures. Chapter 3 detailed the centrality of humanity in formulating a binary moral geography of "bush" versus "home," dividing spaces of humans and animals. It showed how this spatio-moral binary was torn apart by rebels. Chapter 4 considered the way in which humanity was deployed to discredit rebels and their violence-without-goals as irrational, even as rebels transcended reason by uniting logic and faith. This outcasting of rebels from humanity was explicitly formalized through reintegration programs—discussed in the interlude—that took rebel experiences in the "bush" as outside the human, prescribing "curative" treatments to "rehumanize" them on their return "home." Chapter 5 examined how humanity became an analytic for ignoring forms of kinship and relations forged in violence, relabeling them as morally inadmissible or backward. Chapter 6 considered how humanity was utilized by well-meaning scholars to point to the obscuring of LRA "politics" through humanitarian regimes and discourses, discounting the ways in which rebels themselves understood and experienced both politics and ethics.

The effects of the discourse of humanity not only obscured the "truth" of rebels' experiences, memories, and narratives; it also opposed the ways in which rebels often tried to transcend, ignore, resist, or dissolve humanity insofar as it concerned their struggles toward enacting and living existing presents and alternative futures. Rebels dissolved binaries between humans and animals, in both their simplicity and their morality. They exposed and diminished racist colonial legacies inherent to the modern moral concept of humanity, including its implicit teleologies of development, time, and reason. They transcended reason as an analytic of life and action, and fashioned lived experiences outside humanity, surpassing the false divisions made between lives lived "human-ly" and those lived "inhuman-ly." They brought violence and kinship together, showing ways of forging belonging in and through violence rather than in opposition to it. They disowned humanity of its power by suggesting its role as a mere placeholder for a politico-ethics yet to come, functioning in an ultimately irrelevant way. Rather than presenting as inhuman enemies in need of reforming humanization, LRA rebels organize social life and experience in ways that transcend the analytic of humanity. To be "against humanity," therefore, is to recognize its limits and problems as it simplifies the complexity of lived experience.

In James Ferguson's (1994) groundbreaking work on a Lesotho aid project, "development" was an anti-politics machine that *etatized*. Here, among the LRA, "humanity" was an anti-politics machine that moralized. If it failed in its attempt to humanize rebels whom it had to construct as irrational, violent, undeveloped, and ideologically disoriented animals in order to intervene, it nonetheless exercised and expanded the power of the moral as an instrument effect. In other words, despite failing, humanity imported very specific notions of the good—shaped in ideals of modern violence, technology, modernity, reason, and so forth—in ways that did violence to the common good.

The common good is about justice for all, but humanity is very much about what a specific vision of the world judges as good. This vision claims to align with justice, but it often contributes to injustice by distilling complex lives into simple moral judgments in ways that often—as in the case of the LRA—reproduce racist modern imaginaries. Humanity misrepresents lived realities and experiences as it attempts to assign moral value. It hegemonizes what counts as good in ways that are difficult to question or challenge. It prescribes a narrow vision of the good rather than being open to the possibilities of and meaning found in forms of life outside of it. For those who find freedom and meaning in life beyond humanity, humanity rejects their lives because of the way it reads their violence, irrationality, animality, and so forth. At its heart, humanity seeks not to democratize access to the good, but rather to monopolize control over it—doing violence to the very concept by dictating the parameters of what counts as good.[1]

Challenging "humanity" offers the chance to denaturalize and disrupt normative moral assumptions about ways of life otherwise positioned outside its borders. This challenge might open new philosophical and practical paths to the emancipatory outcomes toward which humanity aspires.

Where does this leave us? Although this book is concerned with the lives of LRA rebels, it is at heart a journey toward new ways of healing social and biomedical suffering. This is not a primary focus of rebels themselves, who, as noted in the interlude, largely rejected the idea that they were sickly, dehumanized, and in need of healing. Rather, I am concerned with the practices of a diverse group who might identify as healers in some fashion—many of whom have relied on humanity as a philosophical bedrock for their work. The previous chapters suggest a need to venture beyond humanity. Yet how might this happen? If we are "against humanity," what are we "for"? This conclusion is an experiment in thinking about new, radical prescriptions for healing life beyond "humanity," performed in the name of something other than humanity. To do so, let me first step back and discuss more personally how I came to this project, and indeed, this conclusion.

A PERSONAL TRAJECTORY

It may strike some as odd that a surgeon in training studied the Lord's Resistance Army and became interested in questions of violence, humanity, and rebellion. At a glance, these questions seem distant from medicine, and, to a certain extent, the discipline of medical anthropology. This was an unexpected path for me, one I could not have envisaged when I began my first year of medical training at Harvard Medical School in 2008. I arrived with a strong interest in global health and social medicine, determined to become a doctor providing care to the global poor. I was excited about the possibility of working with doctors Paul Farmer and Jim Kim and their organization Partners in Health (PIH), which had arisen as one of the most innovative programs providing preferential health care treatment for the poor across the world.

But on learning more about the organization, I came across a troubling bit of history—that the Maoist rebel group Sendero Luminoso had targeted and bombed a PIH clinic in Peru. I could not quite believe how the rebels could find PIH objectionable, knowing that Farmer was a socially conscious, critical medical anthropologist influenced by liberation theology and Marxist theory. On further analysis, it seemed that the PIH clinic had been inserted into a counterrevolutionary policy by the Fujimori government to reduce civilian support for the insurgency.[2] PIH were reformers, not revolutionaries, as Paul Farmer reflected: "Sendero's analysis [of PIH as reformers in the pejorative sense] . . . was less easy to dismiss. We *were* patching up wounds. Such interventions would not, it's true, alter the overall trends [of poverty] registered in the slums of Lima, settlements growing at a rapid rate. With a certain degree of angst, we continued our modest attempts" (2001, 30). Yet they were not merely delaying the radical transformation of society through piecemeal health care provision— they were concretely aligning themselves with the government against the Sendero Luminoso that, at least in the spirit of Farmer's reading, genuinely sought radical equality for the poorest indigenous groups in Peru.[3] They had unwittingly become counterrevolutionaries, ignoring history and politics as so many humanitarian interventions before them had. As Slavoj Žižek describes of Sendero Luminoso violence on taking over villages:

They did not focus on killing the soldiers or policemen stationed there, but more on the UN or U.S. agricultural consultants or health workers trying to help the local peasants. . . . Brutal as this procedure was, it was sustained by the correct insight: they, not the police or the army, were the true danger, the enemy at its most perfidious, since they were "lying in the guise of truth"—the more they were "innocent" (they "really" tried to help the peasants), the more they served as a tool of the United States. It is only such a strike against the enemy at his best, at the point where the enemy "indeed helps us," that displays a true revolutionary autonomy and "sovereignty." . . . If one adopts the attitude of "let us take from the enemy what is good and reject or even fight against what is bad," one is already caught in the liberal trap of "humanitarian help." (2004, 512–13)

And so, finding my own path toward a revolutionary medicine blocked by a disillusionment with all kinds of liberal humanitarian action, including PIH's, I returned to anthropology to think about how to do good in the world in ways that promoted rather than hindered wide-scale, systemic change. How, I wondered, could we align our goodwill with a politics of justice rather than a politics of compassion, avoiding the humanitarian trap of claiming neutrality or impartiality? How could we reverse the trend in place since roughly 1968 of taking care of "victims" in the ethical name of human rights or psychiatric harm,[4] and return to the practice of joining "freedom fighters" in their liberation struggles in the political name of revolution?[5] How could we construct a revolutionary, rather than a reformist or humanitarian, medicine from our desires to "help" the poor and marginalized?

My attention soon shifted to the war in Uganda, a situation not too dissimilar from that in Peru. Here was a war between a group of rebels and an oppressive government that had captured humanitarian attention—primarily because of the spectacular violence of the LRA. Yet, as discussed in chapter 1, it was the structural violence of the humanitarian-government apparatus—the so-called internally displaced persons camps, a form of social torture—that had statistically caused more suffering for the poor. How could these humanitarian organizations in Uganda, like PIH in Peru, become complicit with government action and ultimately thwart the kind of justice that they and the rebels sought for the people of the north? Perhaps, I thought, this was because they could only see and be moved by the spectacular violence of the rebels.

When I began my fieldwork in 2012, I intended to explore the tension between structural and spectacular violence through certain questions about the development of and contestation over an ethics of violence. I sought to understand what kinds of violence both rebels and humanitarians saw as moral and immoral; how they came to these understandings; and when and how they reformulated or reexamined these ideas in the context of conflict and demilitarization. Might rebels see their violence as liberatory and thus morally good? Might humanitarians confronted by the statistics about the concentration camps think differently about what "violence" was and what their responsibility was for it? What was at stake here was a way of seeing and diagnosing suffering that, I felt, ultimately guided the way that people with goodwill formulated their own forms of action or intervention.

It quickly became clear that such a philosophical-anthropological project was impossible, at least to the depths that I felt necessary to explore. I found it practically difficult to explore questions on the ethics of violence in the way I had originally formulated them. Few people were interested in comparative debates on the ethics of violence. Former rebels, fearing persecution in an ongoing war, were initially reluctant to openly speak of the physical violence they committed. Humanitarians denied their role in structural violence, with many—including The Resolve—incorrectly placing the blame of camp displacement and mortality at the hands of rebels rather than the government or humanitarian organizations. Spaces of engagement between humanitarian NGOs and former rebels had grown fewer, as the physical conflict had shifted beyond Ugandan borders and the humanitarian migrant sovereignty had largely zoomed off to another "emergency" (Pandolfi 2000).

So, as any grounded anthropologist would do, instead of starting with my original research questions, I started with where my interlocutors—former LRA rebels—were. And they were full of life and memories—memories of fighting, of living in the *lum*, of miracles and prophecies and spirits. They were living lives on their "return" from the *lum* in which love and politics were deeply enmeshed with their identities as former rebels. It became clear to me that their narratives, their memories, their lives, practices, and discourses offered important lessons about an ethics of violence—one in which existing concepts of humanity excluded their rich and meaningful experiences, often because these experiences were forged in and by violence.

Behind the question on structural and spectacular violence, then, stood a more profound question: How and why did violence become a moral gauge as humanity's other? And if life emerged, indeed thrived, in violence, what—if anything—could be done with the concept of humanity that would seem to deny life itself? What was at stake in this ethics was not relative degrees or forms of violence, but the relationship between ethics and violence itself, between the moral-philosophical good of "humanity" and the evil of violence.

Given my background, bringing humanity and its boundaries into question is not merely a philosophical or historical question about a discourse. It is a high-stakes excavation to and razing of the unsound foundation of humanitarian action and medicine, among many other forms of care for the Other. I hope that by exposing the messy, complicated political and ethical lives of former LRA rebels, this ethnography will give pause to the ways in which humanity is used today, offering reasons not to take humanity at face value. Carrying forward Nancy Scheper-Hughes's (1992) vision for a militant medical anthropology, I offer the reader this ethnography as a form of resistance against the "truth" of Enlightenment forms of knowledge, most of all that concept known as humanity. In this sense, this book aims to deepen and extend existing critiques of humanitarian practice or reason by digging down to the roots of humanitarianism—that is, to humanity itself. It builds on the work of generations of critical medical anthropologists—including Nancy Scheper-Hughes (1990), Hans A. Baer, Merrill Singer, and Ida Susser (2003), and Paul Farmer (2001), to name just a few—concerned with the political economy of health and, in particular, lessening the burden of the often unintentionally iatrogenic forms of violence inflicted by medicine and its forms of knowledge. Humanity, as the philosophical underpinning that structures humanitarianism and much of biomedicine, is one of these forms that violence now takes. It has at present outlived its utility.

Talal Asad critically asks, "If there are limits to what constitutes the human, what are they, and why, indeed, are there limits? If, however, there are no limits, how does this affect humanitarianism that is supposedly concerned to defend the sanctity of human life?" (2015, 426). Seeing the ways in which humanity did more harm than good begs the question: In what other name, beyond or against humanity, could we act in ways that encompass the possibilities for more radical political change? How can we move beyond humanitarian practices of moral good to reach the heart of the matter when it comes to treating sick societies? What are concrete ways of thinking beyond or against humanity?

WHAT IS TO BE DONE?: POST-HUMANITY AND THE POSSIBILITIES OF ANTI-HUMANISM

I join Ilana Feldman and Miriam Ticktin, who, in echoing Faisal Devji (2008), tentatively warn of the danger of "humanity" and its deployment: "Humanity is a difficult—sometimes dangerous—category. . . . We may not be able to do without it—both because there does not seem to be any way to make it go away and because it seems to provide a necessary mechanism for imagining a global condition—but we have to remain uneasy with its deployment" (2010, 25). There is good reason to be against humanity insofar as it prescribes and legislates rigid notions of what constitutes the good life. However, I do think we can and should do without it.[6] What remains to be developed is a robust alternative to humanity.

What I want to offer is the possibility of life beyond humanity—a certain kind of post-humanity as a way of thinking, and, indeed, recognizing, the significance of forms of life that exist outside certain historically and politically constructed moral boundaries. It is a way of attending to what Alexander Weheliye refers to as "the interrupted dreams of freedom found in those spaces deemed devoid of full human life" in a movement "toward another kind of freedom (which can be imagined but not [yet] described)" (2014, 12, 138).

We—scholars, humanitarians, and terrorists, among others—are, I think, envisioning and articulating different kinds of realms beyond humanity.[7] These visions of life beyond humanity add to an existing, politicized scholarship on and for the post-human in the "ontological turn." Much as Africanist thought has long been concerned with rethinking or thinking beyond the human, particularly on the question of race, there is more space to think about antiracism and decolonization together with ontology.[8] In being "against humanity," there is the possibility of a union of radical politics and ontological studies.[9] An ontological approach "chipping away" at humanity as an essentialism through the revelation of alternative worlds[10] can and should work alongside an Africanist deconstructive approach attentive to the historical, racial, and colonial dimensions of the concept of humanity as a way of cultivating knowledge production that deals with radical difference by being what Achille Mbembe might call "open to epistemic diversity" (2016, 37).[11]

Life beyond humanity is not only a critique of the abstract nature of humanity as a form of real membership.[12] Nor is it merely a critique of the liberal concept of humanity, of the way in which a universalized humanity has become the monopoly of Man. Alexander Weheliye, Lisa Lowe, Saidiya Hartman, and Sylvia Wynter have been at the forefront of these kinds of critiques, pushing us to think about different kinds of humanities that would include enslaved, colonized peoples. They and others ultimately want to salvage humanity, to find alternative versions of it, because—as Wynter puts it—"of the possibility of our eventual emancipation, of our eventual full autonomy, as humans" (Scott and Wynter 2000, 195).

Although I deeply respect their and many of my rebel friends' attempts to reinvent the human, to liberate a concept of humanity from the prison of liberal Man, I remain skeptical of the future of humanity. It seems that even when we arrive at forms of humanity from perspectives beyond Man,[13] we remain stuck in distinctions between good and evil, hegemonized in a way that continues to deny and do violence to movements toward true emancipation. After all, it was not only liberal Western humanitarians but also Acholi civilians who cast rebels outside of humanity. Similarly, as discussed in chapter 3, it was rebels who inverted the terms of humanity in the context of the anthropo-moral space of the *lum*. They claimed *gang* rather than the *lum* as the space of social discord, laziness, and faithlessness—as the pejorative space of dogs. Were rebels to seize power, would they not use humanity in a similar way, as a mode of delimiting and hegemonizing a particular version of the good as its universal form? Perhaps not. But I am concerned that as power over humanity passes from one set of hands to another, there is the risk of simply inverting or replacing moral orders through its name. Would humanity not find itself in the same miserable fate as postcoloniality—still struggling for freedom as power moves from one elite to another? By contrast, life beyond humanity is a life open to the moralities of the marginalized and oppressed, rather than being synonymous with the good itself, as defined by the powerful.

There are naturally several concerns about moving toward a life beyond humanity. But perhaps moving beyond humanity does not necessarily mean being against it. At a practical level, of course, claims for belonging and recognition are often successfully and strategically made in the name of humanity. To the extent that its calculated use as a method can meet marginalized people's calls for recognition, it may yet have life, even if it comes at a price.

Another concern is that in the current climate of ethno-nationalist xeno-phobia, turning to anti-humanism may seem quite dangerous. Clearly, however, the form of anti-humanism called for here does not mean to absolutely negate the other as impure and in need of cleansing. At the same time, neither do well-intentioned responses to xenophobia that grasp onto an abstract, universal, common humanity allow space for a real, non-liberal recognition of the other—a space from which to truly honor difference. A radical leftist anti-humanism holds the potential to transcend the limits of this xenophobia/anti-xenophobia binary dominating contemporary politics.

There may yet be the possibility of envisioning humanity in a way that forsakes the dialectical game of constructing moral binaries, oppositions, and exteriorities that divide humans and nonhumans, good and evil, self and other, and so forth. For example, Samera Esmeir references the dream of an alternative humanity articulated by the mystical Egyptian Islamist Tantawi Jawhari in the early 1900s, which does not divorce the inhuman from the human, which is not concerned with making boundaries between good and evil, life and death (2012, 96–105). In the present historical con-juncture, however, it seems difficult to escape that normative dialectical notion of humanity structured by moral (among other) boundaries. Instead of directly pursuing an alternative humanity, I explore anti-humanism as a rich ground from which to productively loosen this power-ful grip that humanity has on the moral.

Humanity as Destination, not Journey?

Many critiques of humanity (including Wynter's) have taken issue not with the vision of the equality of beings, but rather with the erroneous assumption that such equality already exists. In these critiques, there is the possibility for salvaging humanity by constructing a better iteration of it.

In this way, humanity compares unfavorably with the idea of a post-racial society—a concept that has been widely and correctly ridiculed for falsely declaring the end of racism. This comparison crystallizes well as "All Lives Matter," the reactionary slogan to "Black Lives Matter." All lives should matter, of course, but they empirically do not. Declaring that they do at this moment in history is to negate the inherently exceptional value of the lives of the subjugated. One cannot simply declare that all lives matter or that racism has ended and thereby bring a post-racial or just society into existence. To do so prematurely suffocates the journey toward that society, doing more harm than good.

Like post-racism, humanity is a violent idea or concept insofar as it is used as a characterization of the present rather than an aspiration of the future. It claims control over the good in the present, stifling attempts to reach the common good of the future. Yet it is precisely through those attempts, those ways of life that live beyond its moral confines, that we might journey toward the kinds of equality to which humanity gestures. To hold onto humanity or to seek to purify it of its genericity as Western, modern, white Man is to hold onto a universality-yet-to-come, mistaking a destination for a journey or method.

By contrast, anti-humanism is a way of opening up the tightly controlled and regulated moral spaces constituted by humanity. Giving anti-humanism a chance is giving a chance to the kinds of experimental life that just may help us reach the common good. In the remaining pages, I discuss the potential of anti-humanism in moving toward an emancipatory medicine. But before doing so, it is important to consider what anti-humanism means with respect to the LRA and their violence. In other words, what kind of ethical engagement does one take with the LRA through an anti-humanist stance? To be clear, this is not a stance in favor of producing or reproducing nostalgia for the LRA, nor a suggestion that we join them. An anti-humanist approach to the LRA, contrasted to a humanist approach, does not merely dismiss them as an inhumane force through the lens of humanity; nor does it re-humanize them in the abstract sense of being or in a way that reinscribes the dictates of a particular form of moral life. Rather, it recognizes that even as so-called "terrorists," the LRA are stuck in the same binds as the rest of us in attempting to open up and move toward new realms of freedom. Freed from the tortured, dualist, overdetermined, and historical form of relationship designated by humanity, anti-humanism creates space for a different kind of mutual recognition.[14]

HOW WE CAN HEAL: TOWARD THE FREEDOM OF AN ANTI-HUMANIST MEDICINE

I am against humanity. Yet I care deeply about social inequalities that bring about pain and suffering for the poor, people of color, and other marginalized groups. As a physician, I treat patients with humble respect and care as I strive to alleviate their ailments. I want to contribute to emancipation and equality, but I do not believe that humanity is the name under which to do so.

What is the alternative to a humanist medicine? I conclude by introducing the concept of an anti-humanist medicine and detailing some of its liberatory potential. Rather than focusing on diseased individuals who manifest social problems, an anti-humanist medicine focuses on social diseases that manifest in individuals. This shift, which may appear subtle, reorients the clinician to the problem at hand—not only a patient, but also a social structure, policy, or practice. In this form of medicine, patients would not be treated simply as individuals who manifest social problems, but rather, more radically, as social problems manifesting in individuals, or, to revive Louis Althusser, "carriers of structures." By seeing disease as the reification of disturbed social relations (see Taussig 1980), we can reinvent biomedicine as a micropolitical practice on sick societies—and thereby begin to denaturalize the depoliticization of clinical practice.[15] As Vicente Navarro and others point out, the practice of modern biomedicine arose as the result of a bourgeois victory in a class conflict over the construction of "natural" order. That is to say, clinical medicine developed as a branch of medicine "to study the biological-individual phenomenon," distinguished from social medicine and public health, which "studied the distribution of disease as the aggregate of individual phenomena" (Navarro 1988, 62). The result has been to divest power and structure from the clinical gaze, outsourcing it to social workers, public health specialists, and others, while biologizing and anti-politicizing clinical biomedicine.

Perhaps anti-humanism is not an obvious solution to the problems of biomedicine. After all, many think that anti-humanism is precisely what is wrong with medicine today.[16] Many doctors look more at computer screens than at their patients. Patients are shuffled in and out of exam rooms and operation theaters, cases of diseases like pneumonias and hernias that come and go—rather than human beings with stories, emotions, and histories. The increasingly technological character of American biomedical practice, including electronic medical records, has led to discontent among patients that their doctors treat them like robots instead of human beings, and the corporate restructuring of health care delivery has led many practitioners to feel unable to care for patients in the way they want.[17] What we need, many say, is more caring attention to patients and their suffering—in other words, we need more humanism, not less. In "humanism in medicine," they find a form of opposition to the kinds of approaches that treat patients as disease cases to be processed through clinical algorithms and technologies that seek to extract surplus value from the power of the disease in a corporatized system. Humanism in medicine is a moral response to these problems.

What we need, I think, is an anti-humanism to provide a structural response, outside the bounds of what we simply feel to be "good." This anti-humanism is patently not the technological and factory-like anti-humanism present in much of American clinical biomedicine today.[18] I am not interested in transforming caring clinicians into bureaucratic agents, unmoved by the suffering of patients and forsaking bedside manner. But at the same time, I am wary of the alternative that asks physicians and other medical professionals to be more "humanist," to show more care for their patients and their suffering as "human beings"—as though this would bring justice to them. Humanism is not synonymous with care, but only constitutes a specific ideological construction of it. One can be try to be more kind and loving toward patients, yet still function as a reformist corporate bureaucrat unable to see the forest for the trees, fixated on individual instead of collective good.

By treating individuals who manifest social problems, instead of social problems manifesting in individuals, humanism misdiagnoses the signs and symptoms of a sick society as those of a sick human being, and thus offers ultimately ineffective, downstream treatments directed at the bio-logical-individual. In other words, while attending to humanist care is certainly a key part of improving the patient-clinician encounter, center-ing this iteration of care obfuscates the more radical and widespread ori-gins of disease in both language and action (in other words, the root causes of the absence of care). When humanism becomes the moral medi-ator of the kinds of changes we would like to see in the practice of bio-medicine, we are left with a specific prescription for change aimed at the care of the individual patient that often disengages from other ways of caring aimed at the societal patient. The figure of the human comes to dominate progressive action, undermining the possibility for more radical forms of collective political medicine.

The structural approach of an anti-humanist medicine builds on other approaches to structural change in biomedicine. Leading physician–social scientists have more recently sought to address the social determinants of illness through the concepts of structural competency and structural vul-nerability, as a way of working on social, economic, and political problems in the space of the clinic and the clinical encounter (Metzl and Hansen 2014; Bourgois et al. 2017). These approaches, which inquire about patient's social histories, housing, (un)employment, and so forth, are practical in their attempts to identify and show how social structures make people sick. Building on their work, I am calling for a deeper excava-tion of the roots of disease and illness and a fundamental reimagination of disease itself.[19] Rather than recognizing the structural causes behind medical symptoms, we must strive to see disease as the embodiment of these structures. In doing so, we can avoid reproducing the biological-individual model of suffering in which the patient-clinician dyad remains central to our imagination of disease and subsequently limits the possi-bilities of intervention.

An understandable risk of proposing an explicitly political medicine is that it may be co-opted by the right. In an age of vocality of right-wing nationalism and the so-called "alt-right," it is not difficult to imagine the notion of an anti-humanist medicine being used to refuse treatment to immigrants or racial minorities, among other possible conservative political uses. Although medicine has and always will be politicized, an anti-humanist medicine would inevitably magnify the scale of the ideological and political struggles taking place at the realm of the body, requiring more careful vigilance to maintain its practice within a radical leftist framework.

Visions of a Structuralist Medicine in Practice

What would an anti-humanist medicine look like? A patient will no longer be treated merely as "a case of osteoarthritis." But nor will she only be seen as "a pleasant old Mexican farmworker who's had a hard life," a human being with individual stories, emotions, and histories. Rather, she will also be recognized as "a case of structural adjustment, racism, and surplus value extraction," among other forms of social discord and conflict manifesting in individuals—"a case of unemployment" (for instance depression following job loss) or a "case of capitalist accumulation" (for instance lung disease following years of addictive smoking secondary to active corporate advertising to increase tobacco consumption), among others.[20] Thinking about the patient as a manifested structure expands the orders of recognition of violence, better attending to the multiple ontologies (Mol 2003) constituent of the complex reality of that violence.[21]

There are still lessons to be learned, it seems, from the Zambian Ndembu doctor made known by Victor Turner. This doctor saw his task, as Turner describes it, "less as curing an individual patient than as remedying the ills of a corporate group," and read "the sickness of a patient . . . [as] a sign that 'something is rotten' in the corporate body" (1967, 392). Taking its cue from this form of social healing, an anti-humanist medicine will work not only on individual human beings, but also on the collective social problems and structural conditions that manifest in them. Practicing this kind of medicine will require a new language that exceeds the existing discourse of biomedicine, a way to make visible otherwise-unrecognized forms of disease, its etiologies, and its possible treatments on the body of the individual patient. It will require that clinicians and patients alike break the hegemony of individualistic or biomedical models of care and disease and open themselves to new, more collective ways of thinking and naming disease and treatment.[22] When today an acute care surgeon performs an exploratory laparotomy after a bullet perforates the bowel of a young Black man in Oakland, her operative report may indicate a postoperative diagnosis of "perforation of transverse colon secondary to gunshot wound," and her operative repair may include a colectomy or colostomy. Within an anti-humanist medicine, we might see this surgeon add an additional diagnosis ("gentrification and unemployment secondary to racist legacies of slavery"[23])—one that reveals *why*, rather than simply *how*, social disease manifests in an individual—and suggest an additional possible treatment ("referral to Black Lives Matter").

To think beyond anatomical or physiological imaginaries is not an easy task for clinicians (nor, sometimes, patients) to accomplish on their own. They require help in transcending biological-individuating discourse and reformulating their worlds as also social ones. Moreover, they are more often entirely focused (and justly so) on the acute biomedical emergency, lacking the necessary time and space to craft alternative imaginaries. What is needed is a form of reunification of social medicine and public health with the clinic—in other words, a reunification of collective healing with individual healing. Practically, this means the integration of those other expert diagnosticians and healers of (social) disease—social scientists, community members, psychologists, activists, patients and their families, public health workers, progressive social workers, and so forth—into clinical teams. When the surgical team rounds on the hospitalized Black man above, it is the anthropologist or historian or Black Lives Matter activist on the team who is able to point to the legal, historical, political, and social diagnosis (if the patients and their families cannot) that is incorporated into the operative report, who is able to provide the referral to a radical organization for political action that aims to fix the social conflict that manifested as a perforated colon in the patient. When a radiologist reads the brain MRI of an American soldier who served in Iraq, became addicted to heroin as a way of coping with PTSD, and suffered a stroke after an overdose, it is the radical economist or sociologist or veteran activist who provides the sociopolitical impression on the read, suggesting the image of hypoxia is consistent with a diseased military-industrial complex operating together with a broader imperialist politics of oil.[24] While the physician diagnoses and heals the biological body, other healers diagnose and attend to the collective disease carried by the body.

This kind of reimagination is not only a theoretical or philosophical practice, nor merely a form of everyday resistance against the hegemony of biomedical discourse. It is also a fundamental intervention in the documentation of and subsequent action on social ills within the paradigm of evidence-based medicine. It provides the opportunity to create radical data that reconceptualizes diagnoses, mechanisms of disease, treatment, and so forth in the sociopolitical imaginary.[25] Given the importance of evidence-based medicine in health policy and transformation, radical data may provide an opportunity to effect real change by pointing concretely to social ills.[26] For example, a hospital examining its annual report on diagnoses might find something like "30 percent of our emergency room visits were due to the new Jim Crow." Health policy, research, and community engagement carried out by the hospital might then be directed toward understanding and solving the problem of the mass incarceration of Black men. Similarly, treatment plans might extend the apolitical recommendation for "lifestyle modification" (commonly called upon in algorithmic biomedical treatment of hypertension and obesity) to include prescriptions for activism, conscientization, political protest, and civil disobedience, to more properly root out the social ills that manifest in patients. To be able to act on social disease differently requires that we see the world differently, which itself necessitates a language distinct from the biomedical-individual form.

An anti-humanist medicine is an explicitly leftist political medicine that first and foremost abandons liberal humanity as an ethics of medicine. That is to say: it requires the idea (radically jarring to some) that not all human beings are equal and that therefore not all patients deserve the same amount of time, attention, and care.

But perhaps this is not such a radical idea. After all, countless studies (and indeed, entire academic disciplines) point to the ways in which racism and poverty contribute to ill health. If our scientific data show that certain groups of people are struggling with more health problems, then it seems logical to offer them preferential treatment and care in hospitals—first access to beds, longer appointments, care by the most highly qualified physicians, preferential OR booking times, and so forth. By virtue of structural discrimination against them—the subtle and not-so-subtle forms of exclusion in the culture and space of the hospital; the arrangement of appointment times during working-class hours; and so forth—it is hardly as though we treat all our patients equally in the first place. The friends of middle-class physicians ask for a favor and magically get an appointment for their mothers the very next day. Poor people of color do not normally have access to these kinds of social resources and capital. Much as we proclaim that we treat all patients equally, it is obvious that we do not.

Many leftist physicians already practice this kind of anti-humanist philosophy, dedicating their lives to serving "underprivileged populations" in community health centers or county hospitals across the country. In choosing what kinds of patients they want to see, they are already subtly challenging one philosophy of humanism in their practices of medicine. Why not declare their practices openly?

Beyond a discursive and philosophical change, this political medicine requires a reapplication of biomedical labor within the milieu of radical social movements. Rather than working under the auspices of Doctors Without Borders (MSF) or other organizations acting in the neutralizing name of humanity (including universities and nonprofit hospitals), we may do better to revive the practice of putting biomedicine at the service of explicitly political leftist social movements, parties, and organizations. What if we could work outside the confines of humanity for a surgery department of Black Lives Matter, or a psychiatry department of Strike Debt, or—as was historically done in the 1970s—for the medical clinics of the Black Panther Party?[27] Canadian thoracic surgeon Norman Bethune embodied this kind of work well. Arguing that "charity must be abolished and justice substituted" (Gordon and Allan 1973, 96) he did not practice medicine in the abstract, apolitical service of the "poor." Instead, he went to the front lines of war to save the lives of soldiers fighting imperialism and fascism. He applied his skills in the service of politics rather than a "neutral" or "impartial" ethics.

It is not only clinicians who might see their work differently. Patients of a political medicine could likewise reimagine their conditions collectively and socially rather than suffer from them as individuals. That is to say, they will recognize themselves as progeny of the same social diseases, opening the possibility for radical biosocialities, including disease unions. Modeled on debt unions, which in part seek to reduce the individual stigma of debt by reimagining debt as a social condition rather than a person's own moral failing, disease unions could unite patients in ways that combat the root causes of their illnesses in a process of collective healing. What if, instead of conceiving of obesity as a personal failing, a politicized obesity union tackled the problems of the capitalist tendency toward overproduction and of food deserts as a broader question of gentrification? What if clinical treatments included not only surgical gastric banding and gastric bypass, but also food justice activism, campaigns against product advertising, and reflection on the crises of capitalism?

We are at a crossroads when it comes to healing our sick societies. One road—the road that most have already chosen and traveled down—is the road of humanism and humanity, a never-ending recourse to the idealism of some future equality as though it existed today. The other—a road with the dangerous name of "against" or "beyond" humanity—scares most away, but only because its signs are misread. One is "against humanity" not because he or she feels nothing for or thinks nothing of other creatures; wishes death upon them; and/or enjoys mass violence, as one might think being against humanity might connote. Rather, one is against humanity because one takes the radical and liberating step of refusing to be duped by an ideology that offers a bandage as a cure for a rotting abscess. One is against humanity because he or she is not inspired by the vacuous gesture that all are deserving of equal treatment; rather, he or she is inspired to move beyond humanity with the radical notion that the oppressed deserve more than the oppressors, and thus that their lives will be preferentially valued.

In opening up a space to learn from rather than merely condemn the Lord's Resistance Army, I have attempted to concretely detail the need to move against and beyond humanity as a politically dangerous ideology that monopolizes control over the good. Above all, this book seeks to alter the course of both scholarly thought and everyday common sense about humanity. It suggests the need for alternative conceptual bases of action for humanitarian, political, medical, and other interventions. My hope is that it will become a starting point for thinking and rethinking radical alternatives not only in medicine, but also in practices of scholarship, development, humanitarianism, human rights, and beyond.

Notes

CHAPTER 1. INTRODUCTION

1. See also Finnström (2013, 127).

2. See for example the use of "humanity" in Scheper-Hughes (1992), Garcia (2010), and Livingston (2012). The affective dimension, Thomas Laqueur (2009) points out, was integral to the early uses of "humanity" as a combination of "human" and "humane."

3. See Holbraad, Pedersen, and Viveiros de Castro (2014) on the politics of an ontologically inflected anthropology.

4. I would not class ontologists among this group given their general openness to alterity, although there are important debates about the coloniality of the ontological turn. See for example Todd (2016).

5. Saba Mahmood articulates a similar stance in which I situate my work, as part of a broader body of literature questioning "liberal assumptions about what constitutes human nature and agency" (2005, 5).

6. I position my work with Samera Esmeir's critique of juridical humanity as "an opening of a space for rebellion and struggle: for texts, events, and practices that articulate another concept of the human or lose the human in politics" (2012, 17).

7. Here I join Alexander Weheliye, who conceptualizes the human as "a heuristic model and not an ontological fait accompli" (2014, 8).

8. For the classic critique of "rationality" see Evans-Pritchard (1976). For the classic critique of "development" see Ferguson (1994).

9. I am alluding to Harri Englund's (2006) excellent critique of human rights as imprisoning minds to a specific kind of freedom.

10. See also Asad (2015).

11. Fifty-six of these groups were listed in the 1995 constitution; another nine were added in a 2005 amendment. See Constitution of the Republic of Uganda (1995) and the Constitution Amendment Act (2005).

12. For more on Acholi people, land, history, and politics, see Girling (1960) and Finnström (2008). For more on class in and beyond Acholiland, see Mamdani (1976) and Branch (2011). For more expansive context and research on the Lord's Resistance Army, see in particular Behrend (1999), Allen (2006), Finnström (2008), Dolan (2009), Allen and Vlassenroot (2010), and Branch (2011).

13. See Atkinson (2010a), from which the ethnicized history presented here is drawn.

14. The timeline that follows is based largely on Allen and Vlassenroot (2010). Atkinson (2010a) also provides a useful reference summary of the LRA war.

15. See Branch's (2011) excellent work on the camps and the politics of humanitarian intervention in the war, in particular chapter 2. Andrew Mwenda, a highly respected Ugandan journalist, calls IDP camps "concentration camps" (2010, 55).

16. Ministry of Health (2005), quoted in Branch (2011, 97), and Atkinson (2010a, 304–5).

17. Chris Dolan (cited in Nibbe [2010]) estimates that 90 percent of the suffering lay at the hands of the government for creating camps and forcibly displacing people; the remaining 10 percent caused by the LRA, he suggests, became the standard narrative: "While the Aboke abductions gained global attention and condemnation and became synonymous with LRA brutality, the extreme deprivation and multiple forms of violence inherent in the camps, and the mass social dysfunction which they generated, drew remarkably little international reaction" (2009, 109).

18. Especially Finnström (2008), Dolan (2009), and Branch (2011).

19. Ronald Atkinson, Julian Hopwood, and Father Joseph Okumu have been studying and following the land question, and in particular the commodification of customary land. See Atkinson (2010a, 328–35).

20. Technically, the LRA and the RUF are blacklisted on the Terrorist Exclusion List, while the others are designated Foreign Terrorist Organizations. By comparison with the Foreign Terrorist Organizations list, the Terrorist Exclusion List uses broader criteria for inclusion and cannot be contested in court. See Cronin (2003).

21. On the ICC question, see Allen (2006). Almost all of my ex-rebel friends and I disagree with the ICC actions, which Allen generally supports. For a more sophisticated analysis of the ICC, see chapter 6 of Branch (2011) on ICC and

human rights enforcement. Note that the charges against Raska Lukwiya and Okot Odhiambo were dropped following their deaths. Despite all indications that Vincent Otti was killed in 2007, the charges against him stand at the time of this writing.

22. United States Cong. Senate (2010); Obama (2011).

23. See for example Agger (2013).

24. The Resolve LRA Crisis Initiative (2013).

25. See for example Mwenda (2010), Finnström (2013).

26. Sverker Finnström speaks of the human terrain mapping done to track the LRA as a "hunt for characters who are no longer fellow human beings" (2013, 131).

27. These moralistic works about the LRA include de Temmerman (1995), McDonnell and Akallo (2007), Dunson (2008), Eichstaedt (2009), and Otto (2011), among others.

28. I did not speak extensively to rebels who had settled outside Ugandan Acholiland in places like Lango, Kampala, Juba, London, or Nairobi, except with Amony, the ex-wife of my friend Otto. Nor did I speak to non-Acholi former LRA rebels.

29. I refer to former rebels as "friends" instead of "interlocutors," "informants," or similar monikers because this more accurately reflects how I see them, both philosophically and in practice, in the sense of my respect toward and connection to them.

30. *Rupiny* is published by the New Vision media group and distributed primarily in Acholiland and Lango. It contains articles in both the Lango and the Acholi languages.

31. In particular, I primarily use *Acholi* instead of *Acoli*, which is more orthographically correct. As the Acholi language was primarily oral and only written into the Latin or Roman alphabet through encounters with the Other, I am not sure that it is ultimately a very meaningful form of resistance to insist that the Acholi alphabet contains no *h*. For phonetic convenience and to avoid a kind of disingenuous resistance, I therefore use "Acholi" on most occasions, except with *tic Acoli*. On Acholi orthography, see Crazzolara (1938).

32. God the Father, purportedly speaking through the medium of Severino Lukoya, also falsely accused me of being a spy. This allegation led me to cast serious doubt on Lukoya's claim to be a medium of an omniscient spirit.

33. I have no immediate familial ties to Uganda, as is often assumed of me as an ethnic Gujarati. Distant, deceased relatives worked on sugarcane plantations in and around Jinja, a fact I only discovered after beginning to work in the country.

34. See Nader (1972).

35. "Home" appears in ersatz quotes because for some ex-LRA, particularly those who spent a majority of their lives in the "bush" as rebels, where and what "home" is comes under question.

36. "Bush" appears in ersatz quotes here because, though it is widely used in English when referring to the LRA war, I consider it to be a poor translation of the Acholi *lum*, which literally means "grass." "Bush" carries with it preexisting colonial and postcolonial meanings that in some instances add an excess of meaning to *lum*. This is explored further in chapter 3.

37. See for example Laqueur (2009), Festa (2010).

38. Thanks to Jason Price for suggesting this last section of the introduction.

39. Cited in Weheliye (2014, 21). As Alexander Weheliye describes it, "*Demonic ground* is Sylvia Wynter's term for perspectives that reside in the liminal pre-cincts of the current governing configurations of the human as Man in order to abolish this figuration and create other forms of life" (21).

CHAPTER 2. HOW VIOLENCE BECAME INHUMAN

1. The remaining twenty-one counts were for "war crimes." On the distinction made between "war crimes" and "crimes against humanity" see for example Jia (1999).

2. For other treatments of humanity and violence, see also Asad (2007), Devji (2008), Laqueur (2009), Feldman and Ticktin (2010). For a sharp critique of the ICC intervention in northern Uganda, see Branch (2011).

3. See for example Amnesty International (1997), Gersony (1997), Pham, Vinck, and Stover (2008).

4. I recognize a minor but important theoretical distinction between "inhu-man" and "inhumane." However, in the narratives I present, these two words appear interchangeably, and as I am interested in the deployment of these terms, I do not address the distinction here.

5. See for example Dwyer (1972), Mamdani (1976), Atkinson (1994).

6. See for example Dwyer (1972).

7. This was indeed how many subsequent colonial encounters played out—as missionaries labored to spread the gospel.

8. See "Improvement of Physique in Negroes" (1946) in Bell (1885–1946, 4).

9. Grogan (ca. 1908–11), "A Safari through the Soudan and Upper Egypt," *Rev-eille*, MSS.Afr.S.1949/4., p. 47, emphasis added.

10. Bell (1906–9), letter titled "1906. 31st August. At Nimule."

11. Ibid.

12. The divide commonly translated as East versus West Acholi is also some-times referred to as upper versus lower Acholi. See for example Sverker Finnström's (2008) discussion, especially on the ways in which this divide splits along lines of tradition and modernity.

13. This alienation is perhaps, I speculate, due to their distinct Central Sudanic origins. John Orr Dwyer suggests that the Lamogi were possibly of

Madi origin, and cites a British officer serving during the Lamogi Rebellion who said that the Lamogi did not belong to "any definite tribe" (1972, 130–31). See also Atkinson (1994, 217–21). Nonetheless, the Lamogi Rebellion is today claimed as part of Acholi history.

14. There is, of course, a long tradition of thinking of violence and humanity as compatible rather than oppositional, particularly in the discipline of biological anthropology. Because I take "humanity" as a mythical discourse of recent construction, I am skeptical of this claim that violence might be considered part of humanity or a human condition. In focusing on this opposition, I am not making claims about the "true" relation between violence and humanity. Rather, I am elucidating a genealogy of thought, one produced and reproduced through parameters of modernity.

15. *Cen* should be treated as a multiplicity. It is also, for example, a lived phenomenology of civilians fearing it, and a way in which "trauma" is understood in "indigenous terms" by Western biomedical experts. I address only one of these multiples of *cen*—as a moral discourse on modernity and violence. Adrian Yen's forthcoming work on *cen* as an "ontological insecurity" addresses *cen*'s unstable multiplicity as a precondition for its singularization in various regimes of care and governance.

16. Talal Asad offers a similar assessment of violence in assessing the shock value of death by machete compared to death by missile: "The interesting point is that being hacked by a machete (or blown up by a suicide bomber) is regarded as *inhuman*, a notion that presupposes there are *human* ways of killing and dying as well as inhuman ones. Indeed, ways of killing and dying are part of how we define the human" (2015, 412).

17. On this belief, see also Soto (2009, 65). However, Oyengo suggested that if *cen* feared guns, he would be able to just borrow a gun and shoot in the area where *cen* is staying in order to chase it away. But, he pointed out, chasing away *cen* is a much more complex process involving admissions of guilt, payments, and reconciliation.

18. Some qualify this by suggesting that the strength of the *cen* determines whether or not it will haunt the killer. If the killed had a strong spirit, that spirit will be more likely to haunt as *cen* than someone killed who had a weak spirit.

19. These conclusions recall those of Talal Asad, writing on liberal thought on violence: "What seems to matter is not the killing and dehumanization as such but how one kills and with what motive" (2007, 4).

20. *Lakwena* here refers to the LRA. It was also used to refer to Alice Lakwena's Holy Spirit movement (see Behrend 1999). Civilians encountering rebels were less likely to distinguish those of Alice Lakwena from those of Joseph Kony or Severino Lukoya (Alice's father), and the name *Lakwena* persisted to refer to the LRA. *Lakwena* means "messenger" in Acholi.

21. Compare with Talal Asad: "It is not cruelty that matters in the distinction between terrorists and armies at war, still less the threat each poses to entire

ways of life, but their civilizational status. What is really at stake is not a clash of civilizations (a conflict between two incompatible sets of values) but the fight of civilization against the uncivilized" (2007, 37–38).

22. Compare to the way in which KAR violence using modern weapons was similarly pitted against the primitiveness of savage enemies without modern technologies of killing. As described by Hubert Moyse-Bartlett, KAR *askaris* in Burma "used for the first time a multiplicity of modern weapons and equipment against an enemy more stubborn, savage and implacable than any they had yet encountered" (1956, 681).

23. Note that Labwor's explanation contradicted Ogweno Lakor's, which suggested that those killed by landmines simply could not haunt their killers, regardless of whether the killers contemplated the killings. Such a disconnect illustrates the complexity of *cen* as a discourse and concept.

24. Thanks to Adrian Yen for bringing this to my attention.

25. This is starkly contrasted to, for example, the remote drone warfare being employed by the American military. On the ethics of drone warfare, see for instance Sharkey (2012).

26. It should, however, be noted that anyone can meet *cen* along the road or in the *lum*, particularly at night, and that they could become haunted by a *cen* in a situation in which they had no responsibility for the killing of the spirit's body.

27. See also Ferguson (1999) on expectations of modernity.

28. For more on the concept of *jok* and its relation to the Christian concept of God, see Seligman and Seligman (1932), Boccassino (1939), Wright (1940), p'Bitek (1963).

29. "RV" ("rendezvous") was a pseudonym she chose because it was a meeting point for rebels in the *lum*. She wanted it to be used here, she said, because it would remind her of the way in which she and I met to chat, as they did in the *lum*.

30. See Behrend (1999).

31. See p'Bitek (1974, 177–79) for examples of *nying moi*, or "warrior's titles," as p'Bitek calls them.

32. "Human rights" (*twero pa dano*) is here understood in its Western framework. Through the course of the war, and as a result of exhaustive work done by humanitarian organizations, "human rights" has become a ubiquitous term in Acholi.

33. Indeed, in describing this ceremony, one says that they *camo* (eat) *nying moi*. "Eating" implies a celebration rather than a mourning. For example, the standard practice referring to the celebration of Christmas is *camo karama* ("eat" Christmas).

34. For more on the LRA relationship with *tic Acoli*, see chapter 4.

35. While some LRA women did acquire ranks, it should be noted that traditionally, Acholi women generally did not receive *nying moi*.

36. "Pips" are decorations designating one's rank, typically adorning the military uniform.

37. His rhetorical stance remains similar today. In an East African Legislative Assembly meeting in 2013, Museveni said that Africa suffers from an "ideological disorientation whereby the reactionaries fragment the African people into sectarianism of tribe, religion and gender chauvinism" (quoted in Arinaitwe 2013).

38. See for example Bayart (2009 [1993]).

39. Kiswahili for "enemy," but used in Acholi to refer to "rebel."

40. On the spatial configurations of the camps in relation to UPDF "protection," see Branch (2011), Nibbe (2010).

41. See "Land Dispute Costs Woman Arm" (2013), Ocowun (2013).

42. On a similar note, in February 2013 members of the Acholi Parliamentary Forum revived the threat for the secession of the Nile State after the embezzlement by the NRM government of donor aid money meant to fund the Peace, Recovery, and Development Programme (PRDP) for postwar northern Uganda. Museveni had recently said, "Corruption is small compared to unlawful killing of people"; by contrast, the Acholi parliamentarians showed up at a press conference wearing black T-shirts reading "Architects of PRDP Theft Worse Than Kony's LRA." See "Corridors of Power" (2013), Nalugo (2013), Naturinda (2013).

43. Note, however, that modern anxieties fueled condemnation of mob justice. A 2012 op-ed appearing in the *New Vision* suggested that "supporting such acts [of mob justice] exposes our barbaric and inhumane instincts, which have no place in civilisation" (Senganda 2012).

44. Quoted in Kazibwe 2014, emphasis added.

CHAPTER 3. GORILLA WARFARE

1. This is largely in the Christian sense, and a meaning made clear by the history of British colonial intervention, both secular and missionary. In the Acholi spirit world, it is certainly true that dangerous or bad spirits are not desirable in *gang* and should be contained or driven elsewhere, including but not limited to the *lum*.

2. The theory that this term was given to the Acholi by their neighbors, rather than Europeans, is endorsed by Okot p'Bitek (1980, 3–4), Angelo Negri (1984), and Sverker Finnström (2008). Another less likely origin theory, proposed by J. K. Russell (1966, 2) and endorsed by Heike Behrend (1999, 128), is that A. B. Lloyd is the one who mistakenly called the Acholi "Gang" after they answered "Gang" when he asked where they came from. This almost certainly overplays the importance of a historically insignificant missionary's encounter with the Acholi in 1903, decades after initial colonial encounters and independent of other regional interactions, especially with Arab traders.

3. For similar descriptions, see also Moyse-Bartlett (1956, especially 85–86).

4. For more on were-lions and shape-shifting, see chapter 9 of Bere (1990). Note that animal totems and taboos were once quite common and well-known in Acholiland, and, as Rennie Bere (1990, 100) suggests, people of certain clans sometimes had the ability to shape-shift into their totem animals. I heard very little of this discourse during my fieldwork, however. When a man-beast (*nguu dano*) began to raid livestock in an area well-known to me, I was told that only Madi or Sudanese tribes like the Dinka could shape-shift. Some elders mentioned that Acholi witches (*lujogi*) were also capable of it, but the blame for the raid known to me was placed on an unknown Madi *nguu dano*. One can, incidentally, draw suspicion of being a *nguu dano* by refusing a sour leafy vegetable commonly eaten in Acholi (*malakwang*) that is said to dull the sharp teeth that *nguu dano* need to chew on flesh and bones.

5. Gulu Support the Children Organisation (GUSCO) (n.d.A, 17). This point is discussed further in the interlude.

6. This clearly evokes Mary Douglas's description of dirt as "matter out of place" (1966, 36).

7. Note that *Dwog Cen Paco* broadcasts, in Acholi, are intended for Acholi rather than international audiences, but are funded and influenced by NGO and government interests, whose discourses are often broadcast in literal and symbolic translations. For an insightful analysis of the construction of politics and other concepts in ostensibly local narrative forms on radio airwaves, see Englund (2011).

8. For more on *gemo*, see Negri (1984) or p'Bitek (2011, 38).

9. E. T. N. Grove (1919) discusses *jok tim* (a hunting *jok*) who, in recognition of offerings made by hunters and left in the "bush," will gather animals together for a successful hunt. It is unclear whether the *jok tim* was considered "bad," although it was regarded as a snake, an animal generally feared for its magical powers and involvement in witchcraft.

10. Much as it is often denigrated as a wilderness, the village is sometimes also celebrated or romanticized as a space in which "Acholi culture" has been "preserved." See for example Sverker Finnström's point that many regard the upper or eastern Acholi as either "'more traditional' (a positive statement) or 'more backward' (a negative statement)" (2008, 33).

11. Church Missionary Society (CMS), "The Case for the Village Bush or Sub-Grade School," Papers of Rev. Henry Mathers, no author nor date. For more on CMS bush schools within CMS missionary policy and ideology, see for instance Cave-Browne-Cave (1931), Kitching (1926, 1936), and Church Missionary Society, *CMS Historical Record. The Upper Nile*, 1945–46, 109. A. B. Fisher, who served in Gulu with his wife from 1913 to 1914, played a key role in creating the "bush school," which he imagined to be making a "deadly attack on illiteracy" and driving "out darkness and superstition" (Fisher ca. 1890–92, Acc. 84 F3/1, Book 4, p. 24).

12. For more on *jok* names, see Seligman and Seligman (1932, 120) or Girling (1960 161), among others. The LRA did not give *jok* names to their children, considering *jok* to be a profanity. This is examined in more detail in chapter 4.

13. See for example Nile (1946) on the naming of children born during a hunt.

14. For comparison with other accounts of LRA yards, see Dolan (2009) and Titeca (2010).

15. *Kac* and *abila* are used interchangeably (see p'Bitek 1980, 104).

16. Sachets were banned in Gulu District by late 2016.

CHAPTER 4. BEYOND REASON

1. For more on Cilil, see Dolan (2009, 43–44) and Behrend (1999, 25–26).

2. See for instance Heike Behrend's descriptions of Latek and his relations with Alice and Kony. According to Behrend, Alice and Latek met to negotiate a possible unification, but "no unification was achieved because Odong Latek refused to recognize the Holy Spirits Tactics and demanded the use of classic guerrilla tactics" (1999, 61). Latek joined Kony in 1988 and persuaded him to "adopt classical guerrilla tactics instead of the Holy Spirit Tactics" (1999, 182).

3. This was, I stress, his understanding. Others spoke of collaborators and intelligence officers who quickly passed information to the front lines.

4. See for example chapter 4 of p'Bitek (1980).

5. A traditional courtship dance (see pa'Lukobo 1971).

6. Note of course that in the aftermath of the Holocaust and in particular Nazi "science," reason was brought into question as a cold killer of humanity, rather than necessarily constituent of it. See Horkheimer (1947) and Finkielkraut (2001). These debates have largely been absent from discussions about rationality and Africa.

7. See Branch (2005) and Finnström (2008).

8. A *lajok* is a powerful type of witch whose sorcery is inherited. See chapter 7 of p'Bitek (1980).

9. One friend of mine, however, who had just left the LRA, noted that they had begun to drink alcohol. Upon hearing this news, my friends had different reactions. Benjamin said that there was no point in the LRA continuing to fight now—they are finished, and could even end up shooting each other under the influence of alcohol. On the other hand, Matayo suggested that the *tipu* had previously issued rules that forbade drinking, but that the *tipu* often changed its rules, and now it had begun to allow it.

10. I am referring to the Enough Project, cofounded by John Prendergast and Gayle Smith.

11. Okot p'Bitek explains this adage as "Too many cooks spoil the broth" (1985a, 21).

12. See also Behrend (1999, 143).

13. Among the forms of LRA *tyer* was the sacrificing of sheep, narrated to me as akin to the biblical sheep Abraham sacrificed to God in place of Isaac.

14. See for example the discussion of priests in Hebrews 7–8 in Bible Society of Uganda (1985, 1210–11).

15. This practice of translation was particularly important as missionaries sought to find an Acholi concept by which potential converts could accept a Christian God. See p'Bitek (1963) and Behrend (1999, 116–19). Interestingly, in place of *abila*, Otto could have but did not use different Christian translations of "shrine" or "altar," including *ot woro* (literally "house of worship"), *altare* (used by Catholics), or *keno tyer* (used by Protestants). See the latter two used differently in Exodus 30 in Acholi Bibles, including the Catholic Archdiocese of Gulu (2007, 101) and the Protestant Bible Society of Uganda (1985, 79).

16. Of course, the fact that Kony prayed at all distinguished him from *ajwagi*, who did not pray to *jogi*.

17. Night-dancing is a feared form of wizardry attributed to witches who come outside one's hut and dance naked, putting their objects under a spell that makes them feel drowsy, bringing them sickness and sometimes slow death. See p'Bitek (1980, 123–26).

18. Born-again Christians also refuse to give *jok* names to their children. Increasingly, Acholi youth find *jok* names as stigmatizing, whereas they previously carried respect for the spirit-child and his or her powers.

19. For more on mimesis, see also Benjamin (1933) and Benjamin and Tarnowksi (1979).

20. The Banyankole are a people inhabiting parts of southwest Uganda. Museveni is often thought to have favored the development of the Banyankole because they are his own tribespeople.

21. Kacoke Madit (meaning literally "a big meeting place") was an effort made toward ending the war and creating lasting peace by Acholi in the diaspora. See Pain (1997) and Poblicks (2002).

22. Indeed, as Sverker Finnström argues, many of the rebel manifestos sought actively to deny or play down the spiritual nature of the rebellion (2008, 123).

23. This is not to say that such duplicity did not exist. Indeed, I heard stories of how some rebels used the pretext of the war to enact revenge or justice in personal feuds, using the violent sovereignty of the LRA to settle old scores. This practice was the modus operandi of *boo kec*, thieves who paraded as rebels while stealing, raping, and committing other acts. Rebels themselves also sometimes doubled as *boo kec*. See Finnström (2008, 5).

24. In particular, they both go beyond and remain within the constraints of the conjuncture. "The engineer is always trying to make his way out of and go beyond the constraints imposed by a particular state of civilization while the

'bricoleur' by inclination or necessity always remains within them" (Lévi-Strauss 1966, 19).

INTERLUDE

1. Other reception centers included Caritas (in Pajule) and Kitgum Concerned Women's Association (KICWA). The organization of reception centers was considered an informal kind of disarmament, demobilization, and reintegration (DDR) process.

2. "Reintegration" is also a discourse evoked in prison "reentry" industries. See for example Wacquant (2010). Thanks to Cole Hansen for pointing this out, and for his invaluable input regarding the idea of this interlude.

3. Personal interview, hotel manager, Gulu, November 2012.

4. Personal interview, AVSI Uganda—Gulu, May 2013.

5. James Navinson Kidega, then Gulu RDC, radio interview on the Amnesty Program, Mega FM, June 2013.

6. Others have questioned the dominant narrative of reintegration in various ways. Some reveal the stories and experiences excluded by this narrative (Verma 2012); others critique its linear trajectory, especially as a source of capital in a global humanitarian economy (Edmondson 2005). Many point to the fact that in this process, rebels often went straight from the front lines to the poverty of camps—hardly the "home" that "reintegration" philosophy posits (Borzello 2007, 401; Allen and Schomerus 2006, 5).

7. Church Missionary Society (CMS), *Annual Report of the Committee of the CMS for Africa and the East*, see especially "New Tasks in the New Africa" (1944–45, pp. 2–15); "Africa on the March" (1945–46, pp. 4–17); and "Understanding the African" (1946–47, pp. 4–18, in particular the subsection titled "Understanding the Returned Soldier").

8. Church Missionary Society, *CMS Historical Record*, 1946–47, Upper Nile Mission, p. 68.

9. Church Missionary Society, *CMS Historical Record*, 1947–48, Upper Nile Mission, pp. 66, 74.

10. See for example Mudoola (2013), Araali (2013).

11. Though this phrase is widely used in different forms, this particular iteration was specifically mentioned by Lacambel on the June 20, 2013, broadcast of *Dwog Cen Paco* in reference to the reasons why recently returned "children" from the LRA were staying at the World Vision rehabilitation center.

12. Labwor and his wife reunited and stayed together in town after leaving the reception centers, but she later left after encountering problems with her mother-in-law, who had encouraged Labwor to become a heavy drinker.

13. Note that not all former rebels passed through reception centers. See for example Allen and Schomerus (2006, 27–29).

14. For other mentions of the burning of old clothes, see Oringa (n.d., 60), Allen and Schomerus (2006, 36), Amone-P'Olak (2006, 102).

15. The somewhat invented tradition of drinking the bitter root (*mato oput*) is a good example of a ritual that seemed more helpful to civilians in reasserting different forms of power over former rebels than in aiding returning rebels themselves. See Finnström (2008, 228–232), Allen (2010), Branch (2011).

16. See for example Gulu Support the Children Organisation (GUSCO) (n.d.B, 6), Calibre Consult Ltd. (2009, 14).

17. Indeed, while on operations, rebels would not bathe, often for days at a time, until their return to base or when they set up camp. Mohammed's claim was supported by a former CARITAS reception center worker, who agreed that education on hygiene and toilets was unnecessary for rebels who already knew these things (personal interview, 2013).

18. This was precisely the kind of practice that was taken to avoid the spread of diseases like Ebola. My friends told me various stories about the 2000–2001 outbreak of Ebola in Gulu, including that: the LRA had prayed and fasted for God to send Ebola to the UPDF; that the *tipu* informed Kony of the outbreak of Ebola in advance; and that a mixture of camouflage (a holy soil) and speargrass roots would protect against Ebola. Many asserted to me that no rebel died of Ebola thanks to protective medicine and the advance warning given by the *tipu*.

19. Aliya suggested that if one were to accidentally use another's basin, the basin would be discarded, considered too unhygienic to be returned to its initial owner.

20. Many friends recalled how they or others were taken abroad by NGO officials, who used them to lobby for funds before corruptly eating the money to build their own homes. RV recalled that one NGO collected ex-LRA women and called them "prostitutes" in order to use them to lobby for more money for their own coffers.

CHAPTER 5. REBEL KINSHIP BEYOND HUMANITY

1. A version of this chapter appeared as "Rebel Kinship and Love within the Lord's Resistance Army," *Journal of Peace and Security Studies* 2, no. 1 (June 2016): 20–32.

2. See also for example Mariane Ferme's (2013) description of similar arguments made by prosecutors at the Special Court for Sierra Leone regarding RUF rebel wives. Note also that the LRA did not practice indiscriminate rape as a standard war tactic, with punishments (often from the *tipu*) said to await any rebel who committed such a crime. Many of my friends insisted that I correct the

misconception that the LRA raped, a misconception that Tim Allen and Mareike Schomerus (2006, 24) and others also try to clarify. Here, so-called rape is considered from a legal perspective in the context of a forced marriage.

3. McKay and Mazurana (2004), Allen and Schomerus (2006), and Annan et al. (2009), among others, offer such nuanced but ultimately moralizing accounts of LRA wives. Erin Baines (2014) is a rare exception in dropping, as I do, ersatz quotes around the term "wife." It is worth noting that although wives were generally given to men, there were also cases of courtship within the LRA.

4. The Lotuko are a tribe in South Sudan. My friends spoke of times when they would raid food from the Lotuko, with whom they had generally antagonistic relations.

5. Palik is a fictitious name used in place of the actual name of Onen's family's rural village.

6. Widow inheritance in the LRA worked quite differently. A wife whose husband died in battle would, especially if she had been a member of the LRA for some time, be left alone for a certain time. After this period, courting would be allowed between her and other men. However, younger wives would generally be given to new husbands instead of being courted. Sometimes, consecutive husbands of a certain woman would die, leading to accusations that the woman had a "hot chest" (*kori lyet*, literally "your chest is hot"). The LRA might pray for such a woman to cool her chest and ensure that her next husband would not die like the others before him.

7. In this ceremony, elders would acquire a rooster with mixed-colored feathers (*gweno latwol*), swinging it at the door of the new husband's hut (where the widow will be staying) before swinging it around both the widow's and the husband's necks. The rooster is then slaughtered and eaten by the elders. *Buku gweno* must be performed before the widow sleeps with her new husband. If the *buku gweno* is not performed, such a relationship might be considered illicit (*lukiro*), and the deceased's children may die as punishment meted out by the clan's *jogi* until another form of cleansing is performed.

8. This is a kind of *awar*, a compensation for the bride price paid by the husband's family.

9. In fact, Labwor's family thought he had died in the *lum* and had even conducted last funeral rites for him, and were surprised when he returned from the front lines very much alive.

10. Ker Kwaro Acholi is the official organization of Acholi chiefdoms.

11. See also Dolan (2009, 296) and Baines (2014). The LRA is also sometimes referred to as the LRM/A, the Lord's Resistance Movement/Army. Some rebels refer to the group simply as the Movement.

12. See for example chapter 5 of Thiranagama (2011), from which the title of this section, "militant kinships," is drawn.

13. See also Thiranagama (2011).

14. Here I follow Lubkemann (2008), Thiranagama (2011), and Ferme (2013) in questioning Nordstrom's (1997) argument.

CHAPTER 6. REBELS AND CHARITY CASES

1. The video can be viewed here: https://www.youtube.com/watch?v=Y4MnpzG5Sqc, accessed June 16, 2017.
2. See for example Malkki (2010).
3. This chapter builds on Dubal (2013).
4. See for example Boltanski and Chiapello (2007, 350), Fassin (2008), Fassin and Rechtman (2009), Feldman (2009), Pupavac (2010).
5. See for example Fassin (2008), Feldman (2009).
6. See for example Hopwood and Atkinson (2013).
7. Of note, Uganda and Cuba maintain strong diplomatic ties. Some of Museveni's guerrillas had undergone military training in Cuba in preparation for his 1986 coup. Comparisons are often made between Museveni's coup and Castro's Cuban Revolution. See for example Museveni (2008), Adhola (2012).
8. See also Finnström (2008, 3).
9. For more on the comparisons between Moses and Kony, see Lavik (2010), Nambalirwa (2012).
10. For instance Van Acker (2004, 336).
11. For instance Branch (2005), Finnström (2010, 74).
12. For instance Ehrenreich (1998), Blattman and Annan (2010, 154–55).
13. A better but less literal translation might be "playing with people's heads."
14. It was also said that Kony simply did not do "politics" in the sense of governance. Many of my friends stressed that he did not want to become president or take power—he would merely overthrow Museveni then let others take control of a new government.
15. Indeed, "politics" in this sense is alive and well in postcolonial Uganda. Rebellion has been far from passé as an attempted mode of social change, even as the number of development and humanitarian NGOs proliferated in the country. From the NRA to the LRA, the WNBF to the ADF, rebel groups have dominated the country's landscape of postcolonial "political" history.
16. "Politics of the belly" could be used to describe this phenomenon in a less pejorative sense, but it is not one that my friends, decrying uneven development and corruption, shared, except to the extent that they too used "eating" or "chewing" to describe corruption. See Bayart (2009 [1993]).
17. *Atuku*, a praise or pet name for beautiful girls, is one of Bigombe's Acholi names.
18. Museveni was monikered a "cattle raider" because his army stole Acholi cattle in and during the course of the war, either directly or through indi-

rect support of Karamojong cattle raiding. See for example Finnström (2008, 71–72).

19. These economies were introduced through the course of the war, primarily through supply of food aid to government-created camps for internally displaced persons. For a detailed description of the humanitarianism-violence complex, see Branch (2011).

20. Other friends of mine did find fault with this kind of "politics." Benjamin claimed that former rebels engaging in such "politics" were lazy and wanted to get money easily without working hard. "For these two reasons [money and laziness], their life changes completely, and they start living as if they didn't know Kony," he lamented.

21. On ethics and subjectivity, see Foucault (1998). On hegemonic notions of and debates on humanitarian ethics, see Anderson (1999) and Terry (2002).

22. On the "affect economy" see Adams (2013). On a similar concept, the "compassion economy" or the "political economy of trauma," see James (2010).

23. See, among others, Annan et al. (2006, 80–81), Baines (2011, 488), Perrot (2012).

24. See also Allen and Schomerus (2006, 39).

25. Most official figures, including Allen and Schomerus (2006), list the standard amount given as around 260,000UGX. I could find no mention of the graduated pay scale based on time spent in the *lum* that Aliya discussed.

26. In a twist of historical irony, the Acholi word used to refer to a biblical chapter, *cura*, is derived from the Arabic *surah*, referring to Quranic chapters.

27. I follow Erica Caple James (2010, see especially 25–26) and her notion of "compassion economies," together with the idea that interveners extract and commodify suffering as a source of profit.

28. My friends did not make distinctions between "pity" and "compassion," as Hannah Arendt (1963) does, nor between a "politics of pity" and a "politics of justice," as Luc Boltanski (1999) does. I read this as an effect of both the different forms of politics and ethics they employed, as discussed above, and the interchangeability of these terms in Acholi as *kica*, defined by Alexander Odonga as "pity, compassion, mercy, forgiveness" (2005, 101).

29. This concept comes from Pandolfi (2000).

30. There is a parallel here between my thinking and that of Erica Caple James and her trouble with the transformation of *militan* into *viktim* in Haitian compassion economies (2010, 20).

31. During a broadcast on Mega FM on April 11, 2013.

32. The only significant discontent over being seen as a *lapeko* was that for many women from Eternal Salvation, it tended to hurt their chances at courtship. It was well known that many ex-LRA who had enlisted with the UPDF would court ex-rebel women from Eternal Salvation. RV claimed that being called "vulnerable" was something that scared men away.

33. Indeed, this is precisely how and why concepts like *ubuntu* have been invented as traditional African humanities—as a way of aligning with the post-modern turn to humanism and its promise of transcending, for example, racial difference in post-apartheid South Africa. See Mbembe (2011).

CHAPTER 7. CONCLUSION

1. Questioning humanity here is a way of unsettling widely accepted models of the good that have been entrenched as the figure of humanity in, among other places, what Joel Robbins (2013) has referred to as "suffering slot ethnography."

2. For more on the counterinsurgency campaign, see Weinstein (2007).

3. Of course, given some of its factions' involvement in narco-trafficking, among other controversial practices, it is unclear if the group truly embodied Maoist praxis. This is, however, secondary to Farmer's reading of the group as Maoist revolutionaries.

4. This characterization is well made by Didier Fassin (2008, 532).

5. This trajectory draws on a more detailed explanation provided in Dubal (2012).

6. Being against humanity does not mean that one should evade the word at all costs; rather, it is to recognize and engage humanity as a site where multiple moral codes are contested.

7. Faisal Devji (2008) describes militant action as essentially rooted in a search for humanity, which can take different, varied forms, including Islamic scripture and legal discourse as well as human rights. That terrorists and humanitarians (together with scholars) search for the post-human together seems to reflect a common response to a global condition.

8. There have been strong arguments put forward by, among others, indigenous scholars such as Zoe Todd (2016) that in drawing on indigenous knowledge in the "ontological turn," the Euro-Western academy has effectively colonized native knowledge systems as their own without attribution, making it seem as though Western philosophical toil has produced nuanced views about the multiplicity of worlds that Africans and other indigenous peoples have known for many years as part of everyday knowledge. Achille Mbembe, in referencing epistemic coloniality in his argument toward the decolonization of knowledge, similarly critiques the production of theory by Europeans who do not fully acknowledge their Others as thinking subjects (2016, 36). It is interesting to note how discussions of race are often absent from mainstream ontological work. However, I suspect that this is a historical artifact of the origins of ontological work in science and technology studies (STS) and need not necessarily be the case moving forward. Much as Africanists and other scholars have developed and are comfortable thinking and theorizing race and difference in their own

disciplinary discourse, there is ample room to develop antiracist, decolonizing ontological approaches.

9. See for example Marisol de La Cadena (2010), particularly her discussion about pluriversal politics.

10. Morten Pedersen quoted in Gad, Jensen, and Winthereik (2015, 74).

11. My deepest thanks to Adrian Yen for his insights into and discussion about ontology and humanity. A more detailed, in-depth discussion of the place of my argument vis-à-vis the "ontological turn" is beyond the scope of this book. I am less interested in theoretical discussions of ontology than in what an ontological approach offers in this ethnography—a way of seeing and dealing with radical difference.

12. See for example Ferguson (2015, 216).

13. Or, as Alexander Weheliye puts it, "how humanity has been imagined and lived by those subjects excluded from this domain" (2014, 8).

14. David Napier's (2017) discussion of xenophilia offers an important glimpse into another way of engaging difference between self and other.

15. I follow Frantz Fanon in his critique of French biomedical approaches to Algerian suffering that conceptualized that suffering as a result of neurological and/or psychiatric disease ("the consequence of how his nervous system is organized"), rather than "the direct result of the colonial situation" (1963, 233).

16. Surgery is seen as a specialty in which this kind of anti-humanism is particularly strong, as Liisa Malkki encounters in her fieldwork. Some of her informants perceive certain surgeons as emotionless cutters who fail to see their patients as fellow persons (2015, 187–88).

17. See for example Pine (2011).

18. For another vision of an anti-humanist medicine, see Jeffrey Bishop's (2008) argument that humanism reproduces dualisms of Western metaphysics.

19. Anti-humanism offers the possibility of fundamental intervention on fundamental causes. For more on fundamental cause perspectives in medicine, see Reich, Hansen, and Link (2016).

20. This follows the imagination of the surgeon Norman Bethune, who, on being inundated with patients with tuberculosis, "wondered whether their charts should be labeled 'pulmonary tuberculosis' or 'economic poverty'" (quoted in Gordon and Allan 1973, 66–67).

21. This is not to say that an anti-humanist discourse should monopolize or totalize the process of recognition in a way that would either exclude or obscure other relationalities or essentialize that violence as purely and only structural.

22. For more on the individual and other assumptions inherent to biomedicine, see Gordon (1988).

23. Joy DeGruy (2005) encapsulates this approach in discussing the emotional trauma of Black Americans as "post-traumatic slave syndrome (PTSS)."

24. See for example Dubal and Lieberman (2015).

25. Indeed, this is a project already in action. ICD-10 diagnostic codes include "social determinants of health" such as unemployment and food insecurity, though more complex diseases like racism or capitalism are not yet incorporated. See for example Gottlieb et al. (2016).

26. The Radical Statistics Group, or Radstats, provides an excellent model for this kind of work.

27. See Nelson (2011).

Glossary of Terms

abila (n) ancestral shrine associated with *tic Acoli*; targeted for destruction by LRA

adoko gwok (phrase) "I have become a dog"

adwii (n) or *adui* (n) rebel; sometimes "enemy"; originally a Swahili term meaning "enemy" or "foe"

ajwaka (n, s), *ajwagi* (n, pl) spirit's priest or witch doctor

aleya (n) type of collective farming work, done in turns

apoya (n) madness; see also *lapoya*

apwoyo (v) thanks; also used as a greeting

askari (n) guard or soldier; originally a Swahili term, now used commonly in Acholi

awal (n) calabash

bal (n) Christian sin; wrong

bal alaka (n) inherited wrong or sin

balo cawa (v) to waste time

bim (n) baboon

boda boda (n) motorcycle taxi

bolo (n) tent-like, temporary shelter made for (among others) traveling guests visiting the homestead overnight for a special event or occasion

boo (n) black-eyed pea or cowpea leaves, eaten as a vegetable

boo kec (n) thieves parading as rebels; literally, "boo is bitter"

buc (n) jail, prison

buku gweno (v) a type of *kwer* ceremony; literally, "to whirl the chicken"

bwami (n) bad behaviors or actions

calo (adv) like, as

camo (v) to eat

can (n) suffering; poverty; *deno can* is to "endure suffering"

caro (n) rural area or rural village

cen (n) vengeance spirit or ghost

cik (n) rules

cilo (n) dirt

culo kwor (v) to pay reparations

cura (n) chapter, used to refer to biblical chapters; originally derived from the Arabic *surah*, referring to a Quranic chapter

dako (n) wife, woman

dano adana (n) real human being

dano mager (n) a ferocious, fierce, wild person

del (n) flesh, skin

dong cen (adj) left behind; undeveloped

dul (n) club, log (of wood)

dwog cen paco (phrase) "come back home"

dyekal (n) compound in a homestead; may contain several huts, granary, drying racks, and other household structures, often identified from afar by mango trees, which are commonly planted in the compound

gang (n) village or home

gemo (n) evil spirits that move from place to place; traditionally thought to be responsible for infectious diseases such as measles, plague, and smallpox

ger (adj) ferocious, fierce, wild, threatening

gero (n) ferocity, fierceness, wildness, cruelty, harshness

goro (n) weakness; disability

got (n, s), *godi* (n, pl) hill or mountain; rock, stone

guci (n) slave

gunya (n) chimpanzee

gwok (n) dog

ido (v) to possess (as done on a person by a *jok*)

jok (n, s), *jogi* (n, pl) spirit; seen pejoratively as demonic by staunch Christians

kabedo maleng (n) holy or clean place

kac (n) ancestral shrine; see also *abila*

kaka (n) clan, lineage, tribe

kal (n) millet

kare (n) time

kica (n) mercy, sympathy, pity, compassion

kwac (n) leopard

kwer (n)   religious ceremony or rite, conducted as *tic Acoli*

kwero merok (n/v)   cleansing ritual for someone who has killed a *merok*

kwon (n)   dough-like bread

kwor (n)   enmity; see also *culo kwor*

labwor (n)   lion

lajok (n, s), *lujogi* (n, pl)   a feared wizard or witch, known to dance at night

lako (v)   to inherit; *lako dako* is "to inherit a wife," a now-infrequent practice of a deceased or absent man's brother inheriting his wife/wives

Lakwena (n)   literally "messenger" (lowercase); more commonly used (capitalized) as a name for both Alice Lakwena's Holy Spirit movement (HSM) and Joseph Kony's LRA

lakwo (n)   thief

lamego (n)   sister

lamo dog (v)   to curse

lamone (n, s), *lumone* (n, pl)   form of enemy; see also *mone*

lamony (n)   soldier

lapeko (n)   person with problems; a poor person

lapoya (n, s), *lupoya* (n, pl)   mad person; see also *apoya*

larakaraka (n)   traditional courtship dance

latim aranyi (n, s), *lutim aranyi* (n, pl)   a person who performs chaotic violence; today often translated as and for "terrorist"

latin mony (n, s), *lutino mony* (n, pl)   privates; soldiers with low or no rank; the direct translation as "child soldiers" is incorrect

latong (n)   ax

lee (n)   animal

lee tim (n)   wild animal

lee tim mager (n)   fierce wild animal

lik (adj)   frightful; ugly

Lubanga (n)   Christian God, spelling used by Protestants

luk (n)   payment for illicit forms of courtship and sexual practice, including unsanctioned elopement

lukiro (n)   illicit relationship or sex, as in incest

lum (n)   space where humans are not supposed to live; poorly translated as "the bush"; literally, "grass"

lwii (v)   to flee

lworro (v)   to respect; to fear

lyek (n)   area of burned grass

malakwang (n)   sour, leafy vegetable not eaten by *nguu dano* for fear that it will erode the sharpness of the teeth

merok (n)   highest form of enemy, with whom no reconciliation can be made; can refer to either animals or humans

ming (adj)   stupid

miya miya (imperative)   "give me, give me"; synonymous with "dependency syndrome"

mone (n)   quarrel or bitterness between or among peoples, at a serious but not irreconcilable level; see also *lamone*

mony (n)   war; see also *latin mony*

muno (n, s), *muni* (n, pl)   white person

muranga (n)   beans

mwodo (v)   to chew, to eat

mzee (n, Swahili)   elder, old person; used almost only for older men, also called *ladit* ("big person") in Acholi; older women are often referred to affectionately as *mego* ("mother")

ngolo (v)   to cut

ngom kwaro (n)   ancestral or customary land

nguu dano (n)   shape-shifting man-beast

nono (adv)   without reason, for no reason or cause

nyek (sometimes *nyeko*) (n, s), *nyeggi* (n, pl)   jealousy; co-wife

nying moi (n)   killer or hero name

okono (n)   pumpkin

olik (n)   bat (winged mammal)

omin (n)   brother

opii (n)   slave

orongo (n)   *cen* of a wild and fierce animal that can disturb someone who kills such an animal and is not ritually cleansed; see also *cen*

ot (n)   house or hut

oyoo (n)   mouse

paco (n)   home, village; see also *gang*

panga (n)   machete

rac (adj)   bad; ugly

remo (n)   blood

roco wic (v)   to repair the head; used as translation of "to rehabilitate"

rok (n)   a foreign land (e.g., England)

Rubanga (n)   Christian God; spelling used by Catholics

rwot (n, s), *rwodi* (n, pl)   chief; lord

rwot ineka (n, s)   puppet, in the pejorative sense; originally from proverb, "Chief, you're killing me with laughter" (*Rwot, ineka ki nyero*)

tic (n)   work

tic Acoli (n)   traditional Acholi religious practice; literally, "Acholi work"

tic pa Rubanga (n)   Christian religious practice; literally, "the work of God"

tim (n)   large expanse of *lum*, often used for hunting; also refers to a foreign land (e.g., England); see also *lum, rok*

tim gero (n)   violence; literally, "a fierce act"

tim gero lataya (n)   brutal violence; literally, an "endlessly fierce act"

ting ting (n)   name given to young girls abducted by the LRA, who often served as babysitters or maids until they were given as a wife to a male rebel

tipu (n)   spirit; shadow

tipu maleng (n)   holy spirit

tipu marac (n)   bad or evil spirit

tum (n)   sacrifice, often in the context of *tic Acoli*; see also *tic Acoli*

twero pa dano (n)   human rights; literally, "the capabilities of people"

two gemo (n)   plague, among other infectious diseases thought to be caused by *gemo*; see also *gemo*

tyer (n)   Christian offering

wang (n)   eye

wang oo (n)   compound fireplace, around which a family gathers at night and shares stories and conversation

wat (n, s), *wadi* (n, pl)   relative (as in a clan member)

yot (adj)   easy

Bibliography

"Acholi Cautioned." 2013. *Daily Monitor*, January 16, 24.

Adams, Vincanne. 2013. *Markets of Sorrow, Labors of Faith: New Orleans in the Wake of Katrina*. Durham, NC: Duke University Press.

Adhola, Yogi. 2012. "Museveni Finally Admits He Was Wrong." *Independent*, July 22. https://www.independent.co.ug/museveni-finally-admits-wrong/.

Adimola, Andrew. 1954. "The Lamogi Rebellion 1911–12." *Uganda Journal* 18 (2): 166–77.

Agger, Kasper. 2013. *Blind Spots: Gaining Access to Areas Where the LRA Operates*. The Enough Project. http://www.enoughproject.org/files /BlindSpots-GainingAccesstoWhereLRAOperates.pdf.

Akaki, Sam. 2012. "Uganda Was Much Better under British Colonial Rule." Op-ed. *Daily Monitor*, October 19, 10.

Allen, Tim. 2006. *Trial Justice: The International Criminal Court and the Lord's Resistance Army*. New York: Zed.

———. 2010. "Bitter Roots: The 'Invention' of Acholi Traditional Justice." In *The Lord's Resistance Army: Myth and Reality*, edited by Tim Allen and Koen Vlassenroot, 242–61. London: Zed.

Allen, Tim, and Mareike Schomerus. 2006. *A Hard Homecoming: Lessons Learned from the Reception Center Process in Northern Uganda*. Washington, DC: Management Systems International.

Allen, Tim, and Koen Vlassenroot. 2010. Introduction. In *The Lord's Resistance Army: Myth and Reality*, edited by Tim Allen and Koen Vlassenroot, 1–21. London: Zed.

Amnesty International. 1997. *"Breaking God's Commands": The Destruction of Childhood by the Lord's Resistance Army*. Report, AFR 59/001/1997. https://www.amnesty.org/en/documents/afr59/001/1997/en/.

Amone-P'Olak, Kennedy. 2006. "Mental States of Adolescents Exposed to War in Uganda: Finding Appropriate Methods of Rehabilitation." *Torture* 16 (2): 93–107.

Anderson, Mary. 1999. *Do No Harm: How Aid Can Support Peace—or War*. Boulder, CO: Lynne Rienner.

Annan, Jeannie, Christopher Blattman, and Roger Horton. 2006. "The State of Youth and Youth Protection in Northern Uganda: Findings from the Survey for War Affected Youth." UNICEF Uganda Report. http://chrisblattman.com/documents/policy/sway/SWAY.Phase1.FinalReport.pdf.

Annan, Jeannie, Christopher Blattman, Dyan Mazurana, and Khristopher Carlson. 2009. "Women and Girls at War: 'Wives,' Mothers, and Fighters in the Lord's Resistance Army." Households in Conflict Network Working Paper 63. Brighton, England: Institute of Development Studies.

Anukur, Luther Bois. n.d. Foreword to *After Living in Darkness, I Am Now Living in Light*. Edited by Brian McDonald. Kampala: World Vision Uganda.

Araali, Geoffrey Mutegeki. 2013. "Prison Turned Him into a Modern Farmer." Seeds of Gold section. *Daily Monitor*, February 27, 4–5.

Archdiocese of Gulu. 2007. *Baibol: Buk Maleng pa Rubanga*. Nairobi: Paulines Publications Africa.

Arendt, Hannah. 1951. *The Origins of Totalitarianism*. New York: Harvest.

———. 1963. *On Revolution*. New York: Penguin.

Arinaitwe, Solomon. 2013. "Museveni Faults Africa." *Daily Monitor*, April 25, 3.

Asad, Talal. 2007. *On Suicide Bombing*. New York: Columbia University Press.

———. 2015. "Reflections on Violence, Law, and Humanitarianism." *Critical Inquiry* 41: 390–427.

Atkinson, Ronald. 1994. *The Roots of Ethnicity: The Origins of the Acholi of Uganda before 1800*. Philadelphia: University of Pennsylvania Press.

———. 2010a. "Afterword: A Perspective on the Last Thirty Years." In *The Roots of Ethnicity: The Origins of the Acholi of Uganda*, 275–335. 2nd ed. Kampala: Fountain.

———. 2010b. "'The Realists in Juba?' An Analysis of the Juba Peace Talks." In *The Lord's Resistance Army: Myth and Reality*, edited by Tim Allen and Koen Vlassenroot, 205–22. London: Zed.

Baer, Hans A., Merrill Singer, and Ida Susser. 2003. *Medical Anthropology and the World System*. Westport, CT: Greenwood.

Baines, Erin. 2007. "The Haunting of Alice: Local Approaches to Justice and Reconciliation in Northern Uganda." *International Journal of Transitional Justice* 1: 91–114.

———. 2011. "Gender, Responsibility, and the Grey Zone: Considerations for Transitional Justice." *Journal of Human Rights* 10 (4): 477–93.

———. 2014. "Forced Marriage as a Political Project: Sexual Rules and Relations in the Lord's Resistance Army." *Journal of Peace Research* 51 (3): 405–17.

Banks, Frederick. 1900. Untitled letter – 54, 7–12–1900. Letters from Uganda. Cambridge University Library: Royal Commonwealth Society Library, RCMS 167/1–43. Cambridge, England.

Banya, Angelo Andrew. 1994. *Adoko Gwok (I Have Become a Dog)*. Kampala: Foundation for African Development.

Bayart, Jean-François. 2009 [1993]. *The State in Africa: The Politics of the Belly*. 2nd ed. Malden: Polity.

Behrend, Heike. 1999. *Alice Lakwena and the Holy Spirits: War in Northern Uganda, 1985–97*. Athens: Ohio University Press.

Bell, Hesketh. 1885–1946. Magazine articles. Sir Hesketh Bell Collection. RCMS 36/5/9. Cambridge University Library, England.

———. 1906a. Commissioner's Report of Uganda Protectorate to Secretary of State. C.O. 536/7.

———. 1906b. Diary. Hesketh Bell Papers Vol. V (ff. 315). Western Manuscripts. British Library. London.

———. 1906–9. Diaries of Sir Hesketh Bell, G.C.M.G. Sir Hesketh Bell Collection. RCMS 36/2/3. Cambridge University Library, England.

Benjamin, Walter. 1933. "On the Mimetic Faculty." In *Walter Benjamin: Selected Writings, Volume 2: Part 2, 1931–1934*, edited by Michael Jennings, Howard Eiland, and Gary Smith, 720–27. Cambridge, MA: Belknap.

Benjamin, Walter, and Knut Tarnowski. 1979. "Doctrine of the Similar" (1933). *New German Critique* 17: 65–69.

Bere, Rennie. 1990. *A Cuckoo's Parting Cry: A Personal Account of Life and Work in Uganda between 1930 and 1960*. Cheltenham, England: Cedar.

Bible Society of Uganda. 1985. *Baibul: Buk Maleŋ pa Lubaŋa*. Kampala: Bible Society of Uganda.

"Bigombe: The Woman Who Dared Kony." 2012. *New Vision*, September 21, 16.

Bishop, Jeffrey. 2008. "Rejecting Medical Humanism: Medical Humanities and the Metaphysics of Medicine." *Journal of Medical Humanities* 29: 15–25.

Blattman, Chris, and Jeannie Annan. 2010. "On the Nature and Causes of LRA Abduction: What the Abductees Say." In *The Lord's Resistance Army: Myth and Reality*, edited by Tim Allen and Koen Vlassenroot, 132–55. London: Zed.

Boccassino, Renato. 1939. "The Nature and Characteristics of the Supreme Being Worshipped among the Acholi of Uganda." *Uganda Journal* 6 (4): 195–201.

Bohannan, Laura. 1966. "Shakespeare in the Bush." *Natural History* 75 (7): 28–33.

Boltanski, Luc. 1999. *Distant Suffering: Morality, Media and Politics*. New York: Cambridge University Press.

Boltanski, Luc, and Eve Chiapello. 2007. *The New Spirit of Capitalism*. New York: Verso.

Borzello, Anna. 2007. "The Challenge of DDR in Northern Uganda: The Lord's Resistance Army." *Conflict, Security and Development* 7 (3): 387–415.

Bourgois, Philippe, Seth Holmes, Kim Sue, and James Quesada. 2017. "Structural Vulnerability: Operationalizing the Concept to Address Health Disparities in Clinical Care." *Academic Medicine* 92 (3): 299–307.

Branch, Adam. 2005. "Neither Peace nor Justice: Political Violence and the Peasantry in Northern Uganda, 1986–1998." *African Studies Quarterly* 8 (2): 1–31.

———. 2010. "Exploring the Roots of LRA Violence: Political Crisis and Ethnic Politics in Acholiland." In *The Lord's Resistance Army: Myth and Reality*, edited by Tim Allen and Koen Vlassenroot, 25–44. London: Zed.

———. 2011. *Displacing Human Rights: War and Intervention in Northern Uganda*. New York: Oxford University Press.

Calibre Consult Ltd. 2009. *Evaluation of Uganda Children of War Rehabilitation Program WVU/CONS/2008-09/004*. Monitoring and Evaluation Report prepared for World Vision Uganda. Kampala.

Carlson, Khristopher, and Dyan Mazurana. 2008. *Forced Marriage within the Lord's Resistance Army, Uganda*. Somerville, MA: Feinstein International Center.

Cave-Browne-Cave, P. 1931. "The Teacher's Opportunity." *Church Missionary Outlook*, September, 183–85.

Church Missionary Society (CMS). 1894. Papers of Rev. A. B. Fisher. Series of foolscap notebooks. Acc. 84 F3/1, Book 4, p. 24. CMS Archives, Cadbury Research Library. Birmingham, England.

———. ca. 1923–33. Papers of Rev. Henry Mathers. Upper Nile Memoranda and Reports. CMS/ACC79 Z2. CMS Archives, Cadbury Research Library. Birmingham, England.

———. 1944–47. *Annual Report of the Committee of the CMS for Africa and the East*. CMS Archives, Cadbury Research Library. Birmingham, England.

———. 1945–48. *CMS Historical Record. The Upper Nile*. CMS Archives, Cadbury Research Library. Birmingham, England.

Constitution Amendment Act. 2005. Third schedule, part 16, p. 48. Amendment of Third Schedule to the Constitution. http://www.parliament.go.ug /new/images/stories/constitution/Constitutional_Amendment_Act,_ 2005.pdf.

Constitution of the Republic of Uganda. 1995. Third schedule, article 10(a).
http://www.track.unodc.org/LegalLibrary/LegalResources/Uganda/Laws
/Uganda%20Constitution%20(1995).pdf.

"Corridors of Power." 2013. *New Vision*, March 13, 14.

Crazzolara, J. P. 1938. *A Study of the Acooli Language: Grammar and Vocabulary*. New York: Oxford University Press.

Cronin, Audrey Kurth. 2003. "The 'FTO List' and Congress: Sanctioning Designated Foreign Terrorist Organizations." Congressional Research Service Report for Congress. http://www.fas.org/irp/crs/RL32120.pdf.

DeGruy, Joy. 2005. *Post Traumatic Slave Syndrome: America's Legacy of Enduring Injury and Healing*. Milwaukie, OR: Uptone.

de La Cadena, Marisol. 2010. "Indigenous Cosmopolitics in the Andes: Conceptual Reflections Beyond 'Politics.'" *Cultural Anthropology* 25 (2): 334–70.

Delmé-Radcliffe, Charles. 1901. Letter to Henry Delmé-Radcliffe. Private papers of Brigadier General Sir Charles Delmé-Radcliffe KCMG CB CVO. Imperial War Museum, London.

de Temmerman, Els. 1995. *Aboke Girls: Children Abducted in Northern Uganda*. Kampala: Fountain.

Devji, Faisal. 2008. *The Terrorist in Search of Humanity: Militant Islam and Global Politics*. New York: Columbia University Press.

District Commissioner's Office Gulu. 1913–14. *Disarmament of Acholi*. Bodleian Library of Commonwealth and African Studies at Rhodes House. MSS. Afr.S.1565/1, Oxford University, England.

Dolan, Chris. 2009. *Social Torture: The Case of Northern Uganda, 1986–2006*. New York: Berghahn.

Douglas, Mary. 1966. *Purity and Danger: An Analysis of Concepts of Pollution and Taboo*. New York: Praeger.

Dubal, Sam. 2012. "Renouncing Paul Farmer: A Desperate Plea for Radical Political Medicine." *Being Ethical in an Unethical World* blog post. http://samdubal.blogspot.com/2012/05/renouncing-paul-farmer-desperate-plea.html.

———. 2013. "From Rebels to Charity Cases and Back?: Ideology and Political Futures in Northern Uganda." *Critical Investigations into Humanitarianism in Africa (CIHA)* blog post. http://www.cihablog.com/from-rebels-to-charity-cases-and-back-ideology-and-political-futures-in-northern-uganda/.

———. 2016. "Rebel Kinship and Love within the Lord's Resistance Army." *Journal of Peace and Security Studies* 2 (1): 20–32.

Dubal, Sam, and Gillian Lieberman. 2015. "IV Heroin Drug Use: A Compendium of Biomedical and Social Radiological Findings." *Lieberman's Learning Lab*. http://eradiology.bidmc.harvard.edu/LearningLab/central/Dubal.pdf.

Dunson, Donald. 2008. *Child, Victim, Soldier: The Loss of Innocence in Uganda*. Maryknoll, NY: Orbis.

Dwyer, John Orr. 1972. "The Acholi of Uganda: Adjustment to Imperialism." PhD diss., Columbia University, New York.

Edmondson, Laura. 2005. "Marketing Trauma and the Theatre of War in Northern Uganda." *Theatre Journal* 57 (3): 451–74.

Ehrenreich, Rosa. 1998. "The Stories We Must Tell: Ugandan Children and the Atrocities of the Lord's Resistance Army." *Africa Today* 45 (1): 79–102.

Eichstaedt, Peter. 2009. *First Kill Your Family: Child Soldiers of Uganda and the Lord's Resistance Army*. Chicago: Chicago Review Press.

Englund, Harri. 2002. "Introduction: The Culture of Chameleon Politics." In *A Democracy of Chameleons: Politics and Culture in the New Malawi*, edited by Harri Englund, 11–24. Stockholm: Elanders Gotab.

———. 2006. Prisoners of Freedom: Human Rights and the African Poor. Berkeley: University of California Press.

———. 2011. *Human Rights and African Airwaves: Mediating Equality on the Chichewa Radio*. Bloomington: Indiana University Press.

Esmeir, Samera. 2012. *Juridical Humanity: A Colonial History*. Stanford, CA: Stanford University Press.

Evans-Pritchard, E. E. 1976. *Witchcraft, Oracles, and Magic among the Azande*. Oxford: Clarendon.

Everill, Bronwen. 2013. "Freetown, Frere Town and the Kat River Settlement: Nineteenth-Century Humanitarian Intervention and Precursors to Modern Refugee Camps." In *The History and Practice of Humanitarian Intervention and Aid in Africa*, edited by Bronwen Everill and Josiah Kaplan, 23–42. New York: Palgrave Macmillan.

Fanon, Frantz. 1963. *The Wretched of the Earth*. New York: Grove.

Farmer, Paul. 1992. *AIDS and Accusation: Haiti and the Geography of Blame*. Berkeley: University of California Press.

———. 2001. *Infections and Inequalities: The Modern Plagues*. Berkeley: University of California Press.

Fassin, Didier. 2008. "The Humanitarian Politics of Testimony: Subjectification through Trauma in the Israeli-Palestinian Conflict." *Cultural Anthropology* 23 (3): 531–58.

———. 2012. *Humanitarian Reason: A Moral History of the Present*. Berkeley: University of California Press.

Fassin, Didier, and Mariella Pandolfi, eds. 2010. *Contemporary States of Emergency: The Politics of Military and Humanitarian Interventions*. Cambridge, MA: Zone.

Fassin, Didier, and Richard Rechtman. 2009. *The Empire of Trauma: An Inquiry into the Condition of Victimhood*. Translated by Rachel Gomme. Princeton, NJ: Princeton University Press.

Feldman, Ilana. 2009. "Gaza's Humanitarianism Problem." *Journal of Palestine Studies* 38 (3): 22–37.

Feldman, Ilana, and Miriam Ticktin. 2010. "Introduction: Government and Humanity." In *In the Name of Humanity: The Government of Threat and Care*, edited by Ilana Feldman and Miriam Ticktin, 1–26. Durham, NC: Duke University Press.

Ferguson, James. 1994. *The Anti-Politics Machine: "Development," Depoliticization, and Bureaucratic Power in Lesotho*. Minneapolis: University of Minnesota Press.

———. 1999. *Expectations of Modernity: Myths and Meanings of Urban Life on the Zambian Copperbelt*. Berkeley: University of California Press.

———. 2015. *Give a Man a Fish: Reflections on the New Politics of Distribution*. Durham, NC: Duke University Press.

Ferme, Mariane. 2013. "'Archetypes of Humanitarian Discourse': Child Soldiers, Forced Marriage, and the Framing of Communities in Post-Conflict Sierra Leone." *Humanity* 4 (1): 49–71.

Festa, Lynn. 2010. "Humanity without Feathers." *Humanity* 1 (1): 3–27.

Fields, Karen. 1985. *Revival and Rebellion in Colonial Central Africa*. Princeton, NJ: Princeton University Press.

Finkielkraut, Alain. 2001. *In the Name of Humanity: Reflections on the Twentieth Century*. London: Pimlico.

Finnström, Sverker. 2006. "Wars of the Past and War in the Present: The Lord's Resistance Movement/Army in Uganda." *Africa* 76 (2): 200–220.

———. 2008. *Living with Bad Surroundings: War, History, and Everyday Moments in Northern Uganda*. Durham, NC: Duke University Press.

———. 2010. "An African Hell of Colonial Imagination? The Lord's Resistance Army in Uganda, Another Story." In *The Lord's Resistance Army: Myth and Reality*, edited by Tim Allen and Koen Vlassenroot, 74–89. London: Zed.

———. 2013. "Today He Is No More: Magic, Intervention, and Global War in Uganda." In *Virtual War and Magical Death: Technologies and Imaginaries for Terror and Killing*, edited by Neil Whitehead and Sverker Finnström, 111–31. Durham, NC: Duke University Press.

Fisher, Arthur Bryan. ca. 1890–92. Personal diary. In the Papers of Rev. A. B. Fisher. CMS ACC 84 F3/1. Cadbury Research Library, University of Birmingham, England.

———. 1913. "The Nile Province." *CMS Gazette*, January 1, 17–18.

Fisher, Ruth B. 1913. Personal letter. In the Papers of Rev. A. B. Fisher. CMS ACC 84 F4–Gulu 3. Cadbury Research Library, University of Birmingham, England.

———. 1914. "The Awakening of a Nile Tribe." *CMS Gleaner*, June 1, 90–91.

Foucault, Michel. 1998. *Ethics: Subjectivity and Truth*. Edited by Paul Rabinow. New York: New Press.

Gad, Christopher, Casper Bruun Jensen, and Brit Ross Winthereik. 2015. "Practical Ontology: Worlds in STS and Anthropology." *NatureCulture* 3: 1–24.

Garcia, Angela. 2010. *The Pastoral Clinic: Addiction and Dispossession along the Rio Grande*. Berkeley: University of California Press.

Geertz, Clifford. 1984. "Distinguished Lecture: Anti Anti-Relativism." *American Anthropologist* 86 (2): 263–78.

Gersony, Robert. 1997. *The Anguish of Northern Uganda: Results of a Field-Based Assessment of the Civil Conflicts in Northern Uganda*. Kampala: United States Embassy.

Girling, F. K. 1952. *The Traditional Social and Political Order of the Acholi of Uganda*. DPhil Thesis, Exeter College, Oxford University.

———. 1960. *The Acholi of Uganda*. London: H. M. Stationery Office.

Gordon, Deborah R. 1988. "Tenacious Assumptions in Western Biomedicine." In *Biomedicine Examined*, edited by Margaret Lock and Deborah Gordon, 19–56. Dordrecht, the Netherlands: Kluwer Academic Publishers.

Gordon, Sydney, and Ted Allan. 1973. *The Scalpel, The Sword: The Story of Dr. Norman Bethune*. New York: Monthly Review Press.

Gottlieb, Laura, Rachel Tobey, Jeremy Cantor, Danielle Hessler, and Nancy Adler. 2016. "Integrating Social and Medical Data to Improve Population Health: Opportunities and Barriers." *Health Affairs* 35 (11): 2116–23.

Gray, Sir John Milner. 1952. "Acholi History, 1860–1901—III." *Uganda Journal* 16 (2): 132–44.

Grogan, Quentin O. ca. 1908–11. Papers of Quentin O. Grogan. Bodleian Library of Commonwealth and African Studies at Rhodes House. Oxford University, England.

Grove, E. T. N. 1919. "Customs of the Acholi." *Sudan Notes and Records* 2 (3): 157–82.

Guevara, Ernesto. 2008. *Guerrilla Warfare*. Location unknown: BN Publishing.

Gulu Support the Children Organisation (GUSCO). 2002. *Report on a Thematic Consultation with GUSCO*. Internal document. Gulu.

———. n.d.A. *A Proposed Standard Child Care and Protection Procedures and Support Materials*. Gulu: GUSCO.

———. n.d.B. *GUSCO Reception Centre*. Gulu: GUSCO.

———. n.d.C. *A Proposed GUSCO Rehabilitation Program Operational Manual*. Internal policy document. Gulu: GUSCO.

Gulu Support the Children Organisation (GUSCO) and Red Barnet. 1998–2001. "Support for War-Affected Children Phase II." Project proposal. Gulu.

Haraway, Donna. 2008. *When Species Meet*. Minneapolis: University of Minnesota Press.

Hartman, Saidiya V. 1997. *Scenes of Subjection: Terror, Slavery, and Self-Making in Nineteenth-Century America.* New York: Oxford University Press.

Holbraad, Martin, Morten Axel Pedersen, and Eduardo Viveiros de Castro. 2014. "The Politics of Ontology: Anthropological Positions." *Cultural Anthropology,* January 13. https://culanth.org/fieldsights/462-the-politics-of-ontology-anthropological-positions.

Hopwood, Julian, and Ronald R. Atkinson. 2013. *Land Conflict Monitoring and Mapping Tool for the Acholi Sub-Region.* Gulu: Human Rights Focus. http://www.lcmt.org/pdf/final_report.pdf.

Horkheimer, Max. 1947. *Eclipse of Reason.* New York: Oxford University Press.

Horkheimer, Max, and Theodor W. Adorno. 2002. *Dialectic of Enlightenment: Philosophical Fragments.* Stanford, CA: Stanford University Press.

International Criminal Court. 2005. *Warrant of Arrest for Joseph Kony Issued on 8 July 2005 as Amended on 27 September 2005.* Public redacted version. ICC-02/04–01/05. http://www.icc-cpi.int/iccdocs/doc/doc97185.pdf.

James, Erica Caple. 2010. *Democratic Insecurities: Violence, Trauma, and Intervention in Haiti.* Berkeley: University of California Press.

Jia, Bing Bing. 1999. "The Differing Concepts of War Crimes and Crimes against Humanity in International Criminal Law." In *The Reality of International Law,* edited by Guy Goodwin-Gill and Stefan Talmon, 243–71. New York: Oxford University Press.

Justice and Reconciliation Project. 2010. *As Long as You Live You Will Survive: The Omot Massacre.* JRP Field Note 11. Gulu: JRP.

———. 2011. *The Lukodi Massacre: 19th May 2004.* JRP Field Note 13. Gulu: JRP.

Kalyegira, Timothy. 2012. "Uganda at 50 Years, Part 4: A Nation of Perpetual Teenagers." *Sunday Monitor,* September 30, 20.

Kanana, Penlife. 2012. "We Would Be Better under Colonialists." Op-ed. *Daily Monitor,* October 3, 12.

Kasozi, A. B. K. 1999. *The Social Origins of Violence in Uganda, 1964–1985.* Kampala: Fountain.

Kazibwe, Kenneth. 2014. "UPDF Speak Out on Kony 'Death' Rumours." *Chimp Reports,* May 6. http://www.chimpreports.com/19899-updf-speak-out-on-kony-death-rumours/.

Killingray, David. 2010. *Fighting for Britain: African Soldiers in the Second World War.* Woodbridge, England: James Currey.

Kitching, A. L. 1906. Extract from untitled letter. *Church Missionary Intelligencer,* May, 372–73.

———. 1926. "A New African Diocese." *Church Missionary Review,* 319–28.

———. 1928. "Charge to the Annual Conference of the Elgon Mission at Ngora." *Upper Nile Mission Correspondence, 1927–34.* G3 A10/P1. Church

Missionary Society Archives. Cadbury Research Library, University of Birmingham, England.

———. 1936. "The Diocese of the Upper Nile." *East and West Review: An Anglican Missionary Quarterly Magazine* 2: 228–36.

Kohn, Eduardo. 2013. *How Forests Think: Toward an Anthropology Beyond the Human*. Berkeley: University of California Press.

Lakot, Dorine. 2003. "Report on Community Needs Assessment." GUSCO internal document. Gulu: GUSCO.

Lan, David. 1985. *Guns and Rain: Guerrillas and Spirit Mediums in Zimbabwe*. Berkeley: University of California Press.

"Land Dispute Costs Woman Arm." 2013. *Daily Monitor*, June 4, 23.

Laqueur, Thomas. 2009. "Mourning, Pity, and the Work of Narrative in the Making of 'Humanity.'" In *Humanitarianism and Suffering: The Mobilization of Empathy*, edited by Richard Ashby Wilson and Richard D. Brown, 31–57. Cambridge, England: Cambridge University Press.

Lavik, Marta Høyland. 2010. "Killing Children with God's Permission?: The Rhetoric of Retaliation in Psalm 193." In *Culture, Religion, and the Reintegration of Female Child Soldiers in Northern Uganda*, edited by Bård Mæland, 193–206. New York: Peter Lang.

Lévi-Strauss, Claude. 1966. *The Savage Mind*. Chicago: University of Chicago Press.

Liu Institute for Global Issues, Gulu NGO Forum, and Ker Kwaro Acholi. 2005. *Roco Wat I Acoli. Restoring Relationships in Acholi-land: Traditional Approaches to Justice and Reintegration*. http://liu.arts.ubc.ca/wp-content /uploads/2016/03/15Sept2005_Roco_Wat_I_Acoli.pdf.

Livingston, Julie. 2012. *Improvising Medicine: An African Oncology Ward in an Emerging Cancer Epidemic*. Durham, NC: Duke University Press.

Lloyd, Albert Bushnell. 1904. "The Acholi Country II." *Church Missionary Intelligencer* 55 (29): 817–20.

Lowe, Lisa. 2015. *The Intimacies of Four Continents*. Durham, NC: Duke University Press.

Lubkemann, Stephen C. 2008. *Culture in Chaos: An Anthropology of the Social Condition in War*. Chicago: University of Chicago Press.

Lugard, F. D. 1892. "Travels from the East Coast to Uganda, Lake Albert Edward, and Lake Albert." *Proceedings of the Royal Geographical Society and Monthly Record of Geography* 14 (12): 817–41.

Mafabi, Nathan Nandala. 2013. "Lets [*sic*] Challenge the Inhuman NRM Leadership." *Sunday Monitor*, February 10, 21.

Mahmood, Saba. 2005. *Politics of Piety: The Islamic Revival and the Feminist Subject*. Princeton, NJ: Princeton University Press.

Malkki, Liisa. 2010. "Children, Humanity, and the Infantilization of Peace." In *In the Name of Humanity: The Government of Threat and Care*, edited by

Ilana Feldman and Miriam Ticktin, 58–85. Durham, NC: Duke University Press.

———. 2015. *The Need to Help: The Domestic Arts of International Humanitarianism*. Durham, NC: Duke University Press.

Mamdani, Mahmood. 1976. *Politics and Class Formation in Uganda*. New York: Monthly Review Press.

Marshall, Ruth. 2009. *Political Spiritualities: The Pentecostal Revolution in Nigeria*. Chicago: University of Chicago Press.

Marx, Karl, and Friedrich Engels. 1848. "Conservative, or Bourgeois, Socialism." In *The Communist Manifesto*. https://www.marxists.org/archive/marx /works/1848/communist-manifesto/.

Mbembe, Achille. 2001. *On the Postcolony*. Berkeley: University of California Press.

———. 2002. "On the Power of the False." *Public Culture* 14 (3): 629–41.

———. 2011. "Democracy as a Community of Life." *Johannesburg Salon* 4: 5–10.

———. 2016. "Decolonizing the University: New Directions." *Arts and Humanities in Higher Education* 15 (1): 29–45.

McDonnell, Faith J. H., and Grace Akallo. 2007. *Girl Soldier: A Story of Hope for Northern Uganda's Children*. Grand Rapids, MI: Chosen.

McKay, Susan, and Dyan Mazurana. 2004. *Where Are the Girls? Girls in Fighting Forces in Northern Uganda, Sierra Leone and Mozambique: Their Lives during and after War*. Montreal: Rights and Democracy, International Centre for Human Rights and Democratic Development.

Merleau-Ponty, Maurice. 2000. *Humanism and Terror: The Communist Problem*. New Brunswick, NJ: Transaction.

Metzl, Jonathan, and Helena Hansen. 2014. "Structural Competency: Theorizing a New Medical Engagement with Stigma and Inequality." *Social Science and Medicine* 103: 126–33.

"Minister Warns Acholi against Starting Another War." 2013. *Daily Monitor*, February 4, 16.

Ministry of Health. 2005. "Health and Mortality Survey among Internally Displaced Persons in Gulu, Kitgum, and Pader Districts, Northern Uganda." Reliefweb.int, July 31. http://reliefweb.int/sites/reliefweb.int/files/resources /461F14718C3CD52885257077006E2350-govuga-uga-31jul.pdf.

Mol, Annemarie. 2003. *The Body Multiple: Ontology in Medical Practice*. Durham, NC: Duke University Press.

Moyse-Bartlett, Hubert. 1956. *The King's African Rifles: A Study in the Military History of East and Central Africa, 1890–1945*. Aldershot, England: Gale and Polden.

Mpanga, David F. K. 2012. "Why Has Independence Dream Eluded Ugandans for So Long?" Op-ed. *Saturday Monitor*, October 6, 8.

Mudoola, Petride. 2013. "Beauty behind Bars: Luzira Female Inmates Get Salon Skills." *New Vision*, June 4, 26.

———. 2014. "Uganda's Rehabilitation Plan Best in Africa. *New Vision*, February 3. http://www.newvision.co.ug/new_vision/news/1337248/ugandas-rehabilitation-plan-africa.

Museveni, Yoweri. 1970. "Fanon's Theory of Violence: Its Verification in a Sub-Sahara African Territory." PhD diss., University of East Africa, Dar es Salaam, Tanzania.

———. 2008. "The Strategy of Protracted People's War: Uganda." *Military Review* (November–December): 4–13. http://usacac.army.mil/CAC2/MilitaryReview/Archives/English/MilitaryReview_20081231_art005.pdf.

———. 2014. "Speech by H. E. Yoweri K. Museveni on the Occasion to Mark 10 Years of the Pan African Parliament, Midrand, South Africa." March 18. http://www.statehouse.go.ug/media/presidential-statement/speech-by-he-yoweri-k-museveni-on-the-occasion-to-mark-10-years-of-the-pan-african%20parliament.

Mwenda, Andrew. 2010. "Uganda's Politics of Foreign Aid and Violent Conflict: The Political Uses of the LRA Rebellion." In *The Lord's Resistance Army: Myth and Reality*, edited by Tim Allen and Koen Vlassenroot, 45–58. London: Zed.

Nader, Laura. 1972. "Up the Anthropologist: Perspectives Gained from Studying Up." In *Reinventing Anthropology*, edited by Dell Hymes, 284–311. New York: Pantheon.

Nalugo, Mercy. 2013. "Northern MPs Revive Secession Call Threat." *Daily Monitor*, February 21, 5.

Nambalirwa, Helen Nkabala. 2012. "There Is No Difference between Moses and Kony: A Critical Analysis of the Contextual Use of Some Old Testament Texts and Motifs in the Early Years of the Lord's Resistance Army." PhD diss., School of Mission and Theology, Stavanger, Norway.

Napier, A. David. 2017. "Epidemics and Xenophobia, or, Why Xenophilia Matters." *Social Research: An International Quarterly* 84 (1): 59–81.

Naturinda, Sheila. 2013. "Acholi MPs Want Kazinda Trial in Gulu." *Daily Monitor*, February 20, 7.

Navarro, Vicente. 1988. "Professional Dominance or Proletarianization?: Neither." *Milbank Quarterly* 66 (2): 57–75.

Negri, Angelo. 1984. *Gli Acioli del Nord Uganda*. Verona, Italy: Centro Comboniano per la conoscenza dell'Africa.

Nelson, Alondra. 2011. *Body and Soul: The Black Panther Party and the Fight against Medical Discrimination*. Minneapolis: University of Minnesota Press.

Nguyen, Vinh-Kim. 2010. *The Republic of Therapy: Triage and Sovereignty in West Africa's Time of AIDS*. Durham, NC: Duke University Press.

Nibbe, Ayesha. 2010. "The Effects of a Narrative: Humanitarian Aid and Action in the Northern Uganda Conflict." PhD diss., University of California, Davis.

Nile, Lucien Upper. 1946. "Out with an Acholi hunt." *African Affairs* 45 (181): 178–84.

Nordstrom, Carolyn. 1997. *A Different Kind of War Story.* Philadelphia: University of Pennsylvania Press.

Nyamugasira, Warren. 2012. "Banish Pessimism at 50." Op-ed. *New Vision,* September 18, 11.

Obama, Barack. 2010. "Statement by the President on the Signing of the Lord's Resistance Army Disarmament and Northern Uganda Recovery Act of 2009." May 24. https://obamawhitehouse.archives.gov/the-press-office/statement-president-signing-lords-resistance-army-disarmament-and-northern-uganda-r.

———. 2011. "Letter from the President to the Speaker of the House of Representatives and the President Pro Tempore of the Senate Regarding the Lord's Resistance Army." October 14. http://www.whitehouse.gov/the-press-office/2011/10/14/letter-president-speaker-house-representatives-and-president-pro-tempore.

Obita, James Alfred. 1997. "A Case for National Reconcilation [*sic*], Peace, Democracy and Economic Prosperity for All Ugandans: The Official Presentation of the Lord's Resistance Movement/Army (LRA/M)." Presentation at 1997 Kacokke Madit, London. Accessed March 15, 2012, http://www.km-net.org.uk/conferences/KM97/papers_htm/casefor.htm.

Ochola, Dominic. 2013. "Diro ma Kony bito ki lulwenye i lum." *Rupiny,* June 5–11, 3.

Ocowun, Chris. 2013. "Pader Police Arrest 24 over Murder, Arson." *New Vision,* June 4, 11.

Odonga, Alexander. 2005. *Lwo-English Dictionary.* Kampala: Fountain.

Ojwee, Dennis. 2013. "Clerics Call for Joint Fight against LRA." *New Vision,* April 26, 8.

Oloya, Opiyo. 2013. *Child to Soldier: Stories from Joseph Kony's Lord's Resistance Army.* Toronto: University of Toronto Press.

Oringa, Patrick. n.d. *In the Name of the Ten Commandments: Children and War in Nothern [sic] Uganda.* Booklet. No further publication info.

Otto, Odonga. 2011. *Tears of a War Survivor.* Kampala: Ikorom (U) Ltd.

Otunnu, Olara. 2005. "Saving Our Children from the Scourge of War." 2005 City of Sydney Peace Prize Lecture. CPACS Occasional Paper No. 05/3. Sydney Peace Foundation. http://sydneypeacefoundation.org.au/wp-content/uploads/2012/02/2005-SPP_Olara-A.-Otunnu.pdf.

Owich, James. 2014. "Youths in Amuru Say Madhvani Sugar Works Will Not Benefit the Region." *Acholi Times,* August 25. http://www.acholitimes

.com/2014/08/25/youths-in-amuru-say-madhvani-sugar-works-will-not-benefit-the-region/.

Pain, Dennis. 1997. *The Bending of Spears: Producing Consensus for Peace and Development in Northern Uganda*. London: International Alert.

pa'Lukobo, Okumu. 1971. "Acholi Dance and Dance-Songs." *Uganda Journal* 35 (1): 55–61.

Pandolfi, Mariella. 2000. "L'industrie humanitaire: Une souveraineté mouvante et supracoloniale. Réflexion sur l'expérience des Balkans." *Multitudes* 3: 97–105.

Parsons, Timothy. 1999. *The African Rank-and-File: Social Implications of Colonial Military Service in the King's African Rifles, 1902–1964*. Portsmouth, NH: Heinemann.

p'Bitek, Okot. 1963. "The Concept of Jok among the Acholi and Lango." *Uganda Journal* 27 (1): 15–29.

———. 1974. *The Horn of My Love*. London: Heinemann.

———. 1980. *Religion of the Central Luo*. Kampala: Uganda Literature Bureau.

———. 1985a. *Acholi Proverbs*. Nairobi: Heinemann Kenya Ltd.

———. 1985b. *Song of Lawino and Song of Ocol*. Portsmouth, NH: Heinemann.

———. 2011. *Decolonizing African Religions: A Short History of African Religions in Western Scholarship*. New York: Diasporic Africa Press.

Perrot, Sandrine. 2012. "Museveni's Best Enemies: Dilemmas and Political Uses of the Reintegration of Former Lord's Resistance Army (LRA) Commanders in Northern Uganda." In *War Veterans in Postwar Situations: Chechnya, Serbia, Turkey, Peru, and Côte d'Ivoire*, edited by Nathalie Duclos, 177–98. New York: Palgrave Macmillan.

Pham, Phuong N., Patrick Vinck, and Eric Stover. 2008. "The Lord's Resistance Army and Forced Conscription in Northern Uganda." *Human Rights Quarterly* 30 (2): 404–11.

Pido, J. P. Odoch. 2000. "Personhood and Art: Social Change and Commentary among the Acoli." In *African Philosophy as Cultural Inquiry*, edited by Ivan Karp and D. A. Masolo, 105–35. Bloomington: Indiana University Press.

Pine, Adrienne. 2011. "From Healing to Witchcraft: On Ritual Speech and Roboticization in the Hospital." *Culture, Medicine, and Psychiatry* 35: 262–84.

Poblicks, Nyeko Caesar. 2002. "Kacoke Madit: A Diaspora Role in Promoting Peace." In *Protracted Conflict, Elusive Peace: Initiatives to End the Violence in Northern Uganda*, edited by Okello Lucima, 62–63. London: Conciliation Resources.

Pupavac, Vanessa. 2010. "Between Compassion and Conservatism: A Genealogy of Humanitarian Sensibilities." In *Contemporary States of Emergency: The Politics of Military and Humanitarian Interventions*, edited by Didier Fassin and Mariella Pandolfi, 129–49. Cambridge, MA: Zone.

Ramos, Alcida Rita. 2012. "The Politics of Perspectivism." *Annual Review of Anthropology* 41: 481–94.

Redfield, Peter. 2013. *Life in Crisis: The Ethical Journey of Doctors Without Borders*. Berkeley: University of California Press.

Reich, Adam, Helena Hansen, and Bruce Link. 2016. "Fundamental Interventions: How Clinicians Can Address the Fundamental Causes of Disease." *Journal of Bioethical Inquiry* 13: 185–92.

Resolve LRA Crisis Initiative, The. 2013. *Hidden in Plain Sight: Sudan's Harboring of the LRA in the Kafia Kingi Enclave, 2009-2013*. http://www.enoughproject.org/files/HiddeninPlainSight_Sudans_SupporttotheLRA_April2013.pdf.

Rieff, David. 2002. *A Bed for the Night: Humanitarianism in Crisis*. New York: Simon and Schuster.

Robbins, Joel. 2013. "Beyond the Suffering Subject: Toward an Anthropology of the Good." *Journal of the Royal Anthropological Institute* 19 (3): 447–62.

Russell, J. K. 1966. *Men without God? A Study of the Impact of the Christian Message in the North of Uganda*. London: Highway.

Sartre, Jean-Paul 1961. Preface to Frantz Fanon, *The Wretched of the Earth*, xliii–lxii. New York: Grove.

Scheper-Hughes, Nancy. 1990. "Three Propositions for a Critically Applied Medical Anthropology." *Social Science and Medicine* 30 (2): 189–97.

———. 1992. *Death without Weeping: The Violence of Everyday Life in Brazil*. Berkeley: University of California Press.

Schmitt, Carl. [1932] 1996. *The Concept of the Political*. Translated by George Schwab. Chicago: University of Chicago Press.

Schomerus, Mareike. 2010. "'A Terrorist Is Not a Person Like Me': An Interview with Joseph Kony." In *The Lord's Resistance Army: Myth and Reality*, edited by Tim Allen and Koen Vlassenroot, 113–31. London: Zed.

Scott, David, and Sylvia Wynter. 2000. "The Re-enchantment of Humanism." *Small Axe* 8: 119–207.

Seligman, C. G., and B. Z. Seligman. 1932. *Pagan Tribes of the Nilotic Sudan*. London: Routledge and Regan Paul.

Senganda, Jaffer. 2012. "Mob Justice Instilling Fear among People." Op-ed. *New Vision*, August 15, 14.

Sharkey, Noel. 2012. "Killing Made Easy: From Joysticks to Politics." In *Robot Ethics: The Ethical and Social Implications of Robotics*, edited by Patrick Lin, George Bekey, and Keith Abney, 111–28. Cambridge, MA: MIT Press.

Soto, Carlos Rodríguez. 2009. *Tall Grass: Stories of Suffering and Peace in Northern Uganda*. Kampala: Fountain.

Taussig, Michael. 1980. "Reification and the Consciousness of the Patient." *Social Science and Medicine* 14B: 3–13.

———. 1993. *Mimesis and Alterity: A Particular History of the Senses*. New York: Routledge.

Terry, Fiona. 2002. *Condemned to Repeat?: The Paradox of Humanitarian Action*. Ithaca, NY: Cornell University Press.

Thiranagama, Sharika. 2011. *In My Mother's House: Civil War in Sri Lanka*. Philadelphia: University of Pennsylvania Press.

Titeca, Kristof. 2010. "The Spiritual Order of the LRA." In *The Lord's Resistance Army: Myth and Reality*, edited by Tim Allen and Koen Vlassenroot, 59–73. London: Zed.

Todd, Zoe. 2016. "An Indigenous Feminist's Take on the Ontological Turn: 'Ontology' Is Just Another Word for Colonialism." *Journal of Historical Sociology* 29: 4–22.

Turner, Victor. 1967. *The Forest of Symbols: Aspects of Ndembu Ritual*. Ithaca, NY: Cornell University Press.

United States Cong. Senate. 2010. 111th Congress, 1st Session. *S. 1067, Lord's Resistance Army Disarmament and Northern Uganda Recovery Act of 2009*. http://www.gpo.gov/fdsys/pkg/BILLS-111s1067enr/pdf/BILLS-111s1067enr .pdf.

Van Acker, Frank. 2004. "Uganda and the Lord's Resistance Army: The New Order No One Ordered." *African Affairs* 103 (412): 335–57.

Verma, Cecilie. 2012. Truths out of Place: Homecoming, Intervention, and Story-Making in War-Torn Northern Uganda." *Children's Geographies* 10 (4): 441–55.

Viveiros de Castro, Eduardo. 1998. "Cosmological Deixis and Amerindian Perspectivism." *Journal of the Royal Anthropological Institute* 4 (3): 469–88.

Wacquant, Loïc. 2010. "Prisoner Reentry as Myth and Ceremony." *Dialectical Anthropology* 34 (4): 605–20.

Weheliye, Alexander. 2014. *Habeas Viscus: Racializing Assemblages, Biopolitics, and Black Feminist Theories of the Human*. Durham, NC: Duke University Press.

Weinstein, Jeremy. 2007. *Inside Rebellion: The Politics of Insurgent Violence*. Cambridge, England: Cambridge University Press.

World Vision Uganda. 2004. *Pawns of Politics: Children, Conflict and Peace in Northern Uganda*. Kampala: World Vision Uganda.

Wright, A. C. A. 1940. "The Supreme Being among the Acholi of Uganda— Another Viewpoint." *Uganda Journal* 7 (3): 130–37.

Žižek, Slavoj. 2004. "From Politics to Biopolitics . . . and Back." *South Atlantic Quarterly* 103 (2/3): 501–21.

Index

Aber (pseudo.), xi, 197—98, 202—3
Acen (pseudo.), xi, 101, 108
Acholi: animality polysemous in, 99—100; early colonial encounters of, 41—48; ethnographic context of, 14—15; glossary of terms, 247—51; had forms of violence seen through colonial eyes as immoral or against humanity, 44—48; humanity of tied to modernity since colonial times, 47; killer or hero names of, 59—63; members of LRA predominantly from, 17; mob justice of, 77—78; Museveni reviled by, 78; naming of children by, 101; night-dancing of, 137, 238n17; shape-shifting belief of, 98, 236n4; violence against thieves of, 77—78. See also *tic Acoli* (Acholi religion)
Aciro (pseudo.), 199
Adorno, Theodor, 139—40
Africa: Museveni on "ideological disorientation" in, 191—192, 235n37; seen in the framework of the "beast," 6; significance of "the bush" in (post)colonial, 98
against humanity (anti-humanism), 219; characteristics of a person who is, 228; as a possible union of radical politics and ontological studies, 217—18; as a way of looking at LRA, 12—13, 220—21; what it is not, 9; what it means, 9—13, 177, 211

ajwaka (spirit-priest; witch doctor), 94; LRA mimed practices of 138—39; question of whether Kony was a, 119, 131, 132, 133, 135, 136—37
Akello Sabina (pseudo.), xi, 90, 136
alcohol, 109, 123, 237n9
Alimocan (pseudo), xi, 195—96
Aliya (pseudo.), xi, 103—4, 108, 155, 157, 175, 199, 200
Allen, Tim, 23
Althusser, Louis, vi, 221
Amin, Idi, 16, 76
Amito (pseudo.), xii, 161—73
Amnesty Act, 19, 149, 199
Amony (pseudo.), xii, 39
animality: association of *lum* with, 94, 95, 97, 98; and boundaries of humanity, 114; exrebel views of, 99; is polysemous, 99—100
anti-humanist medicine: alternate ways to look at, 222; disease unions as example of, 227—28; as explicitly leftist political medicine, 226—27; may describe how medicine operates today, 222; as micropolitical practice on sick societies, 221; is thinking about the patient as a manifested structure, 224—26; treats social problems manifesting in individuals, 222—23; would magnify the scale of

269

www.ingramcontent.com/pod-product-compliance
Ingram Content Group UK Ltd.
Pitfield, Milton Keynes, MK11 3LW, UK
UKHW041941030225
454617UK00004B/89